TIM BOOK TWO

Tim Burgess is the lead singer of The Charlatans and author of the memoir *Telling Stories*.

Further praise for *Tim Book Two*:

'You can't feel blue around Tim. He makes you feel happy, not just about music but about life. Even the most cynical of souls (mine) become infected by his gorgeous energy. Plus he gives good vinyl.' Sharon Horgan

'For a very long time my life revolved around hanging around in record shops, browsing, listening and searching for that vinyl gem. It's a bug that infected many of us, especially Tim! Without it we wouldn't be the people we are today.' Stephen Morris

'What better way to share Tim's irrepressible passion for vinyl than to join him as he goes foraging for that most vital of resources – record stores around the world – revealing fascinating stores behind albums you've heard of and some you haven't.' Cosey Fanni Tutti

TIM BOOK TWO

VINYL ADVENTURES FROM ISTANBUL TO SAN FRANCISCO

TIM BURGESS

FABER & FABER

This edition first published in the UK in 2016
by Faber & Faber Ltd,
Bloomsbury House,
74–77 Great Russell Street,
London WC1B 3DA
This paperback edition first published in 2017

Typeset by Ian Bahrami
Printed in the UK by CPI Group (UK) Ltd, Croydon CR0 4YY

A CIP record for this book
is available from the British Library

ISBN 978–0–571–31474–4

2 4 6 8 10 9 7 5 3 1

The Littlest B & Nik – for everything ever
Nick Fraser – for the road trips, the memories and
all the help

For
Martin Blunt
Mark Collins
Tony Rogers
Debbie Brookes
& Sophie Williams

And for everyone who still works or has ever worked in an
independent record shop, anywhere in the world, for those flying
the flag for vinyl and supporting the bands who make
the records. We thank you and salute you

FOREWORD

I love vinyl, and if you're reading this, you probably do too.

I buy CDs and cassette tapes and even the occasional download, but nothing really beats vinyl for me. Tim Burgess is the same, which is why he's written this book. He looks back at great records and how he first heard them, and great record shops too. For me, it was Bruce's in Kirkcaldy, a cramped dark space where I could loiter of a Saturday, deciding whether my pocket money was best spent on that bargain-bin Doctors of Madness LP or a picture-sleeve punk single. I remember sending my mum along to Bruce's to buy me some Christmas presents, and the shocked look on her face when she returned home. She'd never experienced anything quite like it in her Max Bygraves-loving life.

Wherever I've been in the world, I've always sought out local music, which means finding the best local emporium. There's a certain bittersweet feeling, knowing fewer of these places exist than previously – it's the same with independent bookshops. Yet these were a whole generation's education and escape, places where we could meet kindred spirits, learn from the knowledgeable staff, and begin a lifetime's adventure.

That adventure is ongoing for Tim Burgess. From the first records he heard to his latest explorations, this book charts a world of sound, colour and infinite possibility. So lower your eyes onto the opening track – and start reading!

Ian Rankin

INTRO

So, I'd written *Telling Stories* and the question arose of writing a follow-up. The first book was about pretty much everything that'd ever happened to me.

Well, not everything but, hopefully, everything of significance.

The year since it had come out had involved a couple of huge events in my life, albeit not quite the amount of highs, lows and in-betweens I'd experienced from birth to late 2011, when I finished *Telling Stories*. But I loved the process of writing and enough people were asking if there'd be another book. I joked that *Tim Book Two* would be with them soon, although I had nothing more than a title, and I doubt this is even called that anyway . . .

I needed a something – a subject, a story.

I've always thought that I was defined by records. Not just ones I've been involved in recording but every one I've ever loved, bought, fallen out of love with or that has soundtracked a particular chapter of my life. They are like punctuation marks. If I need to think back to an event in my life, it's easiest to do it with singles and albums. The Cure's 'Boys Don't Cry' transports me to being fifteen and a romance with Helen Birkenhead, who was from the posher part of where we lived. I was the boy from the wrong side of the Northwich tracks, like Cheshire's answer to James Dean, or that's how I saw myself. If I ever hear 'Rain' by The Beatles, the world stops and Rob Collins is in my mind, standing beside me, whispering in my ear, telling me about a melody he'd just come up with that would be the greatest song we'd

3

ever recorded. As clear as day, I can hear his voice and remember our times together.

'The Piña Colada Song', or more technically 'Escape (The Piña Colada Song)', by Rupert Holmes never fails to put a smile on my face. Martin Duffy brought a copy to a Charlatans Christmas party while we were making *Tellin' Stories*. That song, to me, is Martin, beaming broadly and reminding me of why I love spending time with him.

My mate Simon Owen had an older brother, Nick, who was into Wham! and Japan in equal measure. When I hear Japan, I think of Wham!, and the other way round. There are no real rules – you might have the same thing, but with two completely unrelated bands or songs. They don't have to be from the same time, just from when you crossed paths with them. So, in the real world *Forever Changes* by Love came out in 1967, but, for me, it represents the summer holidays in 1983, when Spud Taylor's older brother left it on the turntable at their house. We came in from playing football and were curious as we'd seen the psychedelic logo embroidered on lots of jackets in town. It had made an impression on the world a generation before, but we got Arthur Lee's take on things when we were sixteen, and it defined a time for us – watching *One Summer* on TV, reading *Record Mirror* and borrowing *Smash Hits* from my sister; leading a life that had few responsibilities. Everyone has this – it's what makes songs so powerful. Everyone has their own musical DNA that can stop you in your tracks in the supermarket or make you shed a tear on a flight. Some of that DNA is shared with the people closest to you.

The power is such that a song can be off limits once it has soundtracked a damaging period. A friend's dad would goof around each time 'Shaddap You Face' by Joe Dolce came on the radio, totally embarrassing his son. After his dad died, my mate would not be able to listen to the song without tears streaming down his face. To everyone else it was just an annoying novelty

4

hit, but to this kid it brought back memories of his missing dad. For lots of people, there's a context to songs that's not necessarily linked to the songwriter's original intention.

I became hooked at an early age on the influence that records had. The first time I heard 'Stay Free' by The Clash, I was floored. I was transported from my teenage bedroom in my comfortable suburban home to a pub near Streatham – people playing pool, two lads not much older than me, one about to become a rock star, the other a petty criminal. The poetry we were studying at school never hit me as hard as that song. Records controlled my emotions as a teenager. Within seconds of dropping the needle onto the vinyl I could be celebrating the start of the weekend with Sham 69's 'Borstal Breakout', and two days later the melancholy of a Sunday night would be amplified by 'I Just Can't Be Happy Today' by The Damned.

Record shops were where you could go and dive headlong into this world, like an external hard drive of emotions. In the 1970s every town had one. Market stalls would sell records too. Woolworths still existed and an HMV could be found on most high streets. Even Boots sold records – a chemist's that sold records. Electrical shops where you could rent a TV, they sold vinyl as well. But most towns also had a shop that specialised in records. In 1977 they became somewhere I could spend my increasing independence and free time. They even came with their own in-built form of entertainment, with the guy – it was always a guy – behind the counter and his repertoire of highly unlikely stories concerning most of the bands you ever mentioned. To us kids, he would spin yarns of boozy adventures with the Sex Pistols after their Free Trade Hall gig, or the time The Ramones stayed at his house – 'Joey ate a full jar of Marmite and Dee Dee chatted up my mum,' or some such nonsense. When real grown-ups came in, he invariably served them in total silence, sparking the story back up as soon as they had left.

Maybe he had no tales about the bands who made the records they bought, or maybe we were just deemed gullible enough to be told them. Either way, me and my friends felt at home. It could be argued that my whole life in music came from hanging around in record shops, in particular Omega Records in Northwich – it was owned by The Charlatans' first manager. (If this was one of those classic music biopic movies, there'd now be a scene with my disgruntled parents lecturing me that there was no future to be had from spending all my spare time in record shops – while myself and the audience would share a knowing smile.)

These places had a smell, a feel and a sense of reverence. If you got the name of a band wrong to the guy behind the counter, there would very likely be some mockery headed your way. James Murphy told me of the disdain he received after asking for a record by the Smith Brothers, the guy making sure the whole shop knew he'd goofed up The Smiths. Or they would often correct an errant 'The'. 'It's Sex Pistols, mate. Not *The* Sex Pistols. I'll let you off this time but that's your last warning.'

The names of the bands whose records you loved the most made it onto your school bag, flying a flag that could get you a nod of recognition from an older, cooler kid at school, or a sneer from some dusty teacher who saw it as a portent of the downfall of civilisation.

Record shops became somewhere I could take refuge. Years later, on tour, there would be TV stations, hotels, minibars, parties, drug dealers and other distractions, but where I felt safest and calmest was in a record shop – especially after a heavy day of minibars, parties and drug dealers. There was something that linked people who worked in them all around the world. Regardless of whether they spoke the same language as you, there'd be the same kind of tut, via a nod of satisfaction, as you asked what record was being played. That would be followed by a growing friendship, through little more than band names, album titles and enthusiasm.

Being in a band I've worked with quite a few people who have had to stick to a rigid routine, whether it's the gym or 12 Step – recovering alcoholics or former drug users who have to look for an AA or NA meeting as soon as we hit town. It was a major part of their recovery, but it was also a place of comfort in the world of motorway service stations and tour-bus antics – their beacon that they had to make it to, to keep them from the temptation of transgressing; their lighthouse among the rocks and waves. For me, the comfort came from time spent digging through racks of vinyl while surrounded by gig posters, like minds and the ephemera of band merchandise. I'd head to shops like Amoeba, Aquarius, Rough Trade, Sister Ray, The Thing, Piccadilly Records, Waterloo Records and Groove Store Disquaire. They are the places where you can find others who not only share a love of music but probably share views on films, books and generally opting out of regular life, even if it's just for a short while – like a table of guys grumbling in a pub, but with a more positive slant and a brilliant soundtrack.

I can always remember who gave me which record or who recommended I buy it. If the recommendation is a dud, I question how much they know me and even whether we can remain friends. Maybe it's not that serious, but it might mean a narrow-eyed look next time I see them. There's even a power that can change a record because of who loves it. A tour-manager friend had unerring good taste, and we'd spend hours listening to My Bloody Valentine, The Lemonheads and Spacemen 3 together, but in among this stood an obsession with The Vengaboys. It wasn't to seem off the wall nor was it done with any sense of irony. He genuinely really liked them. Now, I'm not saying I'd ever want to be a passenger on the Vengabus, but if I hear them on the radio I'll listen to the end, wistfully thinking of drives across Europe – without that link, the station would have been changed pretty quickly or something might have been amicably chucked at whoever was guilty of choosing it.

7

Lots of records I've bought a few times over – I think I'm into double figures with *Forever Changes*, *Pet Sounds*, *After the Gold Rush* and *Sandinista!* too. I always give them away and replace them when the need arises. Records are like the Rosetta Stone from which almost everything can be worked out. The girlfriend you went to see Sonic Youth with has broken up with the guy with all the Hootie and the Blowfish CDs? Aw, man, surely that was written in the stars. And there's even a world beyond those with dodgy taste in music: those who don't 'get' music at all – best avoided. I'm not sure what I'd talk to them about anyway.

Record shops have hit hard times, though, and like some endangered species they need our help. Maybe I'm just being selfish but what am I meant to do if they disappear? Did anyone think of that? I'm still an avid collector and I still love what it is that I share with other collectors – from sleevenotes to etched run-out grooves to amazing bargain-bin discoveries. Don't get me wrong – I'm not some kind of Luddite who wants to set fire to the Internet, shouting, 'Witchcraft!' But we need to stick together so that future generations can flick through alphabetical racks separated into genres, from Belgian industrial through to crunk, J-pop and K-pop – so they can eye up the rare, signed box set in the 'these are worth a fortune' bit behind the counter while they take their first foray into vinyl by Talking Heads, Wire, Indoor Life or whoever.

More and more often I'd get to a place I'd not been to for a while and head off to find a record shop, only to discover that it's no longer there: Reckless Records, Selectadisc, Revolver, Replay, Rare Records, Avalanche – all gone. Rising rents, online prices, creeping gentrification – all sorts of reasons are given but the upshot is that lots of towns and cities no longer have any kind of independent record shop.

Recently there has been a bit of a rallying cry and vinyl sales are at a ten-year high. Shops like Pie and Vinyl in Southsea and

Rise in Bristol have realised that a shop maybe can't survive on music alone, but add pies, events and coffee and you can create a thriving new hub – a place to which bands will gravitate, where scenes will germinate and, years down the line, performers may tip their hat for inspiring or assisting them.

Shops like Dig in Liverpool and Rough Trade in Nottingham have opened fairly recently, bucking the trend, and there may be better times around the corner – young kids buy vinyl. Maybe it's Record Store Day, maybe it's some kind of cyclical retro thing, but whatever it is we need it to stick around.

So, a new book. They say write about what you know. And I know about collecting records. I may not know about writing about collecting records, but stick with me and we'll see.

*

I'd never really thought that writing *Telling Stories* had made me into an author. I read the reviews but I definitely didn't count myself alongside anyone else who'd written a book. I imagined other writers to be wearing a frown and a sun visor, hammering at a retro typewriter while knocking back bourbon, sweating in some unforgiving heat under a creaking ceiling fan. (Ironically, that might just be the most author-like thing I've ever written.) Although I had the sun visor, my method of writing was more like chewing on the end of a pencil and scribbling down the longest 'What I did in my summer holiday' essay ever. I'd heard that it'd be cathartic but that it could take over. I even heard advice like 'careful it doesn't start writing you' – I didn't know what that meant but it sounded like something real authors would fear. I felt like I'd got into some exclusive club, but perhaps only because someone had left the door open. Maybe Hunter S. Thompson had left it ajar while whacked out on mescaline. Anyway, I was in but I wasn't sure what to do. I checked and double checked and the reviews in *The Times* and the *Independent* both veered close to what good reviews seem to aim to be: glowing. Either that or I'd selectively read the glowing bits.

After the book came out I got asked to do some literary events. I knew about gigs and music stuff, but I'd kind of left the drink and the drugs behind, so maybe this was going to be my new life. I was imagining reciting chapters in an olde-worlde reading room, with polite ripples of applause at the end.

Onstage we were used to people cheering and losing their minds, or at least losing their trainers, while we performed, and I wasn't sure if the literary world was going to be for me. There's an old saying that giving up drink and drugs doesn't make you live longer, it just seems like it does. Various things had been dubbed the new rock 'n' roll but I was always happy with rock 'n' roll just being rock 'n' roll. But offers came in and old churches and small theatres were booked. I was interviewed in front of audiences by people who were part of the story – Dave Haslam, John Robb and John Niven. I would nervously read a few pages and hope my answers to their questions were entertaining enough. I found a couple of chapters that people seemed to like, and they got laughs or intakes of breath in the right places, which gave me more confidence – from the Isle of Wight Festival to Glastonbury to Aberdeen University via Paris. If this was a film, there'd be a montage bit now with an aeroplane and some photos of me by various city landmarks.

In August 2012 we played a gig at Edinburgh Picture House as part of our *Tellin' Stories* shows – our 1997 album, track by track, followed by an hour of singles and favourites. I'd invited Ian Rankin to the gig via a tweet, and he said he'd love to come along and that we should meet first; he could show me around Edinburgh a little. Now, Ian is the kind of person that is the ideal example of a real author. I bet he has a typewriter and a rickety fan.

We walked around Edinburgh and he told me that he organised events as part of the Edinburgh Literary Festival and that he'd like to invite me the following year. He would interview me in front of an audience. It was about then that I realised that even though I didn't see myself as an author, someone had, in fact, left the door open, and I had sneaked my way in. In some kind of turning of the turntables I invited Ian to DJ before our next Edinburgh gig at Usher Hall. He accepted and was suitably brilliant. You can often get defined by one thing, but it's always good to try something outside of your comfort zone.

*

Two days before I travelled to Edinburgh to meet Ian in 2013 we received the most tragic but, by then, not unexpected news that Jon Brookes, our drummer – a founding member of our band and our brother for the previous twenty-four years – had died. I was asked by *The Times* to write an obituary for him. I'd spent a couple of years writing about our couple of decades together, and I had half a broadsheet page to try to sum him up. Jon had written about his illness, and I'd included some of what he wrote in *Telling Stories*, as it was a first-hand account of what he was going through. Sadly, Jon's fighting spirit wasn't enough. This is his obituary:

I first met Jon Brookes when The Electric Crayons, the band I was in, supported his band, The Charlatans, at Northwich Vics club sometime early in 1989, or it may even have been late 1988. I knew then that he was one of the best drummers I'd ever seen; I saw him play only a few months ago and he was still one of the best I'd ever seen. The first time I spoke to him properly was at what turned out to be my audition to become the singer of The Charlatans, the band he had started with Martin Blunt. I shook his hand and he winced. 'I bust my hand breaking into Dudley Zoo last night. I climbed in with some mates for a party,' were his first words to me. With that, they started playing a song they'd been working on, Jon's drums sounding like 'Tomorrow Never Knows' by The Beatles driving an organ-fuelled garage monster – it sounded like it was going to take off. We called it 'Imperial 109', after a flying boat I'd read about. It became our opening song for the next three years.

It was the perfect introduction. Jon's lust for life shone through in everything he did – from that moment until the recording session Jon came to at the studio a few weeks ago. He spoke about a couple of songs he'd written for the band, and we were sharing ideas for our next album. The very last time I saw him was less than a week ago. We'd been told by his family that they believed Jon could have only a matter of hours before he'd slip away. Two days later, he sat up, asked if some-one could get him a bottle of Chardonnay and chatted with members of his family who had lovingly cared for him since he collapsed onstage in Philadelphia in 2010. But the recovery we all wished for was cut short when I got a call at 6 a.m. confirming that Jon had died at 2 a.m. on Tuesday 13 August.

Jon loved being in a band – he loved being a drummer. He loved being a West Brom fan. He loved being a dad. He was going out with Debbie when I first met him. I never even asked how long they'd been seeing each other – it just seemed like they belonged together. They married and had three beautiful children. They were together on the day Jon died. Watching his kids grow was taken away from him and they lost their dad. However we try and come to terms with what happens in life, the sadness of someone being taken from their family is tragic.

Jon's drums were loud. I always thought they sounded like they had a voice. I always knew his drumming, I'm not sure why – he had style. He was definitely one of the top three drummers of his generation. When hip hop sampled drummers it was John Bonham they went for. When the Chemical Brothers needed beats they called Jon Brookes. Jon just loved to play. Even after his diagnosis he was performing shows with Lew Lewis, the harmonica player who'd recorded with The Clash and The Stranglers. It's just what he did.

In the early days, Jon and I would do all the press interviews – my indie moodiness offset by his genuine love of communicating about our band. When we travelled together to Huntington Beach, LA, just for some interviews in 1990, we felt like the band had gone international. The Beach Boys we were not. The major thing we learnt was that we were definitely from Salford and West Bromwich. But there we were, somewhere we vaguely knew about because we'd seen it in films. We felt like chancers but we definitely wanted to be part of that world. When we came home I'd stay at Jon's. We'd drink in his local, The Village. His dad would come and join us for the last hour. He was so proud when we made it onto the jukebox in there; he'd sing along enthusiastically, seeming like the biggest Charlatans fan – which, he was happy to admit, he was.

Once we started recording, The Charlatans had the perfect start. Our debut album went to number one in the charts. Our second record, *Between 10th and 11th*, came in for a critical mauling, though. But it was Jon who picked up the mantle with the follow-up, *Up to Our Hips* – he'd picked up a copy of the Beastie Boys' third album, *Check Your Head*, from a hapless radio jock who had dismissed it as the bargain-bin fodder of a band past their prime. It was the soundtrack to our US tour in 1992, and we'd dance around the tour bus, mini Maglite torches in our mouths, Jon reminding us of why we'd all wanted to be in a band in the first place. Jon lived for gigs – we became less concerned about reactions to the records, and it definitely helped us as a band. He would arrive at practices telling us he'd sorted a gig in Brazil or Cyprus, anywhere hot – he was always trying to get us a show in Hawaii. Hawaii definitely suited Jon.

Rob Collins's death hit us all hard but it was Jon who was the driving force within the band to ensure that we carried on. We had the Knebworth gig planned and a decision had to be made. He was the first to say, 'We're definitely doing it.' It was a hugely emotional day and we knew we could rely on Jon. Behind his smile he was a rock-solid presence – exactly what you need when the going gets tough.

We travelled the world; we were a family. Members of the band started their own families, but the five of us were like brothers. We had varying degrees of success, but Jon was always undaunted. He was always excited about what we were doing next, just as he was about what we were doing right now. He was solid and reliable; it came through in his drumming as it came through in his character. He led from the back; his drum fills and splashy cymbals often took the lead. Everyone has their own stories of Jon – fans who he remembered at each gig, other bands who'd used his kit instead of having to lug theirs in. We got to work with musicians like Ronnie Wood and Johnny Marr, and Jon always impressed. When we were making *Wonderland* in LA in 2000, Jon had some down time, as we were recording vocals and guitars. Instead of grabbing a piña colada and sitting by the pool, Jon got a music magazine and booked himself some drumming lessons, which he'd diligently attend while *we* were drinking piña coladas by the pool. On the same album, we asked Jim Keltner to record some percussion for us – he was the session drummer favoured by three of The Beatles, along with Bob Dylan and Joni Mitchell. It was amazing to see Jon hold his own with such a legend. Jon was in his element. As brilliant a drummer as he was, he was always looking to improve.

As well as continuing to learn, Jon used the experience he'd gained in twenty-three years of putting out records and touring by setting up a record label, One Beat, and putting on gigs. He managed a couple of bands too. In December I played a solo gig in Birmingham and Jon came along. Duffy from Primal Scream was on keyboards and Mark from The Charlatans was on guitar. The four of us went out for a curry, like we would have done at any point in the previous two decades. I told Jon I was about to become a dad for the first time and we were expecting a boy. The last time I saw him was last week. He was in hospital recovering from a serious brain operation and was fighting his illness with everything he had. His first words as I went into his room were, 'Hey, Tim, how's your little boy?' He had the broadest smile I'd seen on anyone that week. He spoke about recording drums for our new album and his plans to go to the Hawthorns for the new season to watch West Brom.

*

So, Jon had gone and I was a dad. In some ways, the biggest events of my life had happened in the couple of years after *Telling Stories* rather than in the forty years before. We really wanted to do something special so that Jon's family and friends and fans of our band could get together – the funeral was celebratory rather than sombre and even had moments of humour. Jon's coffin was a classic flight case – a drummer to the end.

We were contacted by Simon Moran, who had put on our first gigs. He'd watched the band grow, and we'd seen his company become one of the best-respected concert promoters in the country. He asked if we would like some help putting on a gig, and we knew it was definitely what Jon would have wanted. While Jon was too unwell to play, Pete Salisbury had taken up drum duties for The Charlatans. Pete had been the drummer in The Verve since they formed in 1990, with extended breaks as the band split and came back together. We felt Jon willing us on with the whole project, and it was a sign to everyone that we planned to carry on.

Between us all we decided that the Royal Albert Hall was the most fitting venue – many of Jon's heroes had played there and it was like nowhere else. We knew it would have got his vote.

A date was set for 18 October, which gave us a few weeks to sort out a line-up. Liam Gallagher was the first to get in touch – he'd spoken to Bonehead and said we could count them in. It would be their first performance together since Bonehead left Oasis in 1999, and Liam's first public appearance since a big story had broken about him in the tabloids. He could have easily decided to stay away, but his love for Jon was such that later that evening I watched The Charlatans for only the second time without me as the singer. No disrespect to my predecessor, Baz Ketley, but I think Liam might have inched it.

The Chemical Brothers offered their DJing services. Stephen Morris, one of Jon's favourite drummers, said he would play. James Dean Bradfield volunteered, as did Gillian from New

Order, Winston Marshall from Mumford and Sons, and Freddie and Arni from The Vaccines. Between us, we played solo and formed super-groups for one night only.

Dumb were the first band on. Jon had been their manager. It was tragic circumstances for them to be playing the Royal Albert Hall, but they knew he'd have told them to make the most of the gig and to make sure they got a decent rider.

It was the definitely the kind of send-off Jon would have loved. One of the final songs was 'My Sweet Lord', his absolute favourite. Bonehead and Andy Bell played guitar, and Liam sang lead vocals. Watching from the side of the stage, I felt a sense of pride I had never felt before. I also felt like a fan watching an amazing band put on an incredible performance.

*

Myself, Martin, Mark and Tony met back up after New Year 2014. Big Mushroom, our studio in Cheshire, definitely felt different without Jon.

We had the first draft of what would become 'Emilie' and a nameless song that would end up being 'I Need You to Know'. Jim Spencer, our engineer, even had some drum loops and ideas that Jon had passed on to him to help get us started.

Jon had never written a complete song before, but we were handed a memory stick by one of his friends that contained a song he had not only written but recorded, with lyrics by Jon that his friend had transcribed while he was in hospital. The song was 'Walk with Me', and listening to it was the first step in the making of *Modern Nature*, our twelfth studio album. It was definitely a message that we were to get on with making another record. We included it as a bonus track on a special edition of the album, and it plays after we finish our live sets.

Jon's kit had been set back up in the living room of the studio.

A few days before he died, he had phoned Derrick, our drum tech, and said that he was feeling stronger and would be behind his kit pretty soon. Sadly, he didn't make it. Stephen Morris recorded some of the drums, as did Gabe Gurnsey from Factory Floor, with Pete playing on most of the tracks. But elements of what Jon had left behind made it onto a few songs too.

While all of this was going on I'd take myself off to a record shop and pick up some vinyl. I've always been a fan of a good old quest – Hercules, Jason and the Argonauts, Anneka Rice. Heroic expeditions. But I know my limitations, so rather than wielding a sword against one-eyed winged beasties I'd decided to go for vinyl; and instead of the quest being set by gods on Olympus I would get in touch with people I admired and ask them to suggest a record to look for on my travels, as I took in record shops from Istanbul to San Francisco. I love recommendations; they give you an insight into what makes someone tick. I wanted to discover the strands of musical DNA of people I looked up to, hung around with and owned the records of.

Also, it was a chance to find out where record shops were at – a kind of 'state of the nation'. There were new ones opening, vinyl sales were up, but still shops were closing. I wanted to meet some of the shop owners and see how they were doing. Every record-shop owner has a story to tell, and I wanted to spend some time travelling round and listening to them. I make records, buy records and love everything about vinyl – record shops are entwined in so many aspects of my life that I wanted to spend some time showing them some love! It would be a celebration of vinyl, which has been such an important part of my life since I first played one of my dad's records in 1972. Today, I listen to records with my son, and although he's only two I can see what he likes before he's even started to talk.

I figured that the first job was to assemble the cast whose nominations would augment my collection and tell their story, including Iggy Pop, Johnny Marr, Stephen Morris, Bill Bailey, Paul Weller, Bill Drummond and many more. But these recommendations would not be just for me: anyone would be able to track down some of these gems to fill in the gaps or reignite a love for vinyl; or they could simply be the reason for a satisfying road trip.

Texts, phone calls, emails and handwritten notes went out.

Here's the story of what came back.

The Durutti Column, *Vini Reilly*

Recommended by Tony Wilson

Vini vidi vici

Tony Wilson was an important figure in my life, from being on our TV at home to introducing The Charlatans with some glowing words when we played a TV special at Granada Studios in 1990. With the help of some nifty editing and a little bit of technology, it was the same Tony Wilson that introduced us onstage at our Castlefield Bowl show in Manchester in 2015, with the same words. It was a quarter of a mile from Granada Studios, and in a further nod to the studio our walk-on music for that show was the theme tune to *Coronation Street*.

Had he been around to talk to, I would have definitely gone to him for a recommendation. But the first time I ever met him he held me by both shoulders and told me *Vini Reilly* by The Durutti Column was a record I needed to own.

It was an album missing from my collection, but it hadn't been out long when he told me about it. Tony was always ahead of his time; it's kind of fitting that he kicked things off for this project way back sometime in 1989. He died in 2007, having left his mark on a generation and a legacy in Manchester that will last for ever. It is so hard to encapsulate what he accomplished – on his head-stone it says he was a broadcaster and a cultural catalyst.

Southern Cemetery has more connections with modern music than many cities. The 'cemetry gates' (*sic*) are where Morrissey went on a dreaded sunny day. Legendary producer Martin Hannett is buried there, a short walk from Rob Gretton's resting place – both men key characters in what was one of Manchester's most creative spells.

In keeping with Factory Records folklore, Tony's granite headstone, designed by Peter Saville and Ben Kelly, arrived three years after his funeral. On it is a quote from G. Linnaeus Banks's *The Manchester Man*, including the line 'People drop out of the history of a life as of a land, though their work or their influence remains.' Sir Matt Busby is buried near by. To a generation who were in their teens in the late 1970s and '80s, Tony Wilson's importance cannot be overstated, just as Sir Matt Busby meant so much to Manchester United fans in the 1950s and '60s.

I arrived at the graveyard in the early afternoon, but nothing had been arranged and I'd left everything to chance. Southern Cemetery is the biggest cemetery in the UK and I wasn't sure if I was going to be able to find Tony's plot. I was looking for a piece of granite based on the time-travelling slabs in *2001: A Space Odyssey*, somewhere among the thousands of angels, crosses and statues of the Virgin Mary. It's only fitting that Tony would have a headstone inspired by a sci-fi film.

They don't have guided tours, but I found a hut by the gates and, by chance, Pete, who had worked at the cemetery for over twenty years, came over. He asked if I was looking for anyone in particular, and we started on an impromptu tour. It was remarkably un-macabre, even though we passed a victim of the Moors murderers, gangsters who'd been gunned down, people mistaken for gangsters who'd been in the wrong place at the wrong time, and someone who'd even been murdered at the cemetery. There was also the man who'd started the construction of the Manchester Ship Canal, the aviator Captain John Alcock – but not Lieutenant Arthur Brown – and L. S. Lowry. Pete left me at the final resting place of Anthony H. Wilson and I stuck around for a short time. I was with my son and took some time to reminisce about when Tony had been a part of my life.

With The Durutti Column, Vini Reilly had recorded *A Paean to Wilson* in 2010. It was a bond between the two men. Where Vini was fragile, Wilson was robust. The first Durutti Column record that I'd listened to all the way through was *LC*. I was aware of the band as they were on Factory Records, a label I loved. Alan Erasmus, one of the directors at Factory, was a regular customer at the newsagent's where my mum worked. One day he left some albums after she'd mentioned that her sixteen-year-old son was a music fan, and *LC* was one of them. It was released in 1981 but I didn't get my copy until 1983.

The record opens with Bruce Mitchell's drumming – he was working with the band for the first time alongside mainstay Vini, a partnership that continues to this day. There was something so frail and delicate about the music, almost as delicate as Vini looked in photographs. The whole album has a beautiful simplicity, like sunshine glistening on water – songs about friends: 'Sketch for Dawn', 'Detail for Paul', 'Portrait for Frazier', 'Jacqueline and Danny'. 'The Missing Boy' is about Ian Curtis, Vini's friend who had died the year before. The music was so much subtler than everything I was listening to at the time – it was the sound of summer, the opposite of being punched in the head by clumsy rock music. There was a welcome gentleness that was missing from my other records. I bought every Durutti Column release after that, and in the years since you can hear the huge, often uncredited influence that Vini has had on guitarists and music in general. I found out recently that the title stands for *'lotta continua'* or continuous struggle. Given that Vini recently suffered a series of strokes that threatens his ability to play guitar, it adds a sense of sadness to the beauty.

John Coltrane, *A Love Supreme*

Recommended by Paul Weller

A youth club DJ

One of my first clear memories of a record that has had a lasting effect on me is: 'David Watts'/'A Bomb in Wardour Street' by The Jam.

It was summer 1978 and I bought it from Woolworths in Winsford. I was just about to start senior school and times were carefree. My dad helped out at a local youth club held in a church hall, and I tagged along on the strength of a promise that I could take the new record I wanted.

So, first up was a trip to Woolworths – a traditional handful of sweets from the pick 'n' mix as I headed to where the records were. When you were an eleven-year-old punk, stolen sweets were about as anarchic as it got, and I'm still not sure how anarchic it was, as I'd eaten the evidence by the time I'd got to the 7-inch singles.

My dad was waiting outside in his green Morris Marina, with my record player in the back. I left the shop with my copy of 'David Watts'/'A Bomb in Wardour Street' in hand – and a last scoop of sweets – and jumped in the passenger seat. I took the single out of the bag and inspected it for ten minutes or more. It had a picture sleeve – red and blue arrows, and a tiny passport-style photo of the band.

'Now, it's not punk music is it, Tim?' asked my dad.

'No, Dad, it's . . . melodic, a bit like that Buzzcocks one I played you, the one I thought sounded like The Beatles but you didn't.'

'Ever Fallen in Love . . .?' was the one that had divided our opinions.

'Punk then?' he said.

Things were a bit confusing back then as there wasn't a huge difference between The Jam and The Clash, but one band were mods while the others were punks. My dad's fear was that it would sound like 'Bodies' by the Sex Pistols, whose opening two lines were enough to bring music censorship to the Burgess household for the first and only time.

I'd only heard 'David Watts' twice but I could assure him there was nothing to worry about – I wasn't aware it was a Kinks cover, or even that it was Bruce Foxton rather than Paul Weller singing it. I just knew it was safe for the ears of the youth-club kids and the churchy types who were helping out.

I set up the record player, my Boots Audio 2000, and balanced the record on the centre rod, clicked over the automatic arm (the type where you could play a stack of singles one after the other) and flicked the switch to 'auto'. It dropped onto the turntable, with my dad looking at me with raised eyebrows. 'FaFaFaFaFa – FaFaFa' – definitely nothing offensive in that. He seemed happy enough and got on with putting out chairs.

The song finished and I flipped the record over. 'Where the streets are paved with blood, with cataclysmic overtones' – a perfect song about post-apocalyptic breakdown for a church hall on a Tuesday evening.

After forty-five minutes of playing one side and then the other my dad asked one of the older lads, Ian Cass, to go and find another record. He came back with *Black and White* by The Stranglers. It went to the top of my list of records I needed to buy.

Paul Weller recommends records to me fairly often, sometimes via text message, sometimes with me in a headlock backstage after a gig. I asked him for a specific recommendation above all recommendations, and his answer came almost immediately: *A Love Supreme* by John Coltrane. I hoped I could find it as quickly . . .

The Clash, *Sandinista!*

Recommended by Freddie Cowan

Cold water in the face

For this you have to imagine two parallel worlds: one with me now, and one with the thirteen-year-old me.

Whenever I get the chance, I will often check to see if someone owns *Sandinista!* It was a harder pill to swallow than some of the jacked-up single albums or the comparatively poppy *London Calling*. Lots of people had given up by then, and I find it's my job to point them in the right direction. I am not sure if everyone has an album they'd feel happy recommending, but generally I find that everyone has one that sits above all others, with no rules about coolness or rarity or classic status, and that record is a big clue as to how that person ticks. And for me, *Sandinista!* is it – that's my something.

I bought my first copy in 1980 from Northwich Woolworths, its glowing bright red sign like a sentinel watching over the precinct.

My latest was in 2015 from a shop that's moved around Manchester a few times before settling in its present home. Piccadilly Records currently sits comfortably on Oldham St. in Manchester's Northern Quarter. It's one of the first places I head to whenever I'm near the city. We've played there a few times, and I've got to know the staff over the years. I've bought some of my favourite records in there and their annual chart is one of the highlights of a crate-digger's year.

I'm not sure when the shop moved to Oldham St. but I can remember my first visit to the original site in 1979. I was twelve years old and had just started to get my record collection together.

A trip to town, Manchester city centre, was something that was becoming a more regular treat. Birthdays and Christmas meant that I'd be loaded down with anything up to £25, and this was when albums were around £3 each.

A trip could take all day. Yanks was a basement piled high with imports, corners cut off the sleeves and seemingly no rhyme or reason as to where anything was. A faint smell of 1970s sixth-former and patchouli oil added to the atmosphere. Spin Inn specialised in soul, as did Rare Records near by. It's almost impossible to think that so many independent and specialist record shops could not only survive but most weekends were also where everyone met, discussed music, formed bands, discovered new music and generally hung around. The underground market had Collector's Records, which always seemed to be full of new romantics and Roxy Music obsessives, their numbers offering them some safety from the more ruthless, less tolerant teen gangs at the time, who wandered around town seemingly looking for trouble. There was a Virgin and an HMV on Market St., and even a Woolworths, which meant a whole day could be taken up by looking at records. Not even really listening to them, but simply spending time near them.

Every couple of months a record fair would arrive in town, taking up residence in a nondescript exhibition space in Piccadilly Plaza – the futuristic, out-of-place, out-of-time concrete monolith that was the home of Piccadilly Radio, 261 medium wave, giant grinning profile shots of the DJs down one side of the tower that overlooked 1970s Manchester. There was something especially exciting about these fairs, as they came and went in a day; there was no time to mull over choices, and the legal and copyright concerns that affected the high-street shops seemed not to matter. There were boxes and boxes of professionally produced bootlegs with artwork often better than the real albums.

Piccadilly Records always had something more, though – it

was the place where you could buy tickets. It's hard to imagine now, but every single ticket was bought in physical form, racing into town on the Saturday when a tour had been announced via *Sounds*, the *NME* or *Melody Maker* on the Wednesday. Tickets were bought in the basement and records were on the ground floor. All those record shops and three weekly music magazines, plus a couple of fortnightly ones too. It was pure heaven for this kid living in Northwich, realising the potential that was out there in the world. Well, the potential of gigs and records at least.

*

Christmas 1980 was a watershed for me.

I'd dispensed with getting anything but money as presents from relatives. No games, no toys, no annuals – I'd just become a teenager and had revolution on my mind.

I'd been too young to buy any of the Clash albums on the day of release. By the time I got to own them they'd been out a while. I'd read the reviews, heard the opinions, and they came with a good deal of baggage. Every mate's older brother or sister seemed to own the first album, and I'd bought *Give 'Em Enough Rope* from Rumbelows maybe a year after it was released.

But I had caught up with them and *Sandinista!* was now. It had only come out in mid-December – the band had even set a price of £3.99. Joe Strummer was telling the high street what to do. It was a great time to be thirteen and falling in love with music.

At Glastonbury 2015, The Charlatans were the 'surprise' festival openers, and The Vaccines were playing on the same stage. It gave us a chance to catch up, and Freddie's recommendation was *Sandinista!*

One of the reasons I like The Vaccines so much is that they seem to share the gang spirit that made me love The Clash when I first heard them. Freddie's brother Tom plays keyboards for

The Horrors, who I've known for years, so Freddie and I were friends from before The Vaccines got together. The Vaccines' debut album was an irresistible beauty, and they were unafraid to follow it up with a sophomore record that revealed their more experimental influences.

In 2011 I started working with R. Stevie Moore – I'd loved his music for a number of years and tracked him down in Nashville, where I'd gone to record my second solo album. Freddie heard I was working with R. Stevie and got in touch to say The Vaccines were all big fans and wanted to help as much as they could to introduce him to a new audience.

Get ready for an R. Stevie Moore tangent. He's a tangential kind of guy, so it really fits.

I'd arrived in Nashville to do some writing with Lambchop leader Kurt Wagner in September 2011 – the songs that eventually became *Oh No I Love You*. We met up for coffee and exchanged ideas; I visited his house for dinner and spent time with his beloved dogs.

Nashville seems to have a different view of music than any other place on Earth. Some of the most emotional songs ever were written and recorded there, and music is regarded as being as fundamental as one of the elements. Everyone there has at least a fleeting connection to music; almost everyone plays an instrument, and more than a handful I met had played on hundreds of recordings and were the fourth generation in their family to do so.

In around 2003 I was at a party at Jason Falkner's house and he said he had an album that he thought I'd love. It always intrigues me when someone says that. There's some added pressure: it's maybe the worry that a friend hasn't got a clue about your taste in music or people or whatever they've been recommending. Jason had been in Jellyfish and his band before that, The Three O'Clock, had been signed to Prince's label. We'd met over a shared love of alcohol a few weeks before at Bar Marmont,

27

and had become friends through a shared love of Air, the same jokes and coffee.

So, anyway, he brought in the album *Everything You Wanted to Know about R. Stevie Moore but Were Afraid to Ask*.

He was right. I loved it.

Fast-forward to 2011, and I'm standing in Grimey's, a record shop in Nashville, with an R. Stevie Moore compilation, *Phonography*, in my hand. It was $14 on vinyl and may even have been dropped off by the man himself. I knew he lived in Tennessee but wasn't sure of much more. Rumour has it that he's recorded over 400 albums. What is certain, though, is that his dad played bass for Elvis Presley, Johnny Cash and Roy Orbison. I'd built up a modest collection since Jason had recommended him, and I'd started wondering if I could track him down. Someone told me that he lived in a placed called Madison. I asked Kurt Wagner if he'd come across R. Stevie Moore at all, and he said he was a legendary, if not slightly mythical, figure. Perhaps surprisingly for a sixty-year-old, I found that Stevie had a Facebook account and was as prolific on social media as he was in the recording studio. I sent him a message saying I was a big fan and that perhaps at some point we could work together on something. I got a reply and immediately knew he was someone I should be involved with. His enthusiasm was amazing. He knew of The Charlatans and even asked if I lived anywhere near Macclesfield, where Joy Division were from. He was a big fan of The Durutti Column and told me he'd written a song about Vini Reilly. R. Stevie wrote in a form of jazzy scatty hip speak that I loved. Like a beat poet with a few words seemingly borrowed from a Valley Girl text message.

Phonography had become an instant favourite with me, and the more songs I heard, the more I realised what a genius he was. Everything was done at home before home studios were a thing; everything recorded on tape; Brian Wilson-style harmonies,

McCartney-esque pop sensibilities and Frank Zappa levels of out-there freakiness.

We arranged to meet for pizza. His styling was of a wizardly Father Christmas, and the beat poetry was delivered in a table-shaking baritone. The speed at which he recorded was matched by the speed of his ideas – we should work on some songs, he'd allow me to put out a *Best of . . .* on my label, O Genesis Recordings. He was coming over to the UK to perform some shows, and he asked if I would sing backing vocals and play percussion when we were in the same town. Of course, I jumped at the chance.

By the following Record Store Day, we had a split 7-inch single to release: The Vaccines covering R. Stevie Moore on one side, and R. Stevie performing 'Post Break-Up Sex' on the other. It was a kind of transatlantic lo-fi heaven.

R. Stevie Moore interlude over.

*

The Vaccines had lost a good friend when Charlie Haddon from Ou Est Le Swimming Pool tragically died at a music festival in August 2010. Freddie organised a benefit gig on the anniversary and asked me to play. I practised some songs with Finn and David from Hatcham Social, and we played on a bill with The Horrors and The Vaccines. The next time The Vaccines and I shared a stage was under sad circumstances too: it was our night for Jon Brookes at the Royal Albert Hall. Then came Glastonbury, and later in the summer they swung by the Tim Peaks Diner at the Kendal Calling festival to play some records before headlining there on the main stage.

Freddie's message accompanying his recommendation explained what *Sandinista!* meant to him:

I fell in love with the spread of this record, almost like The Clash's version of the *White Album*.

Sandinista! sounds like the band at the height of their creative powers, taking away all restrictions and embracing full abandon. On 'Ivan Meets GI Joe', the use of the arcade games soundtrack is such an open addition. It sounds like this was the most fun for The Clash to make. Maybe that's why it's so easy to be a fan of. My personal favourite track is 'Charlie Don't Surf'. Far out and close moments, six sides' worth. Very special.

The first song that caught my ears on *Sandinista!* was 'Ivan Meets GI Joe'. A couple of Christmases before, I'd have been getting an Action Man, and here was one of my favourite bands with a catchy number about the superpower Mexican stand-off that was dominating the world at the time.

Like most of the kids I knew, I learnt about politics from songs: Chappaquiddick bridge, Liddle Towers, Steve Biko, Bobby Sands and Sun City were all subjects I first came across on records. Included with *Sandinista!* were lyric sheets featuring cartoons that made it pretty plain where the band stood politically. Even the name *Sandinista!* was a pre-Google invitation to look deeper. The catalogue number of the album was FSLN1, after the acronym used by the Nicaraguan revolutionaries. And everyone seems to think that 1980s music was about hairspray and synthesizers. This was The Clash, and they meant it, man!

'Something about England' was a Mick Jones masterpiece. As was 'Police on My Back' – on investigation I found out that Eddy Grant had written and recorded it in his days with The Equals. They sang other people's songs and even had other people singing songs on their album, with Tymon Dogg weighing in on 'Lose This Skin'. It was the first album I'd ever heard that had absolutely no rules.

A group of children singing one of the band's songs from a different album? Sure, why not?

Alternative versions of tracks on one of the other five sides? Of course.

I think I learnt more about US foreign policy from 'Washington Bullets' than anything I ever picked up at school. I'd heard about Charles Manson, the stand-in for Davy Jones of The Monkees, the unhinged guy that used to hang around with The Beach Boys. I'd heard about *Apocalypse Now* from older kids at school. 'Charlie Don't Surf' just stopped me dead. Even when I listen now I can remember exactly how it affected me over thirty years ago.

These songs were changing me as I was listening to them. I had to keep starting over to keep up.

Ring, ring, it's 7 a.m. Yep, second time through 'Magnificent Seven' is imperious, the green shoots of hip hop vying with the none-more-punk stance. 'Hitsville UK' was a declaration letting us know that the new Motown was being born somewhere closer to home – a homage to Postcard, Small Wonder, Factory, Rough Trade and the burgeoning independent-label scene, coming from a band who were trying to boss their major label.

My favourite tracks are 'Lightning Strikes (Not Once but Twice)' and 'Up in Heaven (Not Only Here)' – both next to each other and both different slants on 'Magnificent Seven' and 'Hitsville UK'. It's brilliant sequencing because that far in, when you listen to the whole thing, they come at you like a breath of fresh air, and it strikes you that these songs sound like The Clash you grew up loving so much.

So, you can no longer buy records in chemists' or TV-hire shops, but Piccadilly Plaza still stands overlooking Manchester – although there are no 1970s DJs grinning from the tower. But somewhere only a stone's throw away a kid will be in Piccadilly Records buying an album that'll change their life.

Van der Graaf Generator, *H to He, Who Am the Only One*

Recommended by Bill Drummond

Nothing like Hawkwind

There's a name that first crops up in the story of pop music sometime in 1977 and stays around in various forms for over two decades, taking in situationism, production, band management, chart-topping singles and albums, and some of the best dance records ever made. Bill Drummond might well be closer to Andy Warhol than anyone else in terms of the role he has had in guiding bands and making spectacular art, but he has also made genre-defining albums, as well as publishing a book offering to help anyone get a record to No. 1.

I'd emailed him in 2012, kind of out of the blue, and asked him what he was up to. I suggested that if he had anything he wanted to release on the label I'd started, then I'd be honoured to work with him. I got a most gracious and friendly reply, but he said he was involved in a project that would be taking up his time for the foreseeable future. That was it. He wished me luck and I heard no more. This is a man who owns a tower, a place where artists can apply to stay in order to create their work. His project The17 was based around soup and humming. He had burnt a million pounds. For me there's nobody like him, and just to receive his email was enough. Then, maybe eighteen months later, I saw that he was setting up an exhibition at a gallery in Birmingham. This was the one he had mentioned. I tried to find out some more. He'd be arriving on a raft that was made out of a bed. He'd be carrying daffodils. It was part of a twelve-year world tour where shoes would be shined, cakes made and a million-stitch blanket would be completed, with visitors being invited to learn to knit. I asked if he'd mind if I came and spent some time at the exhibition, and he said that sounded like a good idea. I arrived with my son in a pushchair – I got the feeling that Bill was a family man. He built beds. He told tales. He arrived at the gallery with his toddler in tow and the youngsters checked each other out as Bill offered me some of his homemade marmalade, spread generously on some toast. I spent time watching videos of Bill telling stories, from taking an unconscious eel home on the bus as a young kid to a disturbing rite of passage he went through as an apprentice on a trawler. He showed me how to knit and I contributed some stitches to his blanket. We went to a nearby cafe for lunch. His passion and drive and love of making art out of what other people might overlook make for such an endearing person – alongside his genius is a love of his surroundings and those he meets. We talked about droplifting books in charity shops. He told me of his adventures managing the Teardrop Explodes and Echo & the Bunnymen. There'd been studios we'd both worked in but a few years apart. I asked him about the final ten copies of *1987*, the album by The JAMs. It was said that they had advertised them for £1,000 each in *The Face*. When asked how many they'd sold, the band had replied, 'Twenty.' Bill laughed at the story but was unsure what was true and what they'd made up at the time.

I was intrigued to know what kind of music Bill listened to, so I asked him to recommend an album. He'd emailed me by the time I'd arrived home: *H to He, Who Am the Only One* by Van der Graaf Generator was his offering.

I'd definitely heard of them but they were never a band that were properly on my radar. I, perhaps foolishly in hindsight, replied that I'd heard of them and 'Were they a bit Hawkwindy?'

Bill put me right on the subject.

'Nothing like Hawkwind, Tim. Nothing like Hawkwind at all. Peter Hammill, the singer and author of their output, was about as intense a songwriter as you can get. That said, I never had any idea what he was on about.'

The album came out in 1970, when Bill was seventeen, and seventeen is an important age for big albums. It was the sound of the dawn of electronic music creeping towards the mainstream, where anything was possible.

The record still sounds oddly futuristic and the intensity hits you from the start. It's the kind of album that never made it past punk's year zero, so its existence was denied when I started to buy records. It's almost a relic, but listening now it's clear they have definitely influenced bands as varied as Muse and The Flaming Lips. Peter Hammill's intensity has lost none of its power, but I'm sure I can hear some Hawkwind in there somewhere.

Echo & the Bunnymen, *Porcupine*

Recommended by Ian McCulloch

Rockie's and Rockfield

So this is one of the records I discussed with Bill Drummond. We had talked about Rockfield Studios for a while, where some of *Porcupine* was recorded. I used to own the album but didn't know whether I still had it. I certainly didn't have it on white vinyl – a Record Store Day release.

I had been trying to find a record shop called Rockie's in Sheffield. Tom Sheehan, who photographed us for the cover of *Tellin' Stories*, had taken me there sometime around 1996. I have vague recollections of a hill. And an afternoon spent in the pub. As it turned out, the day in the pub made the hill seem bigger.

My guide to Sheffield vinyl was Pete McKee, an artist who's worked with Richard Hawley and the Arctic Monkeys, and is as Sheffield as a stainless-steel bottle of Henderson's Relish. We met at his gallery and I mentioned I'd bought *Blah Blah Blah* by Iggy Pop. We bonded over an appreciation of the little-known masterpiece 'Shades' that's tucked away on the first side.

I left with a list of shops, but there was no Rockie's. I guessed it must have closed down. The first was Record Collector. The CDs were banished to a shop next door; the half I was in was vinyl only. There was a John Carpenter soundtrack playing as I went in and I nodded my approval at the guy behind the counter. 'If you like that,' he said, 'just wait till you hear this,' and he took out the soundtrack to a film called *Profondo Rosso* by a group called Goblin.

'It's an Italian horror classic. The band all fell out with each other, so there are two versions with the same name touring around, trying to avoid each other.'

I asked him if they had any Van der Graaf Generator, but they didn't.

The shop felt familiar, but I always kind of feel at home in record shops; they can be very much alike – boxes of vinyl, posters, maybe some sew-on patches.

'You've been in here before,' the guy behind the counter told me. He must have seen me looking puzzled, trying to work it out. 'You were with Tom Sheehan, who used to live near by.' I asked if the shop used to be called Rockie's, and he explained that was Tom's nickname for the owner.

The soundtrack was hitting its stride. I don't know much about Italian horror films but the one name I do know was on the cover: Dario Argento had directed it. Last year, I recorded a duet with his daughter, Asia, who is also a film director, as well as a singer. That's one of the reasons I love record shops so much – whether you record music or not, or just go to gigs or shop for records, you can have an in-depth conversation concerning Italian horror films with someone you don't know. That's why record shops work so well for blokes. You can talk about sleeve designers, catalogue numbers or long-dead bass players without touching on feelings or emotions. It's not necessarily a good thing but it's definitely a thing.

Echo & the Bunnymen played as our special guests recently and, as ever, Mac introduced 'The Killing Moon' as 'the greatest song ever written'. So it wasn't really a surprise when he chose *Porcupine*, one of his own records, as his recommendation.

Joy Division, *Unknown Pleasures*
Recommended by Ian Rankin

In Stephen's shop

Glasgow, and Scotland in general, has always played a big part in the Charlatans' story. There was something about not just us but the whole Manchester scene that struck a chord which rings strongly to this day. Every gig we play at Barrowlands reminds us of this, and every visit to Scotland adds to the story. My trip on this occasion centred around two DJ sets, one in Edinburgh and one in Glasgow, for a night called 'Madchester'. I'm on the poster sitting in a psychedelic van with Morrissey, Shaun Ryder and Ian Brown. We're wearing *Sgt Pepper* outfits. I never checked, but either it was a photo taken while I was drinking and taking drugs or I'm thinking maybe it was Photoshopped. The gig had sold out – the force is strong up there for Paris Angels, World of Twist and Intastella. It was the first time I'd played any of these in a long time, but they've held up well.

I was constantly being told about Stephen Pastel's record shop, Monorail. Some considered it the best in Britain, others the best in the world, but I had somehow never made it along. I hopped in a cab outside Central Station, and the first stop was a piece of public artwork by Jim Lambie commemorating bands that had played at the Barrowland Ballroom – a pathway like a shelf of albums, band names on the spine, from Goodbye Mr Mackenzie to Prefab Sprout and the Manic Street Preachers. We were on there a few times too. The setting was where a derelict building had stood for years, slowly falling apart. It's now a park that celebrates the impression that bands and gigs have left on Glasgow.

The taxi driver had waited, and as we headed off to the record

37

shop we talked about music. I mentioned this book, and he told me about gigs he'd been to at the Glasgow Apollo – Bowie, Bob Marley and Slade – and how Alex Harvey was one of the best but most underrated Scottish artists. He still collected vinyl – he said he loved the fact that a 12-inch album cover was the ideal size for rolling a joint. People wanted different formats and different drugs. It just so happened that a CD case had the ideal dimensions for chopping, dividing and snorting cocaine. I thought back to my CDs scarred by nights of excess – that some might still give a positive drugs test. My copy of Talk Talk's *Spirit of Eden* probably saw as much cocaine as a Viper Room cistern lid in its heyday. Neither myself nor the taxi driver could figure out what relevance this had to anything or what future drug an MP3 could be used for, but we both agreed it had to be written down. For me, the CD years were also the cocaine years; they both faded away with each other.

Monorail is almost like a blueprint for record shops of the future: a coffee shop, what looks like a publisher and a bar, with the vinyl (and CDs – both new and used) in its own room, all overseen by musical genius Stephen Pastel. It was here that I found Ian Rankin's recommendation, *Unknown Pleasures*. A Warner Brothers reissue, I thought it had been put together with loving care, but when I spoke to Stephen Morris about it he was a little more ambivalent.

Hawkwind, *In Search of Space*

Recommended by Stephen Morris

Space is the place

I was ten years old for the first five months of 1977 and eleven for the rest. I was old enough to be aware that punk arrived with a scorched-earth policy, and that all the decks were being cleared. The records that appealed to me the most were by the likes of The Vibrators, Sham 69, UK Subs and The Jam. My interest was in overthrowing things – systems that I didn't understand and *King Arthur on Ice*, talk of mind expansion and guitar solos that went on longer than a Ramones single had been out.

It meant that many bands stayed off my radar until my punk invective had settled a little.

A fourteen-year-old Stephen Morris was being as rebellious in 1972 as I was trying to be a few years later. 17 March 1972. Free Trade Hall, Manchester. Within four years, Peter Hook and Bernard Sumner would be watching the Sex Pistols in the same venue alongside Tony Wilson, at the start of one of the most exciting chapters in Manchester's music history.

'My dad would do a deal with us – we would go to see people like Duke Ellington and then we would all go and see someone of my choice,' says Stephen. 'We went as a family. Yep – me, my mum, dad and sister. There was a topless dancer and a whiff of marijuana, neither of which featured at the Duke Ellington show nor in my parents' idea of what sort of place we should be spending family time. They were dressed like they were going to a meeting at the Masonic Hall. We definitely didn't fit in, but it meant I got to watch Hawkwind.'

There were definitely elements of prog informing the early

days of The Charlatans and the scene known as 'baggy' – we loved Pink Floyd's light shows and Brian Auger's keyboard work. Ecstasy was the musical drug of choice at the time; acid house had just taken over the Manchester clubs, and a wig-out to a Hammond-organ jam and some oil wheels was the order of the day.

Following the release of 'The Only One I Know', we used our own lighting guy when we played live. He went by the name of Captain Whizzo and he stayed with us till the end of the Japanese leg of the *Some Friendly* tour. He'd never left the US before. From what we could gather, he lived in a tree house in San Francisco.

Our manager had found him at the CMJ festival in New York and asked him to come and work with us. He'd done visuals for The Grateful Dead, The Band and The Who at Monterey. We were in the most authentic hands possible – there was a danger you'd go on an acid trip just through osmosis. He was a master of his craft, and before each gig would be stockpiling a dozen bottles of Vaseline and baby oil, which he used for his freaky visuals, much to the confusion and consternation of the Boots cashier in Blackburn or wherever we were playing that night.

Within Hawkwind there was a kind of spiritual handing on of the baton from prog to punk. Lemmy was their bass player for a while before joining The Damned and ending up with the best of both worlds in Motörhead. Barney Bubbles designed sleeves for both Hawkwind and The Damned too. There's also a krautrock seam that runs from Hawkwind to Joy Division via Stephen's drumming. Hawkwind's *Masters of the Universe* has elements of the Joy Division sound.

It's fair to say that Stephen has helped me and The Charlatans as much as anyone, from playing on *Modern Nature* to joining us onstage. He and Gillian Gilbert are two of my musical heroes, and Stephen was insistent that I took in the full glory of *In Search of Space*.

I was as guilty as anyone of having preconceived ideas regarding Hawkwind. My first thoughts were of Lemmy. Second thought: *Warrior on the Edge of Time* – elaborate fold-out sleeve in the shape of a full-size shield. To a fourteen-year-old kid it must have been the best thing ever, and I have to say that I remember the effect seeing it in my Uncle Andrew's collection in 1977 had on me.

Only 'We Took the Wrong Step Years Ago' sounds like I imagined Hawkwind would – Middle Earth wizards that I'd put in the same bracket as Jethro Tull and Tolkien. The rest of the album is equally out there, but in a funky, driving kind of way. Like a Cylon disco.

*

When I started going to see bands play live, it was like entering some kind of portal into the most amazing world possible. Before that it was war films and *Starsky and Hutch* or *The Professionals* that thrilled me, but they were scripted and took place on TV. Gigs had all the excitement of those, but with the added extra that I was actually there, in amongst it all, and with a sense that anything could happen.

I'd seen the names of venues like The Gallery and listings of what was happening at Manchester Polytechnic, and suddenly I'd become a part of it. There was often a threat of violence in the air, but only for those who were looking for it. I always felt strangely safe – like those involved were happy to keep it between themselves. I was maybe fourteen or fifteen and only interested in watching the bands, but slightly older kids would hang around in gangs, keeping an eye out for anyone else looking for trouble. Whenever anything happened, it always seemed a bit like a scene from *West Side Story* – taunts and mates holding each other back, with some exaggerated nods and mutterings.

Over the years, the same faces would be at the same shows – shared tastes and favourite venues meant you would recognise people even if you didn't know them. Jon the Postman was at almost every gig I went to – and I imagine he was at a lot more that I couldn't get to, as well. Big Alex, as we knew him, also seemed to be there watching every band I liked. More often than not he'd be bootlegging the gig. That's how he got to know most of the bands, who would put him on their guest list.

When The Charlatans started playing regularly in Manchester, I was relieved to see those same faces in our crowd. Before long, Big Alex was bootlegging our gigs and on our guest list.

People like Big Alex and Jon the Postman are hugely important characters in determining how live music can take off in a town or city. Pre-Internet, they were a kind of human social media, reading up on bands in the *NME*, *Melody Maker* and *Sounds*, then spreading the word about who people should be watching like some kind of living, breathing music blog.

The world of social media has meant that bands and fans have been brought closer together. I know this as I have a foot in both camps. People who like our music might tweet me and let me know what they thought of a gig or a particular record, and it's great to have that conversation. But I'm a fan too, and I'll often tweet about bands that I like. This can lead to all sorts of opportunities, with support slots and people coming to play with us. Years ago, handily enough, when I'd often be found in the nearest bar before a show, this kind of thing was often done over a game of pool, and I'd talk to Charlatans fans about the times we shared and the songs we loved.

*

I'd played a few gigs in Bristol and been to see a few bands there too. Each time, I would see the same beaming face in the crowd:

the unmistakable figure of Big Jeff Johns – taller, smilier and with more festival wristbands than anyone in the room. The room counts for the smilier and taller part, but the festival wristbands bit is more than anyone I've ever come across.

Having Big Jeff at your gig is a badge of honour. He has great taste in music and most bands put him on the guest list and invite him along. He's always down the front, more often than not dancing, and without doubt he makes the world a better place. Since I first met him, we've talked about music, festivals, bands and good times. Jeff hasn't had a charmed life thrust into his hands – anything but. But he found that music gave him something he couldn't get from anywhere else. To be a part of the world that provides this for Jeff is something that can hardly be put into words. He sent me a poem he'd written, which explained things from his point of view, and it made me think of when I first starting watching bands – the way I was taken to another world that only existed once that ticket got handed in and you made your way towards the stage.

It's meant that whenever we play in Bristol, we have an added element to the show too – those are the things that really mark one gig out from another. Jeff's always been representative to me of each individual person when we play live. It's easy to think of playing the night before, and the night after too, but, for those people in the room at that time, it's a unique moment. Whether it's thirty or 30,000 people, it's a chance for everyone to connect and something amazing to happen.

Every town and city has people I look forward to seeing at the show, but fewer have a record shop to visit. But whenever I think of Bristol and Big Jeff Johns, my next thought is Rise Records – a brilliant example of a shop that keeps on moving to ensure not only its survival, but that it keeps up with some of the best record shops in the country.

We played a gig on the *Thekla*, a converted cargo ship moored in the harbour, when *Oh No I Love You* came out, and we were invited along to Rise, in the centre of the city, to play a few songs. They'd realised that it took more than selling vinyl, CDs and headphones to keep going, so they'd added a deli, got themselves a coffee machine and invited bands to come and play. It all fits perfectly with the time between the soundcheck for a gig and the performance, and it means that people who can't make it to the show, haven't got spare money for a ticket or maybe aren't old enough to get in can come and enjoy a short performance.

So Rise was where I headed on the day The Charlatans played at the Bristol Academy – my wants and needs list firmly in my hand. That day's purchase was the recommendation I'd got from Boy George: unsurprisingly, a masterpiece from a New York original via Cologne by way of Salford chanteuse, androgynous and captivating. In some ways, it was the perfect album for George to recommend.

Nico, *Chelsea Girl*

Recommended by Boy George

Fairest of the season

It takes one to know one. One what to know who, though? In Boy George and Nico's case, there are similarities running right through their lives, from androgyny to drug difficulties and the individuality that was both their muse and their tormentor.

I'd been asked by Culture Club's producer Steve Levine to take part in a gig in Liverpool that he was putting together around a headline performance by Boy George – musicians collaborating with each other for an evening. He'd drafted in Mark King, Bernard Butler, me and Mark Collins, and a couple of up-and-coming singers, Hollie Cook and Natalie McCool. Steve had produced Culture Club's world-straddling hits, such as 'Karma Chameleon' and 'Do You Really Want to Hurt Me?' It was great to see him and George working together again.

We'd not been due to perform together, but we both thought we should, so George and I sat down to work out a song. We threw some ideas around, but we decided it had to be Lou Reed and settled on 'Satellite of Love'. And after one run-through we hit the stage.

We were both big fans of The Velvet Underground, so when I asked him for a recommendation I was pleased he suggested Nico. It's not hard to picture a younger George listening to *Chelsea Girl* and plotting the plans that would see him become famous – and infamous – worldwide.

Boy George first came to my attention in summer 1982. Culture Club seemed to arrive out of nowhere – well, nowhere to a fourteen-year-old kid in Moulton, Cheshire. Maybe to those who frequented Blitz or the underground club scene in London Culture Club had already started to make waves, as George was so striking.

Little captions in big magazines were enough to get people to look twice. Dads would tut, turn over the page, then turn back and shout, 'Have you seen this?!' getting hot under the collar about how someone could even look like he did. The red tops' music sections were reminders of how dull everything had become in pop music since the demise of the Sex Pistols. From where I was looking, only Bow Wow Wow and Adam Ant put any kind of colour into the charts, and although I positively identified with punk at fourteen, I had a watchful eye and very keen interest in all things mainstream. George's striking image made me think of the power Bowie in all his pomp had a generation before.

Culture Club were going to be performing their new single, 'Do You Really Want to Hurt Me?' on *Top of the Pops*. They sometimes used to let you know in the Sunday papers who was going to be causing a controversy on the show the following Thursday. Boy George had a fantastic sense of the subversive, as penetrating as Rotten's hatred of all things Establishment, but he was as glamorous as Debbie Harry – a no-holds-barred, right-between-the-eyes pop star, doing everything a pop star should do.

I liked Adam Ant; I loved Boy George a little bit more, and I smiled at all the hype.

The music world was very excited about this next level of androgyny and it seemed to spiral, with tabloid spats between Pete Burns and George. Who came first with the dreads and the make-up? George's reply to Pete was that 'It wasn't who did it first, but who did it best.' Like an alien landing on *Top of the Pops* on a Thursday in early autumn 1982, he knocked the pop world off its axis.

I remember a girl from school, Sarah Marsh, arriving dressed as Boy George at the end-of-term school disco, where she mimed

'Karma Chameleon'. She'd perfected the moves, the ribbons in her hair, the make-up – all over the world, young girls and boys were identifying with their new-found rebel leader.

Next would be *Wogan*, mainstream TV on which George talked about sex and cups of tea, with grannies falling for his beautiful charm and wit – wit that almost certainly would have protected him on the mean streets of Liverpool when he was growing up.

Then came the riches, the interviews, the fall-outs, the penthouses, the break-ups, the drugs, the handcuffs, the radiators and just about everything else – all forming one of the biggest pop soap operas in decades. We heard from his worried mum, whose own autobiography revealed years of abuse and mental torture from George's father, with whom she had five kids. George's mother's strength and guts famously helped him battle his drug demons and generally helped keep the family together through all the mad circumstances.

I had always wanted to meet him. I had read in *Smash Hits* in 1990 that he maybe fancied me a bit. I thought he was cool. I saw him walking in Soho once in the 1990s. He had a Krishna symbol on his head, adding another texture to his ever-increasing layers of life fabric. He was a DJ then and playing in big clubs. Anyway, I smiled but he didn't notice.

When I asked for his recommendation before the gig in Liverpool, and he answered *Chelsea Girls*, it made so much sense.

'It reminded me of Marlene Dietrich in vocal tone, but spoke of a world unknown,' George told me. 'My mum said, "That's not singing." But I love Nico's voice. She has a storyteller's voice!'

I have always kind of identified with George, having climbed from the unknown to giddy heights, and with drugs to fall back on to soften the landing. And I have had friends who obsessed over Nico. Someone I know used to do heroin while gazing up at a poster of this enigmatic chanteuse. (Another friend of mine who really liked heroin loved Keith Richards and Johnny Thunders.

I think it made him feel more like them. Is that something that happens with drug-takers and heroes? I know when I was doing drugs I gravitated to music that was made by people who did a lot of the same things I was doing.)

I was happy to sign to Beggars Banquet in 1990 mostly because The Fall were with them, but the fact that Nico, too, was part of the roster was a deal-maker for me.

This record is a decent yardstick to use if you're ever going to be friends with someone. If they don't like it, maybe don't bother.

Big Youth, *Dread Locks Dread*
Recommended by Andrew Weatherall

A smoothie with Bobby G

Flashback Records has always provided a safe haven for me. One step from the bustling Essex Road, it throws its arms around you and takes you in. Gone are the hassles of the outside world and the biggest questions become: should I buy this 1970s road-movie soundtrack or the Not Not Fun compilation I'd bought a few times but lent out? It was an east London oasis for me. I loved the walk from Old Street roundabout, up through Angel and Upper Street, and along to the inconspicuous shop front, where you're greeted by bargains outside. Inside, to the right, sit the new arrivals, and downstairs is the biggest treat of all: the singles. There's a coffee shop next door, so when the desire for crate-digging dips, you can get jacked up with caffeine and get stuck in where you left off.

There's a kind of synergy to many of the records in this book and where they were bought. I like a bit of world order, so I'm not sure if it's just me looking for coincidences but the record I picked up one day was the recommendation of Andrew Weatherall – ace remixer and producer, Sabre of Paradise, one of Two Lone Swordsmen and the name behind a huge chunk of records that never left my turntable for a long period of time in the dim-but-not-too-distant past. The coincidence was that the previous time I was in Flashback I had run into Bobby Gillespie himself – had it been ten years before, God only knows what would have happened to the rest of our day. But I have to admit, dear reader, that we went for a smoothie.

Andrew Weatherall's name was linked and inked indelibly on

Screamadelica, and in particular on 'Loaded' – his reworking of Primal Scream's 'I'm Losing More Than I'll Ever Have'. I was intrigued by what his recommendation would be, as his taste in music is about as eclectic as it gets. We share a love of a lot of the same bands and would regularly run into each other at gigs and club nights. I've also seen him take on a two-hour DJ set with records only released between 1950 and 1960. Anyway, his choice was a record I've never owned and knew little about – Big Youth's 1975 album *Dread Locks Dread*.

I first heard of Big Youth just after the Sex Pistols broke up. John Lydon took off to Jamaica in 1978 to scout for Virgin's reggae label, Front Line. Punk and reggae had always fitted well together, both appreciating the outsider nature of the other. Post-punk took much from reggae, and Lydon was something of an expert. Richard Branson saw he was at a loose end and sent him as a kind of envoy. I remember Big Youth being on the list that Lydon drew up while he was there – also on the list was Errol Dunkley, Sons of Jah, Pablo All Stars and Joshua Moses.

The reggae section of my record collection was fairly sparse. When The Charlatans signed to Sanctuary sometime in 2005, we were given the entire Trojan back catalogue on CD – everything from dubbed-out tributes to Bob Dylan, the Trojan Christmas three-CD set, Gregory Isaacs and Augustus Pablo to dancehall compilations. (One of the advantages of signing to a label is that you get to rifle through their back catalogue. At Beggars Banquet, it was The Fall, Cocteau Twins, The Cult, Throwing Muses and Bauhaus. At MCA, we were given the entire Chess back catalogue – Chuck Berry, Etta James, Sugar Pie DeSanto.) I had cassettes of Lee 'Scratch' Perry that friends had made, and we recorded poor-quality tape-to-tape versions of compilations that a mate's dad had brought back from a trip to Jamaica.

Clubs like the Haçienda and their lasting legacy on the Manchester music scene have been well documented, but pretty much at the same time we would spend regular nights at the PSV Club in Hulme – coincidentally, it was the building where Tony Wilson, Alan Erasmus and Peter Saville put on their Factory nights when it was the Russell Club. After they decamped to the Haçienda, it reverted to being a Caribbean club, the older guys listening to dub and reggae upstairs while playing dominoes, with the edgier, younger kids downstairs offering an alternative to the wave of house music that was taking over Manchester. That's where I first heard Big Youth's *Screaming Target* – a patchwork of dub, ska and dancehall.

And now, thanks to Andrew Weatherall, I finally owned a Big Youth album.

Holy Modal Rounders, *The Moray Eels Eat the Holy Modal Rounders*

Recommended by Irmin Schmidt

There's nowhere quite like Deauville

Lots of bands influence those that come later. Led Zeppelin echoed through the new wave of British heavy metal in the early 1980s; Kraftwerk guided the sound of synth pop via Heaven 17 and The Human League. But sometimes it can be just one song that provides the sonic mother lode for future musicians.

One such song is 'Halleluwah' by Can. It was a track that I first heard in 1985, and from there I grabbed *Tago Mago*, *Future Days* and *Ege Bamyasi*. They came from a different direction, with endless jams – repetitive, meditative and almost trance-like. The groove from 'Halleluwah' pretty much set up the Madchester sound. Happy Mondays didn't even bother to change the name of their song that borrows heavily from it. Primal Scream's 'Kowalski' sampled it. 'Fool's Gold' re-evaluated it, rejigged its DNA and propelled it into the future for another generation.

Can had a fairly fluid line-up, with Irmin Schmidt being one of the founder members. His wife, Hildegard, is the band's manager. I got to meet them when I was doing a book reading in Deauville, France, and we spent some time together – he even told me I reminded him of Can guitarist Michael Karoli. I didn't know anything about their relationship. I was hoping he was fond of him, rather than harbouring some long-standing grudge that would be taken out on me, but as we talked I figured that the reminders were positive. Irmin stuck around for my book reading, and he was one of the first people I asked for a recommendation. In some ways, it was from meeting him that I got the idea for this book. I wanted to know what made the people I admired tick, in a musical sense, and asking about an album had the immediacy required, without taking up too much of their time. When I asked Stephen Morris for his recommendation, Can was his other choice – so did Stephen listen to Can and pass the record on to Martin Hannett, who then played it to Happy Mondays? I didn't ask. I should've, shouldn't I? The metronomic sound of Joy Division was definitely helped along by the drumming of Can's Jaki Liebezeit, also loved by Mark E. Smith, and that paved the way for Madchester. Once again I felt like a film-noir music detective trying to piece together some kind of elaborate denouement, and with Can being the Maltese Falcon at the centre of the story.

Siouxsie and the Banshees, *Join Hands*
Recommended by Pam Hogg

Raw power

It was raining, tipping down – or pissing down, if you want to be blunt about it. Northern grey. Perfect record-shopping weather.

Where I grew up is famous for rain, and there's no better shelter than somewhere loaded with vinyl and something to listen to it on, where you can flick through the racks, silently noting whether an album is a 'got', 'not got' or 'need'. Occasionally the shop owner might put something on that is new to those within earshot. I remember hearing *Forty Four* by The Chocolate Watchband in Omega Records. It stopped me in my tracks and within a couple of songs I was asking Steve Harrison, the shop owner and future Charlatans manager, for as much information as possible about them. Rainy days are always good for improving your record collection.

Collecting records kind of found me, more than I found it. I bought the songs I heard as a kid and then fell in love with the designs of the labels, the thud of dropping the needle and the thrill of hearing something that had just been acquired. From there I started to notice the names of producers and sleeve designers, or musicians who had produced records for bands you wouldn't link them with. As much as trainspotters are mocked as the archetypal fans who geek out about steam trains and engine numbers, I wasn't far off myself with vinyl and catalogue numbers, but I was among the racks in Piccadilly Records rather than Platform 5 at Crewe station.

A collection of records, or CDs, kind of represents the personality of the owner. If you knew someone had a Demis Roussos record, you could make a guess about the type of music they liked, but it's within the context of a collection that you can build up a profile of that person. Albums make up the genes and the collection gives you a pretty good idea of who they are. I once had an idea of a renegade detective, like Columbo mixed with *Cracker*'s Fitz – they'd solve crimes by building a character profile just by going through someone's records. Perhaps it's a good job I ended up in a band rather than in TV production.

On a rainy day just two days after the New Year festivities, with all their flamboyance and fireworks and optimism, I was on a road trip to Hull from the Charlatans' studio in Cheshire. From west to east with a list of recommendations from Can's Irmin Schmidt, Lawrence (he of Felt, he of no surname) and Pam Hogg.

I texted Cosey Fanni Tutti to tell her I was on the way to her home town. 'Ooh, twill be dark and dank' – even her texts are thrillingly Hull-ish. I always liked Hull because of Cosey and the Throbbing Gristle connection. The term 'throbbing gristle' came from the language of Hull, as did a lot of their song titles, 'Five Knuckle Shuffle' being the best example. They were writing about their surroundings in Hackney, but they brought a part of Hull with them for added realism and brutal 1970s honesty.

Is 'honesty' the right word?

They were definitely brutal.

I love Hull because of Mick Ronson's voice in the Spiders from Mars documentaries and his brilliant solo single 'Only After Dark', the B-side to 'Love Me Tender' – his fabulously melodramatic stab at the Elvis classic.

I love Hull because The Charlatans had a riotous rescheduled show there in 1995, after a US tour with Menswear. In the freezing cold December I remember Rob's Hammond organ almost exploding, he put so much into it. Afterwards he duetted with Joe Longthorne on a version of 'Winter Wonderland'. Joe was fresh from a performance, resplendent in a yellow suit. It was one of those moments that punctuate a tour, when you're just never sure if what you're seeing is actually taking place – the UK's leading heartthrob for the platinum-rinse crowd running through a Christmas classic with an indie tearaway keyboard superhero. Lots of nights ended up like that – a random generator of bizarre acts, soap stars from local pantos or A-list superstars, all helped along by various substances.

I was looking for Irmin Schmidt's first choice, *The Moray Eels Eat the Holy Modal Rounders*. Or, completing some kind of perfect symmetry, Can's *Tago Mago*. I've owned the Spoon-label release for twenty-two years, having picked it up in preparation for writing *Up to Our Hips*.

While Can were a huge influence on the Madchester scene, I became particularly interested in them when I found a book at Monnow Valley studios, left over from when Johnny Marr was producing an Ian McCulloch album that never saw the light of day because the tapes were lost – or that's the story I heard, anyway. I took the book about Can and fell even more deeply in love with the music. Their story is legendary. In one incident, I'd heard that Damo Suzuki finished singing and went off to the cinema with his girlfriend. When he got back to the studio, the band were still jamming on the same song.

Like many places, Hull has a chapter or two in the story of modern music. Not only Throbbing Gristle and Mick Ronson, but Everything But the Girl and the self-proclaimed 'fourth best band band in Hull'. I really fell for The Housemartins in 1986, when I saw them at the International. 'Sheep' was their latest single and 'Happy Hour' was about to come out. The place was bursting at the seams. Mick Hucknall walked around the venue with a cane – around that time in Manchester, the Simply Red singer seemed to drift into gigs like some kind of Roman emperor, checking out the girls while suffering snarkiness from the boys. Norman Cook DJ'd after the show at the other end of the room. He set his own decks up and played a blinder. Between him and Paul Heaton they'd take care of millions of record sales as Fatboy Slim and with The Beautiful South, but that was one of my favourite gigs in one of the venues that would play a major part in the careers of both The Charlatans and The Stone Roses.

We headed east to a shop called GJM Music. It had been a record shop, under a different name, for the last twelve years, but one that had lost its way. It started opening sporadically and eventually just stayed closed. They were about to clear the racks and auction the stock – another vinyl outlet gone for good – when the new owner, Gary, stepped in. He bought all the records without seeing them and GJM Music was back in business. When we arrived his brother was minding the shop while Gary was off buying stock.

I had my list with me and took to the racks. The first record that struck me was *In the Court of the Crimson King*. I'd never owned a copy. The face on the cover had stayed with me since the very first time I'd seen it, but to me the music was from the generation before, and while Syd Barrett and Pink Floyd had made their way into our hearts, King Crimson had never seemed to find a route in. They were a band for older kids at school, kids who liked Boston and Budgie, but they weren't really for us. It makes it all the more interesting when you get round to spending time with a band that you'd previously shunned. It seems so odd now that you can be listening to the radio on your laptop, and within a couple of minutes of hearing a group for the first time you can own their music – or even just listen to it all and decide whether they are for you or not. The walls between genres are much more blurred, with iTunes even joining in and suggesting what else you might like to listen to. New music is part of everyday life but it used to involve either listening to the radio – which aside from John Peel stuck to fairly narrow parameters on each station – or buying either *Sounds*, the *NME* or *Melody Maker* to see which bands were being talked up, and even then it could be another week or two until you actually got to hear them. In my teens my spending money generally covered the cost of one album or a couple of gig tickets, so choices weren't made lightly. Even our choice of pub was often governed by what was on the jukebox. Today, via streaming sites and YouTube, you can easily hear entire back catalogues of classic bands or someone tipped on twitter. I knew of albums such as *Trout Mask Replica* for a few years until I found someone who actually owned it and would play it to me – before then it was almost mythical. The King Crimson album was definitely filed under that category for me.

Pam Hogg was a name I first came across in *i-D* magazine at some point in 1989. I was a would-be rock star and she was fashion designer, artist and would-be rock star herself. I was in my day job of overseas operations invoice clerk at ICI. Yeah, me neither. I would daydream about not having to wear a tie and hanging out instead with the likes of Pam and Andy Warhol, talking about the New York art scene while sipping cocktails in Soho – a bit like those scenes in *Billy Liar* where he wishes he was anywhere but in the office. Within a couple of years, some of those daydreams became a reality – not involving Pam and Andy directly, but I was serving my apprenticeship in the music world and I was loving everything about it. Then, around the time of Creation's headiest of hedonistic days, my and Pam's paths finally crossed. An exact month or year I couldn't give you, but we shared a lift to get away from a particularly grim festival site – one with a big sponsor and even bigger VIP area. Neither of us wanted to hang around, so we took off back to the real world in a taxi.

I had always wanted to know where Pam's ideas came from – what made her tick, what floated her boat – so her name was near the top of the list for a recommendation. Whether it's art or style or someone's general demeanour, it's always their record collection that gives the biggest clues.

We met again at an awards ceremony, where Pam gave the best speech of the day before awarding a lifetime achievement gong to Siouxsie Sioux. So her choice wasn't a surprise: *Join Hands* by Siouxsie and the Banshees.

Some bands you have to own everything by and some you don't have anything by but you can still love them. When you're a kid you share listening experiences, and with some albums you even share ownership. What I am saying is, I've never actually owned my own copy of this record. I couldn't afford all the records I wanted, so by getting three or four mates together we could have a part-share in a bigger collection. I never personally owned *Never Mind the Bollocks* for years after hearing and loving it, but I used to listen to it every time I went to Panhead's house.

Well, his parents' house.

His brother, Sticker, had it, which meant when Sticker was out, we would play it and throw ourselves round the house, head first, in a punk haze. It was the same with *Inflammable Material* by Stiff Little Fingers. That required a journey to see Jon 'Didger' Davis if I wanted to hear it. Michael McNamara had *Machine Gun Etiquette* by The Damned, and his brother, Kieran, was a mod, so if he was out we had the run of The Who, *Mods Mayday '79*, Secret Affair and lots of 2 Tone classics. The other advantage to this was each set of parents would get rid of us for at least a couple of nights a week. Although when it was their turn there would be mayhem – arguing over what to put on next and inevitably pogoing round someone's room, jacked up on Vimto and the kind of freedom from responsibility that our parents seemed to hold against us.

For some reason I had two copies of 'The Staircase (Mystery)' by Siouxsie and the Banshees, both in generic 7-inch sleeves – either blank or with the name of a record company that didn't match the label the record was on. Much later, Nick Owen – older brother of Simon, my best friend while growing up – had the

Banshees' *Once Upon a Time: The Singles*. 'Hong Kong Garden' and 'Christine' were my favourites initially. 'Hong Kong Garden' was on the radio every day in the summer of 1978 – the summer I was climbing trees and playing in the fresh air. That feeling you only get when you're a kid – like an episode of *The Wonder Years*, if it was set in Moulton, nr Northwich, Cheshire. It was a brilliant soundtrack to grow up to. The Banshees, The Jam, The Stranglers and X- Ray Spex – all playing during what seemed like endless, aimless summer holidays.

I bought the Banshees' debut album, *The Scream*, with my first-ever wage when I was sixteen. Although Siouxsie was around at the start of punk in 1976, and present and involved in the infamous Sex Pistols interview with Bill Grundy, the Banshees weren't signed to Polydor until 1978, and then they took their time putting out their first LP. In hindsight it was possibly the best thing they could have done. A lot of the punk bands that rushed out albums in the fire and brimstone of 1977 often had nowhere to go with the follow-up. By the time post-punk was taking shape, there was a broader, more artistic landscape for bands to exist in, led by the likes of Wire, the Gang of Four and the Pop Group rather than groups like the Angelic Upstarts and 999, who seemed old hat by the beginning of the 1980s.

I almost bought the Banshees' single 'Playground Twist' from Rumbelows. It was on top of the display cabinet, in a picture sleeve, sitting next to 'Stop Your Sobbing' by The Pretenders. I have no idea of the time frame or whether they were battling for chart position, but I just remember them both being there at the same time. I bought neither but was besotted with the titles and the frontwomen, who personified girl power nearly twenty years before it'd be hijacked and neatened up, packaged and diluted by The Spice Girls. In the message accompanying Pam's recommendation, she referred to Siouxsie as 'the dark, magical and terrifying goddess': a better description I have yet to hear.

Pam told me that their first album, *The Scream*, was the record she always listened to in full before heading to Blitz on a Tuesday night. 'It was the perfect album to get ready to,' she wrote. '*Join Hands* is a lot darker and more intense and you can really hear how the sounds influenced so many bands. Like *The Scream*, it's got incredible energy, but this one, with her voice surprisingly tender at times, is even more formidable and really draws you in. Enjoy, m'darling, and let's join hands soon! X'

Pam's message made me really excited to have this on my list. I've read so many varying reports about this LP over the years: from it being the main inspiration for Joy Division's *Closer* to it limping in as a let-down after a brilliant debut. After intense listening and deliberating, I had concluded that *Join Hands* is the goth mother lode, the starting point for a genre that would take in everyone from The Sisters of Mercy via Nine Inch Nails to Marilyn Manson's world-straddling take on the subject.

As with so many pioneers, many missed the potential at the time. Fast-forward thirty years and Siouxsie is admired with an artistic reverence that would have been impossible to imagine when she first appeared in 1976. 'Playground Twist' is a manic masterpiece – incredible, the kind of atmosphere rarely generated on record. The album's themes are based on wartime. It has a white sleeve featuring a wreath of poppies and statues of soldiers from a cenotaph. Pam told me it was designed by John Maybury, who directed the striking video for 'Nothing Compares 2 U'.

After nearly buying this record for three-quarters of my life, I finally picked it up in a second-hand record shop in Hull when I was looking for *The Moray Eels Eat the Holy Modal Rounders*. Pam's choice stared at me from high up on the wall, next to the clock behind the counter. I had flashbacks to the almost-hads, nearly-boughts and shouldn't-have-bothereds of my record-buying past – collecting history flashing before my very eyes.

Thanks, Pam.

When The Charlatans recorded at Mickie Most's RAK Studios in 1991, we found out that Siouxsie and the Banshees were recording their LP *Superstition* in the next studio. It was one of those times when we had to pinch ourselves to make sure it was all real. We ate at the same table as them – Jon Brookes left dinner early one evening to sneak a play of Budgie's ridiculously over-the-top drum kit. He came back shaking, saying it was a dream come true – he'd done it while we'd kept Budgie talking, and none of us were to breathe a word about it.

The rest of us were hypnotised by Siouxsie. I was desperate to not seem like some star-struck fan, but that day she ate pasta salad and a carrot cake – and I kind of sat there, captivated. Exactly like a star-struck fan.

Pam told me, 'I remember the first time I met her. I turned when I heard someone call my name. As she spoke, the lips and eyes were unmistakable. I was so taken aback as she was like one of the untouchables . . . but she'd been to my shop and had borrowed some clothes for a shoot and was chatting away like we'd known each other for years.'

Almost unbelievably, the Banshees recorded five albums in five years. *Kaleidoscope* had the big singles – 'Happy House' and 'Christine'. The follow-up, *Juju*, is such a brilliant record. When bands are pretty prolific, you can chop and change regarding your favourite album. I secretly like the fact that some people write off certain Charlatans LPs. Out of the twelve, people tend to disagree over which are the best and the worst; it's sometimes a case of putting out a body of work and letting people view it from there. There are so many factors that contribute to loving an album – how young you are, how well your plans are working out, how good the drugs are . . . lots of reasons.

John McGeoch was a permanent member of the *Juju*-era Banshees after leaving Magazine. For me he is the post-punk Mick Ronson. He defined a sound.

Just now, my favourite Banshees album is *Kaleidoscope* – maybe because it's been the most played, maybe because Steve Jones features on it, or maybe because of one or a dozen other reasons. 'Happy House' and 'Clockface' are both in my top 100 songs of all time.

For all of those reasons, Pam, the Banshees and Siouxsie in particular will always mean so much to me. I kept in touch with the guys at GJM Music for a while, then I got a message from the owner saying that the shop was closing for good. The landlord was revamping the area and it wasn't worth them carrying on. A sad story.

ABBA, *ABBA Gold*

Recommended by Chris Carter

Adventures in droplifting

Vinyl has always been something that lives several lives. At school, someone's entire record collection would be dispersed among friends when its owner needed to get their hands on some quick cash for a much-needed moped, present for a girlfriend or night on the cider. Kids who had picked up an early copy of *Spiral Scratch* would let it go for the sake of a night with their mates in the pub. Sometimes a classmate would decide they had gone off Adam and the Ants (*Dirk Wears White Sox* era) in order to pledge themselves to the new wave of British heavy metal (Def Leppard, Saxon, etc.) and a slew of vinyl would be offloaded, with dinner money and records changing hands for way less than they were worth, or even swapped for a bar of chocolate at times. My taste in music developed rather than changed – I still listen to lots of stuff I bought when I was fourteen or fifteen. Sometimes I'd sell a record I'd got for cheap that had rocketed in value: I'd picked up singles by The Pack, the band Kirk Brandon was in prior to Theatre of Hate, for 60p each after noticing them in the small ads in the back pages of the *NME* for £5. I moved them on to a friend's older brother, but it just meant more money for records.

After leaving school, reality bites. Cars, holidays, mortgages and the general demands of life meant many record collections were traded in at second-hand shops; a realisation that there was enough vinyl to pay for a new kitchen was a cold hard fact that too many people found hard to ignore. And anyway, that copy of *Sound of the Suburbs* on clear vinyl hadn't made it out of the box for a few years. Rented flats instantly lost inches of floor space as thousands of albums were stored on shelves or got carted around multiple moves and played less and less, often with a partner who didn't have the same passion for vintage rockabilly or whatever. The move to CDs increasingly meant there wasn't the set-up to play vinyl in the house anyway. I'd bump into friends who would all tell a similar story: they had traded their collection in at a second-hand shop, leaving with a handful of cassettes, a fraction of the true value in cash and a feeling that they'd just got a lot older in the space of an agonising session of being told that what they'd spent their life collecting wasn't really worth anything in today's market . . . only to see much of it in the window the next day, with stickers shouting about its rarity and value.

I'm not trying to make out second-hand record shops are bleak, though. There's nothing like digging through the racks to find a copy of an album that's been on your must-have list for a while. And if the other person didn't want it any more, then it's a good thing – plus if it went towards a kitchen cupboard or a few pints with their mates, then everyone's a winner.

Even though vinyl has had a rough time of it over the years, most cities still support a second-hand record shop. London, Leeds, Sheffield and Manchester have quite a few, and among those there are specialist places dealing in northern soul or 1990s dance. Aside from clothes and books, I'm not sure there's another kind of second-hand market that does as well as vinyl. Everyone gets dressed and most people can read, so clothes and books have an unfair advantage. Not everyone has a record player, though, but vinyl is still fighting its corner. Furniture – I've just thought about second-hand furniture shops. There's lots of them too. Everyone has to sit down at some point. But you get what I'm saying, don't you? Good.

But there's another life that records have that perhaps does not receive the credit its due: the amount of money they raise for charity. Not charity records per se, even though Band Aid, Ferry

Aid and Pat and Mick have all made huge donations, but through high-street charity shops like Barnardo's and Oxfam. If some towns and cities aren't able to support a dedicated record shop, then most have charity shops, with albums and singles sitting alongside anything else people have deemed surplus to requirements. They're typically priced at £2 or £3, and a fresh delivery can mean quite a haul for the price of a new CD.

I knew that some of my friends' recommendations were more likely to be found in a British Heart Foundation store than Piccadilly Records. Pretty much at the top of that list was the choice of Chris Carter, who, alongside Cosey in Throbbing Gristle, has been a pioneer and maker of some of the best music of this and the last century. His recommendation? A double album – *ABBA Gold* by ABBA.

It was in Oxfam in Manchester that I found this record and handed over the required £3 asking price for a near-mint-condition copy of the album. I never really appreciated Abba when they were together – to a teenage punk, they represented the enemy. At the time I always thought of them as a girls' band – singing about complex emotions – while the bands that I loved were dealing with borstal breakouts. However, what was being played out on their records was a heartbreaking soap opera not unlike Fleetwood Mac's, but without the cocaine. Björn had written 'The Winner Takes It All' and the lead vocal was by Agnetha. I'm using their first names not because I know them, but because they only really had first names and their initials spelt the name of their band – almost everything about them made them a perfect pop group. So, anyway, Björn and Agnetha were getting divorced at the time, which must have made things near impossible, especially when you consider the lyrics he had written: 'The winner takes it all / The loser's standing small / Beside the victory / That's her destiny'. All the details of a break-up, just as they were breaking up. But Björn said it wasn't about them, so it was OK.

Finding that record in that shop was a partial alignment of the vinyl planets. The reason I was in there wasn't so much to buy something as to leave something. Not in the conventional way of making a donation, but something I'd come across that seemed like a great way to use charity shops to leave records, books and tickets, and then let people know where to find them. The system was called droplifting – a reverse version of shoplifting involving marking up an item and tweeting a message to say where it could be found. I'd been sent some copies of *Telling Stories* a couple of months before it was published, and I wasn't sure about handing them to friends and suggesting they read the book I'd written. I'm not sure why but it just seemed an odd thing to do. I had six or eight copies, in each of which I wrote on the first page: 'This book has been droplifted. Please pay the person at the till £10. Let me know you've found it and I hope you enjoy reading it.' I signed them and tweeted where I'd left them – the first was in Marylebone Oxfam and was secreted between Ross Kemp's book on gangs and Des O'Connor's autobiography. Twenty minutes later someone let me know they'd found it. I left the others in charity shops around the country.

I'd first heard about droplifting as a way for bands and DJs to get their records into shops that wouldn't otherwise stock them. Droplift five copies of a 12-inch into an independent record shop, complete with index divider with the name of the band on. Let friends know it's there and make sure the shop assistant remembers the name when it won't scan and there's no record of it ever having been ordered. One of the most ingenious droplifts was done under the name of the Barbie Liberation Organization by anti-corporate activists the Yes Men, two American pranksters who were highlighting gender stereotyping in kids' toys. They bought talking Barbies and GI Joes and swapped their 'voice-boxes', with the result that the cutesy-looking girl dolls would threaten, 'No escape for the guilty – vengeance is mine,' while the macho soldiers enquired, 'Wanna go shopping? Will we ever have enough clothes?' They then took the rebooted dolls back to the shops and left them on the shelves, with an added sticker giving a number to call if the toy was found to be faulty. The number was that of ABC TV's news desk, which ran the story once they started to get calls and were sent a video by the Barbie Liberation Organization. Banksy also began droplifting artworks into mainstream museums, and the whole thing was reminiscent of Bill Drummond's exploits with The KLF, from culture-jamming posters to burning a million pounds.

None of my droplifting did much towards ending capitalism or putting the brakes on globalisation, but it felt good to join the dots between getting books, records and tickets to people in a slightly more roundabout fashion. I'd mention that it was all done for charity too, but I don't like to go on about it.

I found the Abba album while droplifting some festival tickets – Abba being the band that Bill Drummond drove to Sweden to meet in an attempt to convince them not to make him destroy thousands of copies of an album containing a sample of theirs he hadn't cleared. Like I say, the alignment of the vinyl planets. Kind of.

Guided by Voices, *Bee Thousand*

Recommended by Paddy Considine

Meditating in the van

Alongside playing live and recording, travelling is next on the list of what bands do. Ever since the dawn of video recorders on tour buses, films have been the most helpful way to enjoy time on the road. Don't get me wrong – drinking and making merry are fun while they're happening, but there's a big price to pay for the band and even the audience sometimes when the substances wear off.

Top of my list of travel-friendly directors would be Oliver Stone, Martin Scorsese, Woody Allen, Ken Russell and Shane Meadows. TV box sets were a later addition, with the advent of DVDs of *The Sopranos*, *Twin Peaks*, *Seinfeld* and *The Office*.

I first came across Shane Meadows when we were asked if 'North Country Boy' could be used in the soundtrack of a film he was making with Bob Hoskins, *Twenty Four Seven*. The next film of Shane's I watched was *Dead Man's Shoes*, featuring one of the most breathtaking lead performances I have ever seen. I made a mental note to check the name of the actor in the credits. Paddy Considine's portrayal of brotherly love and retribution stays with you for good once you've seen it. Over the next ten years I looked out for Paddy's performances, and they were never short of masterful.

In 2013 I got a message from Paddy asking about transcendental meditation. He'd read that I practised it and he had a few questions. That same day we spoke on the phone for over an hour, without spending much time discussing either acting or music. We met for coffee at the Charlatans' studio and I played him a few songs from *Modern Nature* that we hadn't played to anyone else yet.

Paddy then revealed he was in a band. I had heard somewhere that he was, and had checked out a few songs. Often the words 'actor' and 'band' in close proximity can send a shiver down the spine – stranded vanity projects on the hard shoulder of music's motorway, featuring the likes of Keanu Reeves, Macaulay Culkin or Juliette Lewis. But Riding the Low, Paddy's band, were one of the rare exceptions, along with Scarlett Johansson, Steve Martin and maybe a couple more.

I invited them to play at Tim Peaks at Festival No. 6, and they were fantastic. Joe Duddell wrote a string arrangement for one of their songs and had a quartet rehearse it in readiness for a performance fifteen minutes after they had all met. They were in good hands – Joe has written string arrangements for Elbow, New Order, James and The Charlatans, so the performance at Tim Peaks in the town hall at Portmeirion was something extra-special.

Whenever we meet I love talking to Paddy about performance and onstage goings-on. Don't get me wrong, I don't have any hidden desires to be a thespian, but there's always something that has gripped me about the process of acting. Paddy has always preferred to just act and direct rather than talk about it, but as part of Tim Peaks we've teamed up with Dave Haslam a few times for an onstage interview. As well as bands, it is things like interviews and the building of scale models of the solar system that are the most thrilling and engaging elements we put on at our festival stage.

Paddy's choice of album is *Bee Thousand* by Guided by Voices. Here's his description:

Bee Thousand – my favourite album from Guided by Voices. The very definition of lo-fi, before lo-fi was hip. Everything great about Pollard's songwriting is here on this record. The fantastic pop melodies, insanely beautiful lyrics. Listening to Pollard is like stepping into another universe. Once you are hooked, you never want to leave. If The Beatles had a song as insanely catchy as 'Echos Myron' maybe they would have been huge. Who knows? Counter that with the fragile sweetness of Tobin Sprout's contributions and you have a remarkable album. This record changed the direction of my mind. It opened up doors that can never be locked. XXX

*

Social media has become a big part of the communication between bands and fans. And in some ways it's caught the big record companies by surprise, with artists talking straight to the audience – going from recording in their bedrooms to arenas, with kids at home doing the job of the A&R men.

When we had our first No. 1 album we stopped by the record label every so often to collect letters and gifts that would have been sent maybe a couple of weeks before. Nowadays, somebody can hear a record on the radio and get directly in contact with the person who made it, which makes the process of writing and releasing songs even more enjoyable.

A few years ago the new social-media kid on the block was Twitter. MySpace had run out of fuel and was broken down on the side of the road, while Facebook was a great way to keep in touch with your actual friends when on tour or recording or generally not being in the same place as they were. But here was another one. I avoided it for a short time, as I was told it was mainly full of pictures of people's cats and lattes. But then I got me a profile. Soon, I had 4,000 people following me and I didn't know what to do. I would post Charlatans songs and upcoming concerts, where I was DJing next. I didn't have a cat but I was fond of lattes.

One morning I woke up at the studio while I was recording there on my own. I tweeted, 'Morning Tweets x Coffee?' I have no idea why, but I knew there were people out there and I was feeling sociable. I got more of a response with that one tweet than pretty much anything I'd said on there in the past. Requests came from Russia, Argentina, Japan and Preston. People told me they were running late and needed a quick espresso; others saw I was up and about and asked questions about the band and gigs and records, as we'd not made one in a while.

It was metaphorical and metaphysical and it became a daily routine, like an upside-down version of the emperor's new clothes. Nobody pointed out there was nothing really there and nobody burst the bubble.

I would tweet each morning and get in a 140-character chat with some regulars. We'd finished *Who We Touch* and I was starting to write *Oh No I Love You*. I'm not sure whether I was missing some of the camaraderie of the band, catching up from the night before and shooting the breeze, but soon enough 8,000 people were following me.

I watched *Four Lions* on TV and noticed that one of the actors, Riz Ahmed, was tweeting as it was showing. I'd seen the film a couple of times before, but it was given a whole new dimension and a fresh insight by Riz's tweets. I wondered if we could do the same thing with a record: anyone who wanted to could take part by pressing play or dropping the needle at a prearranged time, and I would tweet about the techniques we had used in the studio, the antics that went with a certain song, decode the lyrics and offer a general look behind the scenes and a peak under the lid of one of our albums.

The first one we did involved maybe 300 people listening simultaneously all over the world to *Some Friendly*. We did each Charlatans album in order, with more and more people joining in each time. The most recent one was on the twenty-fifth anniversary of the release of *Some Friendly*. We found an online map where people could drop pins to say where they would be listening. A few days later, I checked back to find pins dropped in Canada, Iceland, Nepal, Australia, most European cities, Japan and South America. The only continent that wasn't represented was Antarctica. Half joking, I sent a plea asking if any Antarcticans would be joining in. Now I do understand that most of the population of that continent are penguins, but we tracked down a research station run by the British Antarctic Survey. They got back to tell us that one of their researchers was a fan and would be more than happy to join our listening party. So, without much fuss, I think we had for the first time in history an album that was playing simultaneously on every continent on Earth. Sadly, our message to the International Space Station remained unanswered.

Every morning there was the same clarion call for imaginary caffeine. The whole thing needed a name. Tim Peaks was born.

It's a homage to David Lynch's television show, and with a similar oddness it grew and grew. A designer who followed me on Twitter sent in a logo and we made some mugs – all forty-eight were snapped up in ten minutes, and when we made some more they went too. This carried on until we had sold 500. We needed somewhere for the money to go and we thought the best home would be the David Lynch Foundation. The thought that this was actually doing some good and that beneficiaries would be learning transcendental meditation encouraged us to do more.

Next up was a Tim Peaks blend of coffee. Fair trade and damn fine were the stipulations. I spent a day sampling, describing, sipping and spitting.

The number of followers grew to 10,000. BBC 6 Music rang. They wanted me to do a couple of morning shows on Christmas Eve and New Year's Eve, with an hour of each show dedicated to Tim Peaks. The metaphysical was becoming the physical, and we got a call from a music festival that wanted a Tim Peaks for real. Like *Field of Dreams*, we built it and they came.

I picked up the phone and we got ourselves a line-up to play in our log cabin at Kendal Calling. Edwyn Collins came, and he brought Roddy Frame. They told me they had plans for me to join them on a couple of songs. I sang 'Fantastic Day' with Nick Heyward and played my own unannounced set. It reminded me of the great things I love about festivals – music and people.

Tim Peaks became a bit of a travelling circus. It went to the Isle of Wight Festival, where we had sets by the likes of Sleaford Mods, Nick Heyward and Sean O'Hagan from the High Llamas. I noticed Suzanne Vega was attending, but as an audience member rather than as a performer. Via Twitter and smoke signals, and with more than a dash of cheek, I asked if she would like to stop by and we would rebrand Tim's Diner as Tom's Diner for a few hours. The fee offered was a brownie and unlimited coffee. The following day I was talking with one of the volunteer baristas when somebody came up and said, 'There's a lady here to see you.' I'd presumed somebody maybe wanted an autograph, but they added: 'An American lady. She said you'd promised you'd get her a guitar.' Yep, it was Suzanne. As we tracked down a guitar, she took to the stage unannounced and launched into an a cappella version of 'Tom's Diner'. It was the moment of the festival, and Suzanne loved it so much she came back the following day to perform another set. A day in the life of Tim Peaks – thousands of cups of coffee got served, and the money was donated to the David Lynch Foundation. Then a call came in. David Lynch was to present me with an award for contributing to his cause, and in true Lynchian style it was done with him on set in Poland and me at the Globe Theatre on the South Bank in London.

It's now maybe five years on from the first caffeine-fuelled tweets and Tim Peaks is a regular at some of the best festivals in the UK. And to think it all came from a tweet.

With these good vibes in mind I beamed out a message to David

Lynch via some contacts, and I sat and waited to see if anything came back. A three-word message emerged from the ether, and that message was . . .

Trout. Mask. Replica.

Sergio Mendes and Brasil '66, *Herb Alpert Presents Sergio Mendes and Brasil '66*

Recommended by Anton Newcombe

Same language, different world

Summer 2014, and over a coffee in Leeds, at the nearest cafe to the parked-up tour bus of The Brian Jonestown Massacre, I'm catching up with Anton Newcombe. His band are playing The Cockpit that night, and The Charlatans are at the Brudenell Social Club. Both shows sold out, natch.

I told Anton about the book and asked him for a recommendation. His choice was *Herb Alpert Presents Sergio Mendes and Brasil '66*. It's a mainstay of second-hand shops in the US, but he was unsure whether it was even released here. He said it's the perfect start to any record collection. This made sense and struck a chord with the Anton Newcombe I had got to know since 1995.

Anton was the de facto mayor of good times in LA sometime around 1998. It wasn't an official job, but he did it well. His band defined the slacker cool of the counterculture, representing something old and new – timeless in their sound and how they looked. They had something of the outlaw gang about them and could quite easily have existed in San Francisco in 1968. They were West Coast cowboys, not dissimilar to The Charlatans, the godfathers of San Fran psych – The Charlatans who made us become Charlatans UK in the US.

The Brian Jonestown Massacre's recording methods were something I'd not come across before – renting houses with advances, dragging in their gear, their gang and their influences, and a few weeks later the lease would be up and they'd have a completed album.

I needed them in my life.

The Brian Jonestown Massacre had a fluid approach to line-ups. While not quite at the level of The Fall, personnel changes were regular and not without colourful back stories. Joel Gion, gonzo conjuror, tambourine in hand, a hot mix of Gene Clark and Bez. Matt Hollywood, Charles Mehling, Jeff Davies, Dean Taylor and Miranda Lee Richards completed the vision at that moment, though on another day there would be omissions, additions and possible altercations resulting in another couple of people per night through the membership turnstile.

The movie *Dig!* has shown them to be, or at least portrayed them as, dangerous, a danger to themselves, the real life Spinal Tap – overblown but endearing. Anton is a genius, a tortured genius – a tortured genius wearing a fur coat and roller skates sometimes, but a tortured genius nonetheless. As time goes by the torture seems to diminish as the genius grows.

I moved to LA in 1998, a couple of years after we played Knebworth with Oasis. With Oasis calling the musical shots in the UK, it was a breath of fresh air. BJM were the first band I saw in LA, days after moving there. I was knocked out. To me, they were like The Byrds but with a punk aesthetic.

It was at the Troubadour in West Hollywood, the venue Elton John had used as the launch pad in his bid for stardom in America – the LA stop-off for everyone from Joe Strummer to Coldplay.

Anton sat stage left and at the back. They were so cool. I wanted to meet them after the show – I was secretly hoping they had heard of my band and wishing they would tell me they thought my band was cool. They had heard of The Charlatans. They did like our music, and I was handed a copy of *Strung Out in Heaven*, their new album. We chatted about:

John Peel

Travel

Drugs

Girls

Hair

The Monkees

The Monkees' hair

Family

Jack Nicholson

And a mutual love of Elliott Smith.

When our paths crossed I found I had a lot in common with Frankie Teardrop and Charles Mehling. Frankie didn't join until 2000, but timelines and the BJM don't follow the rules of the regular universe. Frankie kept chickens in his flat and loved Pabst Blue Ribbon – the king of beers, according to Dennis Hopper's character in *Blue Velvet*. He cruised round Hollywood on his skateboard and also roadied for The Charlatans when we came to town. Charles did the lights for Black Rebel Motorcycle Club, who supported us on what would be their first American tour. He also slipped into the role of video director and subsequently directed two Charlatans videos, becoming one of the most in-demand directors around.

There was something about the BJM that was like the perfect leather jacket – a beat-up style that couldn't be faked and that made everything around them look drab. They were my newfound gang – brilliant for introducing me to new ideas. Not so brilliant was their need, love, appreciation and craving for narcotics of every prescription. Ah well!!! You can't have it all, although we often tried to. Every silver lining has some sort of cloud, but we loved ours.

Berlin, 23 May 2013. On a short solo tour of Germany I got a message from Anton to stop by and visit, as he was living in Berlin in an old car dealership converted into a living space upstairs and recording studio below. At the time, he had just checked himself out after a spell in hospital. Fab, his studio engineer and right-hand man, had all the qualities and strength of character to help

Anton through. I arrived at the building to a briefing from Fab. Anton was in a real creative phase, and Fab wanted to capture and document it. While my band read magazines in the van and bumbled round town, I was given a lyric sheet and tambourine, and the desk was fired up. It was like the song already existed fully formed in Anton's head – a cover version of 'The Battle of Armageddon' by Hank Williams – so as I sang each line, I would be stopped in my tracks by Anton holding up his hand to give direction and we'd go back to the start. I picked up on the subtleties and nuances he wanted, and I think we worked well together. In a recording studio I either work as the boss or take 100 per cent direction from the person who is the boss (not the person who maybe thinks they are the boss). That's how arguments are sidestepped and projects actually finished.

Later that evening the song and video were uploaded by Anton and shared with the world. It's my way of working – we met for coffee after breakfast and by dinnertime we were 200 miles away watching what we'd done on the best 3G connection the autobahn could offer.

You'll always read about fights, scrapped sessions, arguments and punch-ups, but studios are like crucibles. There's a lot of heat, but amazing things can happen – coloured smoke, flashes, bangs and things you'll never see or hear of again, so there'll always be ideas that don't make the cut. The good stuff hits the vinyl and the bad stuff hits the newspapers. And in music it was ever thus.

I've been the puncher and the punchee. I've thrown a tantrum and had tantrums thrown at me. I've freaked out at people and people have freaked out at me, and any and all of these at 9 a.m., 10 p.m. and 3 a.m. But there's a moment when, with your feet up on the mixing desk, you press play, and when you've got it right, there's no feeling like it.

When you've got it wrong? There's no feeling like that, either.

I found a copy of *Sergio Mendes and Brasil '66* in Holt, Norfolk, in what I imagine is the only post office/record shop around. Even the sign outside says, 'Yes, we are still a post office.' Andrew, the proprietor, divides his time between cataloguing Incredible String Band albums and sorting out passport applications. Other record shops have branched out with pies, coffee and gigs, but matching up vinyl with assorted postage is surely the most incongruous combination yet.

The Byrds, *Younger Than Yesterday*

Recommended by Grumbling Fur

The North West Coast

In the family tree of music in my head, The Byrds are sitting pretty somewhere near the top. Even though they split in 1973, their sunshine-drenched Californian acid-folk rock still holds strong, all the way from 1964 till now and beyond – through multiple line-ups, always involving Roger McGuinn and always more than the sum of their parts. For a band that emerged on the back of a cover version, they have an astonishing depth to their own skills. Their songwriting has influenced many great bands, from R.E.M. to Hüsker Dü, The Stone Roses, The Smiths and Ariel Pink's Haunted Graffiti.

I was nineteen years old when I tuned in to their jangling jingle-jangle. The older kids who I used to go along to the Haçienda with would spin 'come down' records at parties afterwards – Pink Floyd's *Piper at the Gates of Dawn*, Jimi Hendrix's *Axis: Bold as Love*. But it was always *The Byrds' Greatest Hits* that made everyone gravitate towards the turntable. Disarming and with a sense of togetherness, more Marrakech than Scott McKenzie's 'San Francisco', it chimed with scallies and influenced bands from Liverpool as much as those from Manchester.

The old rules I'd adopted as a naive punk were beginning to fade. Nihilism was replaced by sunshine, and I saw the inherent coolness of a fringed buckskin jacket and an unashamed bowl cut – and of songs written under expansive American skies rather than by frustrated kids from the suburbs. Greeting people with a beaming smile rather than a suspicious sneer – it felt more like me.

Our former manager Steve Harrison asked one day whether I'd

heard that The Stone Roses had ditched their Playn Jayn sound. 'They sound more like The Byrds now' – it seems Ian Brown and John Squire were maybe doing a similar thing.

The Byrds have become an integral part of my life and have definitely seeped into my musical fabric. I think it's really cool when you get inspired by a band and attempt to pick up the mantle. I once heard Roger McGuinn on the radio talking about his life and the music he was currently listening to. He mentioned The Charlatans, saying we were updating a sound not too far away from the one The Byrds created with their first four albums. It was incredibly flattering.

You never really know how your heroes are going to react if and when you meet them, whether to go for the hug or brace yourself for a dressing down or just a big dose of apathy – or even whether they have come across your music, despite the success it may have had.

Much as we could headline a festival or have a No. 1 album, I was still knocked out when I discovered that Mick Jagger and David Bowie had definitely (although almost certainly separately) heard a Charlatans song – and not just through the thin walls of a Portakabin backstage when we went on before them. The first time I realised for sure that Bowie knew about us was backstage at the Isle of Wight Festival. We played on the main stage before his headline set, which would turn out to be his last-ever UK show. He was waiting near by, and I asked if it would be OK to have a photograph taken with him.

As I stood with him I said, 'I'm the singer with The Charlatans. We're on before you.'

He smiled really sweetly at me and replied, 'I know, Tim, I know.'

When Mark Collins joined The Charlatans and first struck up an acoustic guitar I recognised something Byrdsian that made me excited about writing with him. In my most romantic songwriting notions, I see us as the Salford Roger McGuinn and Gene Clark. A few years ago, we made a mini-album called *Warm Sounds* while we were in-between records – reworkings of some of our favourite Charlatans songs. We played them like we imagined The Byrds might have done – y'know, if they decided to reform and do a record of Charlatans covers. Still no news on that just yet, but we liked how we sounded on it. Maybe it didn't open any new doors for us, but it's sometimes nice to be reminded there's a door there.

*

There is so much music everywhere you turn – hotel foyers, coffee shops, songs leaking from headphones on Tube platforms. Occasionally you wish there wasn't. Thankfully, though, every now and again something stops you in your tracks.

On hearing 'The Ballad of Roy Batty' from *Glynnaestra*, Grumbling Fur's second LP, I was smitten and they went to the top of the list of bands I wanted to work with. I started sending Twitter smoke signals out like wildfire, sharing my love of their sound – the natural harmonies of Alexander Tucker and Daniel O'Sullivan, mixed with synthetic modulators. I knew I had to make contact. I eventually did via a friend who casually dropped in the fact that he knew them while I was enthusing about their record. They invited me to a lovely terraced house in Wood Green, an incredibly inspiring place to work – garden at the back, stuffed animals, paintings and artefacts once owned by Coil decorate the rooms. The beds are all handmade by owner, designer and Jhonn Balance's partner Ian Johnstone – goat, sheep or ox heads hang sinisterly above the pillows, as if to warn off any passing Tibetan spirits looking to inhabit an interesting party. Or maybe they're just a wry joke.

The vocals of Grumbling Fur are up there with the best. They're inspired by JJ Cale, Fleetwood Mac, The Beach Boys and Paul McCartney, but are closer to The Byrds and, I think, David Crosby in particular, the undisputed vocal genius of his time.

Daniel and Alexander have come to be an important part of my life. We have written a handful of songs together now, and have sung onstage at least half a dozen times. In some ways it was The Byrds who brought us close – unknown to any members of The Byrds, but music's like that. It's something that started at post-club house parties in the late 1980s and culminated in a recording session in Wood Green, where, during a conversation, a book called *Modern Nature* mysteriously fell from the bookshelf onto my head. But that's another story completely.

Fad Gadget, *Fireside Favourites*

Recommended by Daniel Miller

The first last piece of the jigsaw

Being the singer in a band was an all-consuming ambition, but from the moment I started collecting I developed a keen interest in the goings-on behind the records that I loved so much, and the people working closest with the band were the record label.

Alan McGee was head of Creation Records and also our manager for a time. Jeff Barrett and Martin Kelly were close friends of The Charlatans who also happened to run Heavenly Records. I had seen the good and the bad side of the relationship between bands and the people who released their music.

My favourite labels veered from continent-straddling behemoths to glorious failures that burnt bright but also burnt money. So I thought I would start a record label.

What could possibly go wrong?

Apologies about the drama. Nothing really has gone too wrong, but labels do tend to lurch from week to week and invoice to invoice. I kind of did it to have an affinity with figures I admire, from Tony Wilson at Factory and Martin Mills at Beggars Banquet to Daniel Miller at Mute. I just needed some people who made music and some other, like-minded people to bring it all together. At some point in 2011, O Genesis Recordings was born. It was my chance to try to get things right where other labels had got them wrong . . . or to find out why others had struggled and then possibly make the same mistakes as them anyway.

An exciting time, either way.

We dubbed our artist contract the 'Nontract', as it was a one-paragraph deal that basically said, 'You be nice to us and we'll be nice to you.' And without wanting to appear too above ourselves, there was a desire to shake things up a little.

The first release was by Joseph Coward, and the label found its feet with successive releases by Electricity in Our Homes, Nik Colk Void – one of the partners in the label – R. Stevie Moore, The Vaccines, Inspiral Carpets and upcoming bands like Hot Vestry and Eyelids, who Paddy Considine had introduced me to. It was a pleasure to release their album in the UK and to take them on tour supporting The Charlatans in the US.

I'd recorded my solo album in Nashville but – and I'm not sure why – I'd not given too much thought as to who would release it. That is, until at one meeting it was pointed out that I had spent hours and hours convincing bands to release their records on O Genesis and that it would look a little bit odd if I was trying to find another label to put my own album out. So by accident rather than design I signed myself and became my own A&R man. I got a table for one at a Chinese restaurant and ordered two grams of coke. That last sentence is not true, but it made me laugh so I'm leaving it in. If you know A&R men, it might possibly make you smile. If you don't know A&R men, you know a tiny bit more about them now.

So many labels are vanity projects that are put into cold storage when interest wanes and bills increase, and I didn't want to add my name to that list, so we worked with people we loved and projects that stretched us, keeping the costs low and the love high.

I had been a fan of Ian Rankin's for a long while. I knew he loved vinyl and was a man with great taste in music after he gave me a guided tour of Edinburgh and interviewed me as part of the Edinburgh Book Festival. The interview will stay with me for ever, as it took place in the week that Jon Brookes died. I think I would have cancelled on anyone else, but I knew how sensitive Ian was and the love from the audience and him was overwhelming. I had just written a book, and going from one discipline to another opened some interesting doors. I got a sneaking suspicion that Ian would love to be involved in putting out something on vinyl.

He wrote a short story especially called 'A Little Bit of Powder', set in the music world and based on legendary events supposedly involving Alex Chilton. I wrote and recorded some theme music and we pressed up a 500-copy run.

We joked that it was probably second-hand shops that sold the largest combination of Ian Rankin books and Charlatans records, and thought it would be interesting and irresistible to approach a charity shop. And there was the added bonus that the profits would be put to a good cause.

Oxfam is a place where both Ian and I had dug through endless James Last albums to try and find a hidden gem. We mentioned our idea to Anton Newcombe. He told us he had done some work with Oxfam and gave us their contact details. And that was that.

People really picked up on the buzz. Ian and I did some radio interviews, and the feeling took me back to when The Charlatans were releasing records for the first time. On the day the record was released, Ian sat in his local Oxfam. People there were surprised to see him and got their records signed. I played a gig at the Union Chapel and called in at a couple of the Oxfams near by. We chose to take a slightly different path and we loved it.

The reason for making a record can sometimes be fairly oblique. I met Professor Tim O'Brien at a Sigur Rós show we were both at, which took place beside the radio telescope at Jodrell Bank. I spent the afternoon in the visitors' centre listening to various space sounds and the audio from the crews of long-decommissioned rockets. I got on really well with him and we hatched a plan to work together

OGen 069 ended up as a free MP3 download from the Jodrell Bank site. We paired Tim up with Jim Spencer, one of the four partners at the label and long-time producer of not only The

Charlatans but also Johnny Marr and New Order. Professor Tim brought signals from spacecraft at the dawn of the space age, the death throes of an exploding star and the sounds which flooded through the universe after the Big Bang. Producer Jim took them and made them into a fully formed song.

Tim and Jim came over to Tim Peaks at both Festival No. 6 and Kendal Calling to present it, and minds were blown, including that of Jon Hopkins, who spoke to Tim afterwards about sounds and science, while I looked on like a proud parent. It was a measure of what we had achieved as a label.

What does the song sound like?

It sounds like the planets of the solar system clubbed together and made a dancefloor smash.

One of the first records on which we took a slightly different route was the sixth single, 'Gold E' by Nik Colk Void. Instead of a conventional cover, the sleeve was a polyurethane cast moulded from the test pressing, each one individual by nature of the material and the method used to hand-make it in the warehouse. The sleeve could be played but came with a warning that there would be a scrap with your stylus, with the plastic winning – that didn't stop several people posting films on YouTube of the needle in the grooves.

As a music mogul with a label I thought I'd reach out to a hero in the same field, and got me a vinyl recommendation from Daniel Miller. Like any self-respecting label boss he chose a gem from his own back catalogue – a record I didn't have but one I had once owned and loved for many years.

After I left Hollywood my records weren't far behind me, deported from LA. But you know what? They didn't like it that much there anyway. It was just too damn hot. But when they caught up with me some of the boxes and lots of the records were ruined – rain-damaged and bedraggled. They had been left by a baggage handler on the runway at LAX during the heaviest downpour for three years. Now if I can find a part of my life that is more like the lyrics to a sprawling Jim Webb song, then I am yet to live it.

One of the victims out on that runway was the third LP release by Mute: *Fireside Favourites* by Fad Gadget. An electronic record made by Frank Tovey, it had been a mainstay on my turntable since I first picked it up in 1985. This was the album Daniel recommended.

By various methods you can end up with multiple versions of a record. I try not to be too possessive, which means entering the risky world of loaning. But I am a borrower too. There is a sharing element to music which means that just because you're the owner of a piece of black plastic, you shouldn't shirk your responsibility of giving that music to others. Because of this, multiple copies are an analogue but expensive version of streaming. They come about through general wear and tear, non-returned loans and just the warm feeling of buying a certain record again and again and again.

Many is the time I have arrived at a party with a record, played it a few times, and someone else has left the room with it. Other times, I have arrived at a party with a record, played it once, and been handed it back and asked to put it away. But the thing about music, I suppose, is that it's a way of finding if anyone in a room shares your impeccable taste.

Topping my list of multiples would be:

Unknown Pleasures and *Closer* by Joy Division
20 Jazz Funk Greats by Throbbing Gristle
The Velvet Underground and Nico
A Love Supreme by John Coltrane
After the Gold Rush by Neil Young
Check Your Head by the Beastie Boys
Loveless by My Bloody Valentine

Before Today by Ariel Pink's Haunted Graffiti
Surf's Up and *Holland* by The Beach Boys
Back to the World by Curtis Mayfield
Chelsea Girl by Nico

Numbers of these range from five to twenty, but when I buy one I am on high alert for giving it away. If you see me in a record shop with any of the above, feel free to ask if you can have it, and I'll probably let you – with a short review and a quick rundown on which are my favourite tracks.

I always kept quiet about my multiple-album buys, thinking it might be something that was linked to previous obsessions, like the drink and the drugs. I wasn't sure if it was something that other people did, but I was at an event at Somerset House where I was interviewed by Pete Paphides about vinyl and collecting records in general. It was kind of like a group-therapy session for record obsessives – myself, Bill Brewster, Pete and Jo Wallace talking through our vinyl lives. They all mentioned that multiples were a part of their lives too – phew!

Royal Trux, *Thank You*

Recommended by Lauren Laverne

Wearside Xanadu

In 1983 I was a big fan of Radio 1. John Peel, Janice Long and Andy Kershaw ran free. Laibach would be played on the same day as Frankie Goes to Hollywood and Orange Juice. It was the place where I first heard Half Man Half Biscuit, Ivor Cutler and The Bhundu Boys.

A decade later, outside of Steve Lamacq and Jo Whiley I started to feel less of an affinity for the station, but didn't have anywhere to take my ears. Now I am not going to get all DLT on you and lock myself in a room decrying all modern music while smashing up the gaff. In fact, Radio 1, I think looking back it was me, not you. Around 1999 I was enjoying Nic Harcourt and *Morning Becomes Eclectic* on KCRW, and *Jonesy's Jukebox* on Indie 103.1 – stations in the LA area, my home at the time.

When I came back to the UK I was in limbo somewhere between Radio 1 and 2. The world had got bigger and smaller at the same time. There were hundreds of TV and radio stations springing up, whole channels dedicated to nothing but fishing, cooking, cars, auctions, car auctions, fish cooking – everything but monkey tennis.

People wanted much more choice, while stations were becoming narrower and more specialised. Magazine circulations were crumbling, record sales were plummeting – everything was changing.

In stepped 6 Music at the BBC. The station was a shot in the arm for bands, music and everyone with taste. Eclectic, funny and, most of all, enjoyable, it was made for all of us. Not just me – for everyone who loved music.

New bands were emerging, to the delight of disenfranchised ears all over the world. I even did a couple of shows myself, alongside mainstays Iggy Pop, Cerys Matthews and Jarvis Cocker. Steve Lamacq found a new home and a rightful spot.

The Charlatans were session guests on Lauren Laverne's show, and she introduced me to new music and even new genres in my newly structured days spent writing a book, running a record label and generally being readily distracted. The Charlatans were the first band that Lauren went to see with friends rather than her parents – Newcastle City Hall in April 1992. We have lived some parallel musical lives, from Lauren's experiences with her band Kenickie to her presenting *Transmission*, where I guested with Carl Barât on the Adam and the Ants classic 'Ant Music' – dressed as Adam. I performed solo and with The Charlatans at Lauren's 'Christmas Jumper Jam' at the Union Chapel in London. She interviewed me at Glastonbury, and it was never more than a couple of months that we wouldn't bump into each other.

Not much brightens up a day more than finding out that a new record shop is opening. Via Edwyn Collins, I heard about a band taking over the abandoned Sunderland Tourist Board office – insert your own gallows humour here. Pop Recs Ltd was born. Frankie and the Heartstrings carried in boxes of vinyl and turned rooms into spaces where affordable music lessons were given. Local artists had themselves an instant gallery, and the band's spirit and contagious enthusiasm built a Wearside Xanadu. Friends such as Edwyn Collins, The Cribs and Franz Ferdinand all played live there. I gave them a call and stopped by on a solo tour in 2013. Our parting words were, by hook or by crook, The Charlatans would play there one day.

Fast-forward to 2015, when everything you just read in the last few minutes conspired and came together in a Kenickie vocalist/ace radio-station festival/ex-Tourist Board-now-record-shop alignment of the planets whirlwind.

Lauren's choice of album was *Thank You* by Royal Trux – an album I'd never owned, but a band I'd always liked. As our gear was being set up, I had a search through the racks that had been shifted next door. They had one pristine, unopened copy – Pop Recs had a stall at the Radio 6 Festival in Newcastle, and it was in a pile they were taking along to find new owners.

Royal Trux came hot on the heels of the coolness of grunge – heroin chic mixed with actual heroin and actual chic. They were caught in the middle of the bun fight that ensued after Nirvana broke through to the mainstream, with labels insistent that they didn't want to miss out on the next big thing, despite not having a clue what the next big thing would be. It resulted in a million-dollar deal, kicked habits and a legacy of some great songs.

Lauren was for real. She'd gone from young punkka to multi-media, super-savvy taste-maker and DJ. She still has all the enthusiasm and integrity of someone who really cares – the same spirit that you'll find in Pop Recs Ltd.

In 2014, at the 6 Music Festival at Victoria Warehouse in Man-chester, I played a solo show with my bandmates Hatcham Social and Mark Collins. At the following year's festival, The Charlatans were asked to headline The Sage in Gateshead. It was a sea change and a beautiful moment for our band. I have never shied away from the fact that ending up as a chicken-in-a-basket nostalgia act would be far worse than us calling it a day, and here was the most relevant and radical radio station around saying to the world that we were part of their gang. We had made *Modern Nature* and we knew we loved it. It was a case of seeing what everyone else thought and being asked to hold the torch. Closing the final night was the kind of affirmation we all needed after losing Jon.

I've always loved doing gigs that are out of the ordinary, and the one at Pop Recs was a perfect example. Tickets were £5.00, or £2.50 with concessions, and all of that money went towards the upkeep of the shop. I remember reading about a benefit gig that the Sex Pistols played one Christmas Day in Huddersfield. It was for striking firemen, and the band took presents for the kids. I was eleven at the time and fifty miles away, but the thought of that gig stayed with me for a long time. The Pistols did it without too much fanfare, and it went against the media's portrayal of the band as selfish, sneering yobs, so it was given little coverage.

At our Pop Recs show Dave Harper from Frankie and the Heartstrings made a sweet-potato stew that volunteers, band and crew all shared. There was no stage and we stood eye to eye with the 200 ticket-holders. Young kids sat cross-legged on the floor at the front, and we stuck around signing posters at the end. There was something about the spirit of Frankie and the Heartstrings that captured the essence of what being in a band means to me. We asked them to support us on a tour, where they sold Christmas cakes that included a download of their festive song featuring Edwyn Collins. For two of the nights they swapped places and went on after BMX Bandits and Riding the Low so they could play in front of a larger audience.

*

Like a rare rhinoceros, some things have to be protected when the numbers have started to dwindle.

There is no better power than people power, and there is a musical ecosystem that involves studio labels, venues, pressing plants, shops, manufacturers and a whole host of businesses that would disappear if some of the elements were removed. Shops are the final but visible part of the equation, the people who sell it all for us. If there was no outlet for vinyl, a huge part of the enjoyment of the buying process would disappear. Vinyl needed a helping hand. Step forward Record Store Day.

Then step forward critics of Record Store Day.

I would like to declare myself a big fan.

So, for one day a year labels and artists get together and try and get as many people into record shops and buying records as possible. Limited editions, coloured vinyl, exclusive re-pressings – some people say it's cashing in, but that's almost the point of it. Think of it as Christmas Day for records. The beneficiaries are primarily the shops, but labels get a cash boost, pressing plants are booked solid and artists have an excuse to clear out the closet and do something special. There's an irony to people complaining about this, but the important part is that the record-making machine is working at full capacity.

Sometime around every New Year, I start to wonder what I am going to do for Record Store Day. I feel the pressure that it has to be worthwhile for all involved at the label. In 2011 I had just received the finished mixes for my second solo album. I sent early copies to Lauren Laverne and Paul Weller, and they both chose 'A Case for Vinyl' as a standout track. I'd read about Record Store Day and didn't want it to happen without me, so I mentioned it to our distributor. He said that if we wanted to do something, we needed it to go into manufacturing within twenty-four hours. I got Sam Willis from Walls to remix the track for the B-side overnight, and the following day the buttons were pushed for the first O Genesis Record Store Day single. Since then we have done at least one each year. Queues at the shops have started earlier, and on Record Store Day 2015 I was interviewed live on Sky News outside Piccadilly Records.

Yes, it's getting bigger and maybe less cutesy, but the fact remains that in April 2015 there were not only more record shops than at any time in the last ten years, but also dedicated vinyl single and album charts. It's not perfect, but not many things are. Most music fans possess a healthy cynicism, which makes for active discussions about over-commercialisation and messing with the natural order of things, and general goofing about over how they think things should be done.

There's always some kind of call for vinyl-lovers to march on the gates of eBay with flaming torches to protest that some people have the audacity to sell records on at vastly inflated prices. You might disagree, and I'm sure some people will take me to task when we meet, but in some ways I'm not that concerned with what happens to a record after it's been bought from the shop. I'll not buy a copy of a Record Store Day single from eBay, but I'm not overly bothered if someone else wants to. On each Record Store Day I've spent all day in the shops that stand to benefit, and they are crammed with real music fans buying records for themselves. In 2015 there were upwards of 400 releases, limited to 500 or even 1,000 copies. That is a lot of vinyl, but while I was never that good at percentages it isn't as high as some of the naysayers make out. There are calls to bring in draconian rules to stamp out any kind of reselling, but it's all reminiscent of some kind of Witchfinder General, which goes against the general laissez-faire ways of the music world.

Without Record Store Day, I'm not sure The Charlatans would have worked with Sinkane or Laura Cantrell, and I wouldn't have been live on Sky TV and DJing in Piccadilly Records on a beautiful spring afternoon. So I'm not sure whether the tide has turned, but each year there's younger and younger and more and more kids collecting vinyl. Some of the people arriving at Piccadilly Records had been to a record fair in a hotel function room near by. I was shown a red-vinyl copy of *The Velvet Underground and Nico* by two girls who were maybe fourteen years old. We talked about Warhol and Lou Reed for a little while, and they bought the Honeyblood Record Store Day single. It reminded me of exactly what I was doing from 1982 onwards – spending time with friends in town and excitedly looking through racks of vinyl. Everything changes but everything stays the same. Records and record shops might be an endangered species, but we're going to do everything we can to keep them alive and help them thrive.

T. Rex, *The Slider*

Recommended by Johnny Marr

Johnny, Johnny

My friend Panhead cried when Marc Bolan died. We were on a school trip to Menai in Wales. There were six of us in a dormitory, and David Mills's bed separated Panhead and me. Panhead had two older brothers who would have shown him the ropes with T. Rex, and possibly even Tyrannosaurus Rex. We were ten years old.

In 1983, I was sixteen years old. It was the year I left school – a watershed for anyone, but it was the year after the Falklands War and we were in the midst of the miners' strike, which meant times were particularly bleak. There was not much to hang on to or hope for. At school I had been told that there were no jobs for someone like me, and they weren't sure or much bothered about what I would end up doing once I left. My prospects were as slim as my interest in them.

Only a few miles away there was someone roughly my age – well, three years older – who was about to become the guitarist of his generation, in a band that would resonate around the world.

I had heard stories about Johnny Marr going to Morrissey's house in Stretford, making it seem possible that one day the Keith to my Mick would ring on the doorbell. But in the meantime, it was interviews I was ill prepared for, for jobs on the bottom rung of any career ladder – post-room guy, cleaner, general dogsbody.

Soon, the places where I was my spending time were being name-checked in songs. No longer was it Highway 61, Route 66 and Ocean Boulevard that were the backdrops, but Rusholme, Southern Cemetery and Whalley Range – even Manchester schools.

As 1983 turned into 1984, everyone in Manchester was tracing family trees to try and find a link with The Smiths. Jeff Hunt told me his sister worked with Andy Rourke's mum. Steve Drew had been writing to post-punk nearly men The Hoax. We never thought anything of it until the drummer turned out to be Mike Joyce. We were close to the beating heart of what was what. Even their names were regular: the singer went by his surname, almost like the shout of a disdainful teacher, and the band name was deliberately commonplace. They were kitchen-sink drama in a world of Hollywood movies. We had nothing to stand behind, so we stood behind them.

They allowed you to dress as you wanted. Johnny wore beads one week, and the following one everyone had them, when the week before you wouldn't have been allowed to even think about it. Whereas Morrissey's touchstones were Shelagh Delaney and Oscar Wilde, Johnny brought in some glam, backed up with twelve-string folk – the flourish of Mick Ronson with the discipline of Ralph McTell.

When Johnny first played with The Charlatans was one of those moments when everything stands still and you try and take in what's going on. The first time you play with somebody new isn't the time you walk out in front of a crowd going wild; it's more likely to be that afternoon, with none of the pomp and circumstance. And so it was that Johnny walked into a makeshift rehearsal room at the Lomax venue in Liverpool, and we set about finding our way around 'Weirdo' and 'Right On'.

I was introduced to Johnny at a bonfire party round at his house on the outskirts of Manchester. I distinctly remember the surprised – or was it happy? – look on his face when I told him I really loved his guitar playing on Stex's 'Still Feel the Rain', a 1992 single on Some Bizzare Records.

When we needed help recording at our new studio in 1998, Johnny suggested an engineer he'd worked with called Jim

Spencer. We have recorded at Johnny's studio a few times. He almost produced *Up at the Lake* but that didn't work out, although he did help us with the running order. Shamefully, I have to admit that I think we were all hitting things a little too hard, especially me, and that may well have put him off.

Anyway, it's fair to say that Johnny has helped us out on many occasions. And he helped me out a lot before we ever met.

Hey, Tim – I'm very happy to set you off to find *The Slider*.

It should have lyrics in the inner sleeve, I think.

Howard Kaylan and Mark Volman aka Flo & Eddie on amazing backing vocals. Holy shit. And when I'm sad . . . I slide. Keep a little Marc in your heart. Johnny X

London is a big city. I have lived there on four separate occasions, in Chiswick, Chalk Farm, Camden and Seven Sisters. One of the biggest attractions for me was the record shops in W1, Soho and Camden, especially in the 1990s, when there were dozens of them. Though many have changed, dwindled in floor space or vanished completely, some remain – and in some cases have recently expanded.

Sister Ray just opened a shop in Shoreditch selling only vinyl – it must be the first time in ages that that's happened. I bought *The Slider* second-hand from Sister Ray in Berwick Street, with accompanying lyric sheet intact.

Lou Reed, *Lou Reed*

Recommended by Lawrence

Yes! I met Lawrence

Some days can unexpectedly go from mundane to amazing and right back to mundane with absolutely no warning – just a momentary colourful stitch in life's rich tapestry.

Being in a band means landing in a city, never quite having a sense of belonging but being offered a welcome that means you don't want to leave. Chicago has always had a special place in the heart of The Charlatans. It is always in the middle of a tour, with no jet lag and no anxiety about leaving. We were always in the swing of it, and the people of Chicago live amid an amazing musical heritage. We must have played there fifteen times, and there's just something about it – the Double Door, the Vic Theater, the Aragon Ballroom. And our favourite, The Metro – for some reason it was always the best gig.

When a place is always a highlight for a band, you want to pick it apart and analyse why. So why was Chicago so good?

I've got a theory. I'm not sure if my theories hold more water than anyone else's, but a tour is often a case of a day of not much happening with a firework display at the end. You get a lot of time to mull over the fireworks, so this is my theory. The Charlatans' sound was forged in the crucible of the music of late-1980s north-west England, which was a melting pot of twelve-string Rickenbacker West Coast harmonies and industrial, post-Motown Detroit. But to me, another city was having the biggest effect of all: Chicago, which was responsible for introducing dancefloors and repetitive beats to kids from Manchester housing estates.

Well . . . that and Ecstasy.

I grew up listening to bootlegs. I had vinyl copies of a couple of Joy Division ones, but to me they existed best on cassette. £3.50 from the underground market in Manchester, identikit artwork and a promise from the guy running the stall that this near-legendary gig at the Rayleigh Pink Toothbrush had to be heard to be believed. There is an intensity to a live show that comes through regardless of whether the tape is from the mixing desk or the bootlegger has switched the Dolby on or off. Onstage fights, mass singalongs and glitches are captured for ever. They have something an authorised live album often misses, whether it's the fact that the band were unaware they were being recorded or the lack of pomp and ceremony, with no release dates or reviews – just a moment in time, complete with the guy standing near the microphone constantly shouting the name of the song that you know the band always plays last.

I'd seen Charlatans bootlegs but had never bought or listened to one. I'm not sure if my overly critical ear would allow me to hear them properly, but they were something I associated with other bands.

We played a gig in Chicago in 1991, and there was a definite sense of it being a memorable show. We all had the same feeling when we came off stage. Often, immediately after we've played, there's a period of time when only glitches, mistakes or difficulties are at the forefront of your mind, then that fades and the euphoria of the night hustles its way in. The doubts would be clubbed over the head with a couple of bottles of beer and the enjoyment would take over. That night in Chicago didn't seem to have any of those niggles. We'd been relaxed, on top of our game, and we were all stoked about the show – plus it was the first time we played 'Can't Even Be Bothered' and 'Between 10th and 11th', an unreleased song that became the title of our second album.

A few days later, we got a cassette from the sound engineer – a

C90 with 'The Charlatans live in Chicago 21st February 1991' written on it in felt tip. We had kept away from releasing a live album at that stage – like a *Best of* . . . I think there's a time in a band's career when a live album works. But we had our cassette, and the idea was put forward that we should release our own bootleg. I'm not sure how many bands have bootlegged themselves, but I'm happy to add the name of The Charlatans to the list.

Beggars Banquet assisted with the quasi-illusion of the record being some kind of illegal recording, which we all thought gave it more credence. They pressed up a few thousand copies and sent them to record shops that we knew dealt in 'under the counter'-style releases.

So, yeah, Chicago was always a great show for us, and it became the place where we bootlegged ourselves.

*

I always loved days off in American cities, partly just because they were easy to navigate around. The parallel streets, criss-cross avenues and neatly ordered blocks meant even someone like me with no sense of direction could spend time exploring, knowing that I could find my way back to the hotel, venue or wherever we were meant to be. It's not often that you get time on your own on tour, and because of that these moments were precious.

One such wander took me into Neiman Marcus on North Michigan Avenue in Chicago. I was buying a T-shirt on a Monday morning at 9 a.m., which meant the shop was completely empty. As I was handing the T-shirt to the cashier I looked at him, but he wasn't looking at me; he seemed to be in some kind of trance. I figured that something was happening just over my shoulder, where the server's eyes were fixed, and whatever it was meant I was being overlooked. He was completely unaware that his mouth was slightly open. I tried to lean my head into his gaze but it had no effect. The only thing to do was to turn around and see what the distraction was.

Fire? Advancing bear? Supernatural phenomenon?

What I saw was something much more surprising. Behind me in the queue, the source of the open-mouthery, was Hollywood superstar Steve Martin. He had two shirts in his hand, but no one was going anywhere; this was a stalemate situation until the cashier's hypnotic state was broken. I joined in.

In amazement, and in a rare submission to fandom, I asked Martin if he would be kind enough to sign his autograph and whether I had time to dash to the stationery department for some suitably deluxe paper while he continued with his transaction. He replied with the words 'No need' as he produced a business card from his inside jacket pocket. We had a brief discussion about why he was there. Buying shirts was his reply. I felt like it was my own personal joke from him, with a Woody Allen vibe to it. He signed the card, handed it over, took his shirts, smiled at me and nodded, turned around and left. It was like a scene from *Mr Ben*.

I looked at the signature and found the other side was printed with a message:

This certifies that you have had a personal encounter with me and that you found me warm, polite, intelligent and funny.

Steve Martin's card always struck me as a brilliant take on celebrity culture. This was pre-camera phones, and even though he only used them for a short while, it gave people everything that they would want from an encounter with him. The whole thing came back to me on a trip to Manchester to introduce a showing of *Lawrence of Belgravia*, the Heavenly film that documents the story of the Felt, Denim and Go-Kart Mozart frontman. Lawrence had a fistful of flyers that he was ready to sign when the audience came out; he'd already written his name on them and was ready to add the names of whoever asked him for one.

I told him about Steve Martin's card, and we agreed that some kind of official memento should exist for anyone who had the good fortune to meet Lawrence. He pointed out a colour and font on his flyer, and the following week we sent him his new business-style cards, printed with the four words:

Yes! I met Lawrence.

I got in touch with him a couple of weeks later to see if the cards had arrived and to get an album recommendation.

Hi Tim, *Tim Book Two* is one of the best titles ever! I'd luv 2 b part of it – Yes, I'm in. What is the plot then? Television and Lou Reed is 2 obvious although now I've said that I quite fancy *Lou Reed*, 1st solo LP, which is in my top 5 ever – I love it 2 death and it gets such a bad rep – idontgetit. My choice: *Lou Reed* – Lou Reed.
Thanks. Lawrence.
Oh yeah, by the way, I was handing the cards out last night in Bristol to fans – they go crazy when I casually hand them one, they can't believe it! It's a stunning idea. I love them.

When I'm talking about music with someone I don't really know, I'll often mention Lou Reed. If the other person doesn't like his music or get enthusiastic, then I know I can bring the curtain down on the conversation. I love Lou Reed. I love his music, his bravery and the fact that he seemingly made music more to please himself than to aim for any kind of commercial success.

I love The Velvet Underground too. There's not much that Lou did that I'm not a huge fan of. Admittedly, his album with Metallica sits on top of a pile of records that haven't been played many times, but I'm saying it's my fault, not his – that one day I'll realise what he was doing and love that album too. That day hasn't happened yet, and I think it might still be some time off.

In 1990 I bought an original copy of *The Velvet Underground*, the one with Eric Emerson on the back of the sleeve. I bought it in New York City. I always imagined it had maybe once belonged to someone close to the band, as it was a rare copy that was withdrawn. I listened to 'Loaded' on repeat for several months in 1994, at the height of my Velvets' obsession.

Lou Reed was a hero of mine and I'd seen him onstage a few times but had never had the chance to meet him. If truth be told, I think I might have avoided it, as he was notoriously grouchy. While that wouldn't have spoiled it for me, it seemed like it was something he didn't really like doing, so I never went out of my way to make it happen. Then one day, when and where I least expected it, it happened: fate stepped in and put me fifty feet away from him at Piccadilly railway station in Manchester. He was sitting unaccompanied, drinking a coffee. It was a while before I had to catch my train, so I thought this was a message from above. I quite often get recognised and usually enjoy a conversation, although it can never be too protracted due to the impending travel arrangements for everyone involved.

I knew Lou would like it too, but I just wasn't sure if Lou knew that he would.

Anyway, I fancied a coffee, so I made my way over. In the two minutes I had been thinking about it nobody had approached him – maybe his grouchiness went before him or maybe he just looked like an everyday guy in his jeans and leather jacket. He'd just released *Set the Twilight Reeling*, which I thought was the best album of his later period, but criminally it hadn't really set the world on fire.

I ordered my coffee and in my politest way possible whispered, 'Mr Reed?' in Lou's general direction. He turned, nodded and made quite a New Yorky noise of affirmation in my general direction. So far, so good.

'If at all possible, would you sign an autograph for me?' He looked up to see me holding a card and a pen.

'If I fucking must,' he fired back, and I was filled with the warm glow of receiving the full Lou Reed experience. I let him know that I would be OK if he didn't fancy doing it, but suddenly a smile replaced his grimace and he beckoned me to give him the pen and paper. He signed it and handed it back, and I decided I'd put our in-depth conversation on ice till the next time we met.

A thank you from me, and an honest, genuine 'Have a nice day' from him, and my one and only meeting with Lou Reed was over.

I'd never owned Lou's debut solo album on vinyl. He ended up making around twenty solo albums, but that first record and I never got introduced. I knew a lot of the tracks, as some featured in various forms on the many compilations out there. Without any kind of restriction, I think I would buy every album by every band I've ever liked, but there have to be some rules, and, well, the sheer weight and volume of vinyl make it impossible. As any record collector knows, a stack of vinyl reduces the size of a room by twelve inches on each side. But the biggest factor holding me back was that in my twenties and thirties I was moving around – a few different flats in London, various places in Manchester and Salford. Moving around with a vinyl habit that's not in check comes with a shellac tax. Every record gets boxed up and transported, with some staying boxed till the next move. Maybe I'm settled now. Maybe that's what my records are telling me. They had a trip from LA, but now they're home and out where they ought to be.

*

As part of the *Modern Nature* tour, we took in Japan. Lots of mates were in bands when I was in my teens, and by my twenties it seemed almost everyone I knew had started one. So, a gig at the Rayleigh Pink Toothbrush or Moles in Bath might have been impressive, but lots of our mates had blazed those trails before us. Japan is a different kettle of sushi altogether – you don't get to play there just because you've got a few mates who'll fill up a small venue on a rainy Tuesday. Nope, it meant you'd made it. It didn't mean you were going to last, but who cares about lasting? It was about burning bright, and there's nowhere brasher and brighter than Japan. We've made regular trips over and have lots of friends to catch up with when we get there.

Shibuya is where all the young people in Tokyo shop. I can't really think of an equivalent anywhere else in the world. But Japan is like that; lots of things don't have an equivalent – restaurants where the food is alive, hotels where the rooms are capsules, and places where everyone dresses as cartoon characters.

There's a sense of being further away from home than anywhere else in the world. If you don't read Japanese, then signs are just a series of unfathomable characters, and there are few cultural touchstones that match ours. People are unafraid to walk the streets wearing surgical masks. Rather than another country, Japan has always seemed more similar to *Blade Runner.* In recent times we have caught up a little, but around 1991 it left my head spinning.

One kind of space, though, is always the same. The template for record shops seems universal: 12-inch racks built to accommodate albums, and CD displays with just enough space around them for posters announcing new releases and live shows. The staff, too, have the classic record-shop-owner mix of knowledge, coolness, a bit of geekiness and a touch of musical superiority.

I walked into Disk Union, deep in the heart of Shibuya. I must have been in there half a dozen times, and it's like one of those films where someone ducks down an alley in a chase scene. Our schedule was pretty packed – lots of signings and some radio and a whole lot of people to meet. It's always a meditative experience to replace that with the gentle, repetitive flick through some records. Maybe it's muscle memory, but it's similar to a waking meditation, my left hand on the front of a rack and my right middle finger pushing each LP forward, with a standard three-second pause that could turn into longer, depending on what was revealed. Compared to the chaos of a tour bus or the frantic nature of a gig, it's my equivalent of fishing, or maybe sailing or mending something in the shed. Like someone entering a church, I get hit with some kind of inner peace.

I spent some time among the racks of Disk Union: perfectly presented vinyl originals of all your favourite records. The ones you never knew you needed, and ones that you maybe never even knew existed. In a way, Japanese record shops manage to do things better than anywhere else. That day the records I bought were all second-hand but pristine in appearance. In one of the bags was Lou Reed's debut album – he had died only a couple of months before, so I thought of Lou, Laurie Anderson, Piccadilly station, Steve Martin, autographs, Lawrence and how New York had lost a genius. I stepped back into the street. It was raining hard and looked even more like *Blade Runner* as I made my way to the venue we were playing that night.

The idea of finding something that someone has recommended for the book is fleeting when you walk into a shop with such glistening prizes. It's like an unmade jigsaw in my head, with the pieces scattered around the world, but the road trip, the journey, doesn't get more exciting than finding a record for Lawrence in Shibuya.

Allen Ginsberg, *First Blues*

Recommended by Peter Gordon

'Hey, Ernie, do you think there is too much echo on my voice?'

Sometimes with performances it's easy to get bogged down with agents, managers, promoters and schedules, all jostling and jousting for the alpha-dog role. Details, fonts and meal requirements are pored over, and the actual actuality of the gig can get lost in the fog of emails.

There's nothing better than a flurry of hit-and-run shows. In 2010 Mark Collins and I packed some gear into a mate's car and set off to play a short acoustic tour. We took bookings as we went, and ended up back home nearly two weeks later, having played a handful of small venues, announcing them just a few days in advance and enjoying the experience of minimal people being involved – meaning minimal fuss.

After *Modern Nature* came out The Charlatans took to the road and we played some of the best gigs we've ever done. That's how it happens sometimes with live performances: when the planets align, it's one of the most amazing feelings. While we were setting up for our London Roundhouse gig, I got a call from Peter Gordon asking if I would join him on some of his European dates. He'd put together an amazing set of musicians to play Arthur Russell instrumentals in Paris, Primavera Sound in Barcelona, and London. He asked if I would sing.

We were between commitments with The Charlatans, and I guessed that involving too many people might lead to complications that could scupper things, so we packed a few essentials and headed to Paris on the Eurostar, arriving a couple of days before the scheduled performance.

Being asked by someone like Peter Gordon was too good a chance to pass up. We had a few run-throughs with the band: fellow Arthur Russell stalwarts Rhys Chatham on flute, Peter Zummo on trombone and Ernie Brooks on bass. It felt like what I imagined Birdland would have been like – musicians at the top of their game, creativity above anyone's ego, and all the while being unhindered by the guitar, bass, drums and vocal constraints of the regular rock set-up. If truth be told, I felt a bit out of my depth, but that's a feeling I have always loved.

Like being at the start of a roller coaster.

There was an intuition between the musicians that was palpable, and each artist gave room for the others to stretch their legs, occasionally standing in the spotlight themselves. There was a sense that this was how music had been performed, in a completely natural way, in places like New Orleans, Memphis and New York City at the big bang of music sometime around the 1930s.

Peter Gordon's adopted audience gave themselves over to him, and it didn't take long. There's sometimes a sense of impatience at a regular rock gig: head to the bar when the new album tracks get an outing and go crazy when the big old favourites get wheeled out. But this was different, in that the band went where the music took them and the audience was enthralled.

There were two songs with vocals, and I sang on a Loose Joints number called 'Tell You Today'. After the show, while everything was being packed away, Peter leaned over to me: 'Barcelona tomorrow, Tim. You're coming, right?'

Arthur Russell's *First Thought, Best Thought* – sometimes known as 'The Instrumentals' – is one of my favourite albums; occasionally No. 1, but this is not a numbers game. The best ones circle round, and on any given day it could be any one of fifteen claiming the top spot. But on some days this is the best record ever for me.

The first version, the live version, came out on Crepuscule Records, the one-time European base and sometime home of Michael Nyman, Paul Haig, The Durutti Column and Peter Gordon. Playing on this recording are Peter Zummo, Peter Gordon, Rhys Chatham, Ernie Brooks and Bill Ruyle – all key members of the New York scene in the mid- to late 1970s.

During a conversation, I mentioned to Peter a stage I was curating at a festival. In his measured, honeyed New York drawl he said, 'Of course, Tim, that word "curated" wasn't really used back then. It's a modern word. At the Kitchen Club we just brought our friends over and everyone pitched in; there was no real pretension, but I suppose that's what we were doing. We were curating, but we didn't have that word to hand.'

Peter's recommendation was *First Blues* by Allen Ginsberg.

'You know Arthur used to live in the same apartment block as Ginsberg, in the East Village?'

I thought it best to try and find this record in Barcelona during some down time in the day. I'd often visited a record shop called Discos Castelló in a narrow side street just off the Ramblas – a haven of peace and quiet, one minute from one of the busiest streets in Europe. The shop had been there since 1928, and each time I headed down Carrer dels Tallers I said a silent prayer that it still existed. My few Spanish words didn't really work in there – it was just album titles and artists. I headed back to the venue with my new album.

So for a couple of days I was a member of Peter Gordon's band, spending time getting to know the others and sharing stories from our adventures and otherwise in music. As well as being in the bands The Necessaries and The Flying Hearts, both with Arthur Russell, Ernie Brooks was the bass player for The Modern Lovers. Arthur was a massive fan of ABBA, and Ernie told me his favourite song was 'When I Kissed the Teacher'. I've never really looked for a link between Arthur Russell and Chris

Carter, but a shared love of ABBA is something that made me smile.

Ernie asked when and where I was when I first heard Arthur's music. He really cares about Arthur's legacy and takes an interest in how the rest of the world discovered him – that's just about as much as anyone could hope for after they're gone. Ernie told me stories of how Arthur's apartment was filled with strands of magnetic tape, from floor to ceiling, all different projects that he was working on. From time to time he would bring a bunch of them to Ernie's to work on. Talking Heads' Tina Weymouth lived in the apartment below, and she stopped Ernie on the stairwell, asking how long Arthur was planning to be up there playing the same sections again and again. But here we were, over twenty years after his death, performing his music in Europe – an idea the band said he would have loved. And hated.

The first time I heard an Arthur Russell song was in the car in LA. Two kids from the local radio station played 'Soon-to-Be Innocent Fun'. I was stunned by the vocals, loud and echoey.

'You know, Tim,' Ernie said, 'Arthur once asked me, "Hey, Ernie, do you think there is too much echo on my voice?"

'I said, "Yes, Arthur, I do – but that's what makes it so perfect."'

The second time I heard one of Arthur's songs was after a recommendation from Ed Simons of The Chemical Brothers. And after that any mention of his name to people with good musical taste would bring an outpouring of love for the music he left behind.

I first came across Allen Ginsberg as many other people did – when we declared ourselves beat poets at the age of sixteen and took to cocktail cigarettes, philosophy and polo necks. He arrived in a job lot with Jack Kerouac – King of the Beats and writer of the most famous book of the genre, or at least it was to all my beat friends in Northwich in 1983 – and alongside William Burroughs, who accidentally killed his wife in a loaded-gun

William Tell re-enactment put down to heroin psychosis, and Neal Cassady, Kerouac's hero and the driver of Ken Kesey's bus. I knew Ginsberg through *Howl*, The Clash's 'Ghetto Defendant' and from him being in the background in the alleyway of Bob Dylan's 'Subterranean Homesick Blues' video.

The polo neck was put in mothballs and the books sat on a shelf until sometime in 1991, when Bob Dylan and everything beat-related took over my life during a tour of America. When we first went to the US, tours had an *On the Road* feel about them – no mobile phones or social media, so there was a sense of cutting ties with the world back home. We'd pull into a gas station after leaving a town and the tour manager would phone ahead to the next venue to let them know we were on our way and to check everything was sweet. There was a sense of romance in the never-ending roads: checking newspaper headlines in convenience stores to find out what was happening, then back on the bus with a deck of cards, some guitars, compilation tapes and a feeling that we were in a moment we'd treasure for the rest of our lives, through endless cassettes and miles on the road.

Repeated plays of *Blonde on Blonde* by Bob Dylan gave way to the *Basement Tapes* Volumes 1–5 by Dylan and The Band, bringing Ginsberg back into the picture, first in the name of the song 'See You Later Allen Ginsberg', and then in the film *Renaldo and Clara*, an ad hoc cut-and-paste road movie that I found on videotape in a second-hand shop in Buffalo. We watched it at the back of the bus.

I first came across Peter Gordon through his band Love of Life Orchestra, and in particular one song I heard in Amoeba Music around 2004. I had been listening to his New York peers, such as Rhys Chatham, Liquid Liquid and Glenn Branca, and his name cropped up a lot. It reminded me a little of the Haçienda years – a distillation of Detroit techno, afrobeat and everything that had gone before in New York, particularly Talking Heads and ESG.

The song was called 'Condo', and it opened a door that has stayed ajar, an obsession that remains to this day.

I played 'Condo' to Nik from Factory Floor while they were recording at The Charlatans' studio. It had a similar effect on her as it had on me. She contacted Peter on Facebook and sent him some music. Within a week he was playing on her track – the song was called 'Beachcombing'. They got on really well and arranged to play a show at the Factory Floor artists-in-residence series at the ICA, rehearsing at the warehouse we lived in, in Seven Sisters.

I gave Peter a copy of *Oh No I Love You*, and after a couple of weeks I heard back from him. I don't know whether, like a hypnotist, I had planted something in his head telling him we should collaborate, but if I did – or didn't – it still worked.

I had been putting together a track with Kurt Wagner that was missing something special. I sent it to Peter, with a hint that he might have the final piece of the jigsaw. He did – it was shaped like his saxophone. He is a multi-instrumentalist, and these are always the best people to work with. Peter plays drums, keyboards and could probably muster a tune out of pretty much anything. He added beats, keys, saxophone and atmosphere. What he returned changed the song completely – into what it could have been all along – and I knew we had a writing future together.

We covered an Arthur Russell song, 'I Couldn't Say It to Your Face' – one of the most beautiful songs I have ever heard. The fact that Peter had played on the original was like looking through a window into the room where they first recorded it.

So if these are all the ingredients to the recipe, then the cake is the slab of vinyl playing on my turntable now: 'Oh Men', with me singing, Kurt's lyrics and Peter's musical soundscape.

First Blues by Allen Ginsberg, as recommended by Peter, featuring Happy Traum, Bob Dylan and Arthur Russell; titles include 'CIA Dope Calypso', 'Vomit Express' and 'Stay Away from White House'. When I hear it I see Peter, hear *Howl* and remember 'Ballad of the Lights', polo necks, *Blonde on Blonde*, time in Texas with friends, Joe Strummer, Tijuana, jug music, New Orleans and white robes. Like the mixing together of all the elements you need to make a perfect dream – just like that scene in Michel Gondry's *The Science of Sleep*. They sneak in your ears and end up inside your head, under your skin and part of the fabric of your life. Different records for different people, but when your soundtrack crosses over with someone else's it makes for magical shared moments.

Peter and I have released songs that we have recorded together, with Peter producing and playing many of the instruments, and with one phone call bringing in my musical heroes who recorded with Arthur Russell. Often I just wonder how I got here.

The Beach Boys, *Pet Sounds*

Recommended by Kevin Shields

We need to talk about Kevin

Before they hit the signature My Bloody Valentine sound, Kevin Shields's band could sound like the best thing The Cramps never recorded to something that would sit comfortably on *C86* – not yet 100 per cent defined, but still brilliant.

The DNA. If you break it down into its constituent parts, a little bit of the magic can fall out, but when the ingredients are melodic bass, a drum sound that takes Cabaret Voltaire's *Nag, Nag, Nag* as its blueprint, Celtic riffs that could stir the coldest of hearts, American noise that out Sub Pops Sub Pop and great hair just in case there was any doubt . . .

I asked Kevin's partner prior to the release of their latest record, *MBV*, when there was going to be another album, and she said, 'That's a tough question. Kevin is so meticulous. It can take him up to an hour to choose a sandwich in the supermarket.'

To celebrate the release of *Loveless*, 200 promo cassettes were arranged to be sent out to the anxiously waiting critics and journalists. Kevin listened to each one before giving his approval. I'm not sure how many he sent back to be corrected, but the 200 that eventually did go out were to his satisfaction.

Like footballers who use space to run off the ball, it's not always about what you can see. That's when the genius happens. It's not just the individual members of the band, but how they complement each other, how they overlap and fill the gaps. Great musicians in great bands help each other to be the best they can be. To me, that's how it is with My Bloody Valentine.

Debbie Googe, their bass player, is one of my favourite people in the world, and Kevin is one of the most brilliant, gentle souls, whose outward expression of his inner feelings was manifested in the most perfect, massive noise imaginable. They never asked to be loved, but they're impossible not to love. One of the few bands I use as a yardstick of people's taste. If you like MBV, you're OK with me.

The laws of physics, audiophonics and the passage of time were theirs to bend. In one span of My Bloody Valentine time lasting five years they produced two cover versions, but they are two of the best cover versions ever recorded: their take on 'We Have All the Time in the World' and 'Map Ref. 41°N 93°W' by Wire. I'm not sure whether their Louis Armstrong cover was a message to fans and record-company executives, but knowing Kevin it wasn't just plucked out of the air, and was maybe even a bit of a two-fingers-up to anyone trying to rush them.

I've also heard that two of their songs were recorded in real time, but with My Bloody Valentine comes legend. The music press took a huge interest, but to them it was the process – all eyes and ears were on them, but they would never be hurried. Their eponymous album was pretty much recorded in secret and dropped on the Internet at close to midnight with little fanfare. Like I said, they are not affected by the laws of physics.

I'm not saying The Charlatans blazed any kind of trail when we released *You Cross My Path*, but Kevin told me as far back as 2008 that the next MBV LP would be put out on the Internet – anyway, if it's to do with them, I will take any kind of involvement.

I once asked Kevin if he'd play guitar for me at one of the shows I was doing with Mark Collins at the Union Chapel. He said he would, then I heard nothing for three months. I walked into the venue thinking that maybe it had slipped his mind, and there he was, sitting in a corner restringing his guitar. I was surprised to see him, but he seemed surprised that I was surprised. He'd said he'd be there, and he was. To share a stage with him was a trip and a huge honour that I'm hoping will happen again some day, but no rush as we have all the time in the world.

For a band that's made three albums proper in twenty-five years they've left a footprint on the history of music as relevant as anyone. Of course, Kevin makes it all sound so easy. His innovations were completely natural to him. He shrugged when he told me, 'All I did was tune two strings to the same note and strummed with the tremolo arm – that's how I got my sound.'

I had inadvertently followed them around as a DJ in 1987, and was at their last show in New York in 1991. I saw them at their first nights at the Roundhouse in 2008, when they decided to start playing again. After the Roundhouse, I travelled back to LA to see them at the El Rey Theater, which was being used as their warm-up show for Coachella. The El Ray is a 700-capacity venue in the Miracle Mile area of the city. It's an art-deco beauty that was opened in 1936. We parked the car and crossed Wilshire Boulevard – I was excited to see them in such a small venue. I walked down a side street and was struck by the enormity of the truck that had brought their gear. It was enough for a venue five times the size and was the first sign that Kevin had lost none of his singular view of what the band were there for. The second sign was when I walked round the corner and saw another truck the same size with three guys loading it up with flight cases that had already been unloaded.

Clips of the first Roundhouse gig on YouTube show people with their hands over their ears heading for the exit. Earplugs were available, but crowds had not been filmed leaving a venue en masse like this since *The Exorcist*. Kevin wouldn't have wanted it any other way.

I like the way he thinks.

*

We spent a few years going to shows together – Pixies at Village Underground, The Specials at Brixton Academy, Spiritualized at The Barbican. But most memorable of all was watching Brian Wilson with Kevin while standing in the rain at GuilFest in Guildford. In many ways, Brian Wilson is unique; in so many ways, he was the leading pioneer of the 1960s. He had an awkwardness in regular life that fed his genius. You would not find him touring with the band in the back of a van.

If you were to ask Kevin for an album in the same time it takes a landfill indie band to write and record one, you'd be out of luck. But stand back, give them room to do what it is they need to do, and the results are up there with any album that any band has ever made.

They are astonishing.

Both Kevin and Brian can put you in a trance – Kevin with repetition and noise, Brian with the sun-drenched harmonies and precise arrangements for which he's famous.

It's a well-known story that Brian didn't get out of bed for three years at the height of The Beach Boys' fame. Kevin is all about the sound, and *Pet Sounds* is too. It's the perfect choice for Kevin – one listen to 'Moon Song' by MBV reveals this. *Pet Sounds* was Brian's gateway to *Smile*, and nearly his undoing; *Loveless*, too, at times threatened to derail Kevin. Both artists are visionaries, and their music exists in parallel to whatever else was being made at the time.

The Beach Boys' *Surf's Up* will always be in my top ten records of all time. I listened to it constantly while we were making *Up to Our Hips*, but this is not about my recommendations, so let's stop me right here!

Roxy Music, *Roxy Music*

Recommended by Kevin Rowland

I want you to be me from now on

When I first joined The Charlatans, around the spring of 1989, I'd drive the 140-mile round trip from Cheshire, staying with whichever of the Midlands-based members of the band was nominated. I'm not sure if I was in demand or if they were spreading the burden, but each had their own distinct taste in music. With Jon Brookes we'd listen to some metal and a bit of dance music; at Rob Collins's the emphasis was on Paul McCartney; and at Martin Blunt's place it was a mod tip with the odd Stranglers interlude.

I loved the times we'd spend just listening to records and introducing each other to new sounds. The album that Jon Baker, our original guitarist, played more than any other was *Dionne Warwick Sings Burt Bacharach* – songs I was familiar with but that I'd never stopped and listened to; they always struck me as a bit middle-of-the-road. But listening to them with Jon, I felt I'd been missing out on some of the most beautiful songs ever written. Music is so much about sharing a part of yourself with someone else – as the band progressed we absorbed each other's influences. What we wrote as a band was subconsciously influenced as much by Curtis Mayfield as it was by Deep Purple or The Rolling Stones.

'Do You Know the Way to San Jose' became ever present on mixtapes that I made for friends – alongside Orange Lemon's 'Dreams of Santa Anna', 'No Particular Place to Go' by Chuck Berry, 'You Keep Me Hanging On' by Colourbox and 'Me, Myself and I' by De La Soul. And it's still one of my favourite records of all time.

In 2012 I was asked to present a *Q* award for the song 'Walk on By' to Dionne Warwick. I was flattered when I was asked to present the award to Dionne. I was asked to say a few words. I came up with a couple of pages. Kevin Rowland was in the audience and came to find me after the presentation; we shared a love of everything Dionne had done, and he asked me if he could see the speech as we queued to get our photographs taken. Afterwards, Dionne asked if I would sign the speech so she could take it home with her . . .

Want to know what it said?

You do?

Are you ready?

Here goes:

Today I'm under doctor's orders not to speak. But when I told the doctor that I'd been asked to give an award to Dionne Warwick, he said I was under new orders to definitely do it. He said I could choose five hundred words and that I wasn't allowed to talk for the rest of the day. So I'd best get on with it, as I've used about a hundred already. I've written them down, so it's a mixture of an award presentation and a prescription.

Dionne Warwick's single was released in 1964, so has been a part of my life for as long as I can remember hearing music. But it wasn't until I decided I was a punk that I realised what a perfect song it is. The Stranglers' version was my gateway to discovering not just the beauty of 'Walk on By' but the talent of Dionne Warwick too – and with them came a love of songwriting through Burt Bacharach and Hal David.

When Bacharach, David and Dionne Warwick collaborated they managed to shape life's most heartbreaking elements into a form we would hear on each and every type of radio station. 'Do You Know the Way to San Jose' would be whistled by milkmen the world over, yet it was about shattered dreams and minimum-wage jobs and going back to Mum and Dad's. Knowing where you really belong. Pipe dreams.

'Walk on By' itself involves tears in the street, unrequited love and

Groundhog Day-style heartbreak. And they called it easy listening. If you listen properly, it's anything but easy – utter devastation, but given so much dignity by Dionne Warwick's rich, beautiful voice. One of the most soulful performances ever recorded, the song has been passed down through generations – brothers, sisters, friends, parents and agony aunts might have found it difficult to prepare us for the romantic tribulations that face each and every one of us in our lives, but this song, this performance would be in the manual for broken hearts, the emotions are so raw. Our protagonist hasn't started healing yet and we have a three-minute look into their lives. There's so much grace to the performance. It qualifies as one of the best vocal deliveries ever. It's just one of those songs where the music, lyrics and performance are of the highest calibre – each one complementing the other without taking away from the heartbreaking beauty.

Anyway, that's me and my word count nearly up. I just have enough left to say:

Ladies and gentlemen, the amazing, the beautiful Miss Dionne Warwick.

*

The focal point of Dexy's Midnight Runners was always Kevin Rowland, but the beating heart of the band was Big Jim Patterson – sidekick, co-pilot and trombone player extraordinaire. The two of them worked together to make Dexy's one of the most exciting bands in the world, then took some time out from each other and came back with the immense *One Day I Will Soar*.

I was asked to introduce a showing of their documentary *Nowhere Is Home*. It was a film of their run of live theatre shows in 2013, and Kevin and Jimmy had asked me to compère a Q&A and introduce the film at Festival No. 6 in Portmeirion.

It gave me a chance to catch up with Kevin and Big Jim. We talked about the weather and songwriting. I had sent Jim a rough version of a song The Charlatans were demoing a few months before and had asked him to work his magic on it. I remember buying Dexy's 'Geno' in Northwich back in 1980, and now I was standing there discussing making a record with one of them. He told me he had never done a brass arrangement before and jumped at the chance. What came back blew us away and reminded us of why we'd started a band in the first place.

When I told Lawrence (he of no surname) that Kevin's recommendation was *Roxy Music*, he said, 'That's such a great choice – you can hear in his music that he loves them.'

I walked into Holt Vinyl Vault on one of my regular visits while I was living down the road. I was feeling pretty chuffed, having spotted Irmin Schmidt's recommendation, *The Moray Eels Eat the Holy Modal Rounders*, when Andy, the proprietor, said to me, 'Are you still after the first Roxy record, Tim? I've managed to get a copy.'

'Yes, Kevin told me to buy it.'

'Kevin?'

'Kevin Rowland. It's his choice for *Tim Book Two*.'

'Ahhhhh! Right,' said Andy. 'I saw Dexy's on their "Projected Passionate Revue" tour in 1981. It was very intense. He told the audience to shut up in between songs. Kind of scary – lots of courage.'

To me this is the beauty of buying vinyl – a friend recommending a record, leading to me standing in a shop having a conversation with someone I hardly knew, talking about a concert that took place thirty-odd years before. As often happens in a record shop, the subject switched and whatever records I left with, the Roxy Music album wasn't one of them.

I don't know much about Roxy Music, but I've always loved their exotic sleeves and their even more exotic look. They were always slightly off my radar in the late 1970s, but their feather boas and gold lamé lit up a TV that was otherwise pretty dreary.

Saying that, I have most of Brian Eno's solo work.

And Phil Manzanera's *Primitive Guitars* is up there with the best.

I own hardly anything by Bryan Ferry as by the time I knew who he was, he seemed to have morphed into more of a crooner and, among other issues, my mum liked him, which didn't help. At all.

John, the pipe fitter at Runcorn ICI, was a big music fan and a few years older than me. He used to talk to me like some kind of war veteran about venues and scenes that were no longer around while we passed time in the canteen. I remember him saying that in 1973 there was nothing going on until Roxy and Bowie happened, that it was just the most boring musical landscape ever and it was like everything was black and white before they came along and brought some colour. He made it sound like the Dark Ages.

My musical life began in earnest around 1977, so I was late to the Roxy Music party, though I do remember 'Avalon' in our house. Is that Ferry or Roxy? Anyway, I'm certain Eno was long gone by then.

Fashion is something Kevin Rowland takes very seriously. On opening the Roxy album, the inside of the gatefold is like a big bolt of brightness – postcards almost, of the members all looking like they came from another planet. It's very now, so it must have been incredibly futuristic at the time.

The albums people had recommended were, for the most part, some kind of clue to their musical genealogy. They were often a record that suggested the direction the recommender was moving in. The drums on *In Search of Space* from Stephen Morris; the esoteric bliss of Lawrence's choice, Lou Reed's first album; and Kevin Shields's recommendation of *Pet Sounds*, revealing MBV's often overlooked sense of melody.

The line between Dexy's and Roxy Music is fairly direct, in a roundabout way. Roxy were pushing forward the idea of the aesthetic of a band, and Kevin Rowland took it even further. A band with a uniform, a uniform that changed a couple of times as the band was rebranded. Bryan Ferry and Kevin Rowland are seen as figureheads, both with a team of the most proficient musicians around, and both finding it difficult to hit the creative heights without those people.

I remember when I was kid, standing in my punk gear and a neighbour telling me about the hell he'd gone through as a fan of Bowie, Roxy Music and Marc Bolan in the late 1970s. He seemed a respectable, middle-management, office-workery kind of guy, but he spoke of being constantly chased out of town, threatened and beaten up. Moulton just wasn't ready for guys with eye shadow and feather boas. I'm not sure it even is now, so at the time these young lads would have seemed like a threat to the moral make-up of the universe. *Roxy Music* came out in 1972, when Kevin was nineteen. I can picture a young Kevin Rowland, somewhere in the Black Country, jumping at the chance to ruffle some feathers.

*

I left LA in 2010. Twelve years there had meant my roots in the UK had lost some of their grip. I'd moved to London when The Charlatans took off, and had spent time living in Manchester and at our studio in Middlewich.

There's nothing like packing your records into boxes to signify the end of one era and the start of another.

Me and the records stayed in the studio for a while and I rented a flat in Hoxton. I'd lived in Camden in 1993, just before Britpop hit its heights, when Blur and Suede ruled the waves. It was where everything seemed to happen. Journalists and bands would play pool in the pubs and hang out in the streets that were name-checked in the songs on the radio. Now, the cultural bubble had moved, and when I came back to Shoreditch it seemed to have arrived there. The Macbeth and The Old Blue Last had replaced

Camden Lock and The Good Mixer as places to hang out, and it was bands like The Horrors that were the soundtrack.

A friend told me about a warehouse in Tottenham that was a rehearsal room and studio, with some workspace and even a few residents. The nearest Tube was Seven Sisters and the actual warehouse was hidden amongst some outbuildings surrounding a gated delivery yard containing several clothing factories. Opposite stood a couple of brutalist glass-and-concrete buildings that were home to rival churches, who would battle it out every Saturday night and Sunday morning, with the choirs relying on volume above harmony or timing. There was a simmering hatred between the increasing number of disenfranchised Tottenham residents and the police, which blew up into full-scale rioting and looting in February 2013. Living in a warehouse surrounded by clothing factories and storage while the buildings around us burned was enough to make everyone think about moving on. Within weeks we received a notice telling us the warehouse was to be demolished to make way for new houses.

Our experience seemed to be representative of what was happening to musicians across the city. Rocketing rents and every available space being converted into apartments meant that rehearsal rooms were disappearing, and the paltry fees new bands earned from gigs, mixed with the fact that the labels were a lot less generous, meant that kids without some kind of parental assistance were unable to continue living in London.

When I moved into the warehouse, it was being used as a studio by Factory Floor. They had been recording their debut album for a couple of years, and each day I heard it getting closer to being finished, going from a collection of industrial beats and rhythms to the best album of 2013.

Magazines like *Select* and *Vox* were the big publications during my time in Camden. In the years in between, print sales had taken a hammering, but in their place websites like *The Quietus, Pop*

Justice and *Drowned in Sound* had sprung up – free and brilliantly written, with the advantage of having links to the music they were discussing. The *Quietus* gang moved into the warehouse, and it seemed that lots of what was going on was from our little Seven Sisters base. From being quite detached on arriving back in the UK, I started to feel involved again.

There was one record shop on the high street, Every Bodies Music. They specialised in reggae and dancehall – it was the place I first heard Prince Fatty, who went on to remix one of my solo singles – but they had racks and racks of every kind of music. I bought copies of *Hats* by Blue Nile and *Provision* by Scritti Politti in there, and a record that had all but been ignored since its release but that had started to be seen as a lost gem in more recent times: *Don't Stand Me Down* by Dexy's Midnight Runners, my favourite band by a mile at one point in my life.

Kevin Rowland is a wayward genius who has had more than his share of troubles. He is now someone I count as a friend, though someone I don't see often enough. But he's certainly someone I can phone to talk music, plans, ideas and football.

Dexy's had first struck with 'Geno'. It was their take on the marginalised soul-boy style, and it went to No. 1. Kevin then got some violins and blew everyone away with *Too-Rye-Ay*.

Expectations were high for their third album, and Kevin emerged with the band decked out in a new preppy Ivy League look. It was critically panned. Sometimes, though, you just have to release the record you've made and hope that the world catches up in time. A similar thing happened with Talk Talk's *Spirit of Eden*, and I'm holding out hopes that one day it will for *Who We Touch* by The Charlatans. In a parallel universe, *Simpatico* went multi-platinum.

Anything that's good is worth getting more than once, and I've bought copies of *Don't Stand Me Down* across several formats over a dozen times – whether it's to gently try to convince your friends, to share with someone you love, or simply to replace a copy that's been worn out by the needle on your record player. For me, the sign of the best records is that you want to start playing them again before you've even reached the end. I used to get the same thing with cigarettes and bowls of sugar puffs, but it's a while since I've had either for that very reason.

Kevin didn't want to release a single. As he saw it, you had to have the whole album or nothing at all – the record company would have considered Dexy's a singles band, so it must have made for some interesting meetings. Eventually he was talked into releasing 'This Is What She's Like', edited down from the album's twelve-minute version. It was a gatefold double 7-inch. Heavenly Records' Jeff Barrett told me I had to hear it. I remember being half crashed out and listening to 'Reminisce, Part Two', the B-side, a rolling three-chord trancey piano underneath chatty lyrics about finding the spirit of Brendan Behan in New York City. Jeff was the champion of *Don't Stand Me Down*. It came out in 1985 but I didn't own a copy until 1993 – oddly enough, around the time I moved to Camden.

One of the following stories is true; the other is what happened in a dream.

Salvador Dalí's personal assistant called me and asked me to go to the Savoy. She said it was very important. Salvador needed to speak to me urgently. I walked to the hotel foyer, where I was greeted with handshakes, nervous smiles and laughter. Ushered into the lift, I was led to the executive suite where Mr Dalí was sitting, smoking and waxing his moustache – he looked frail. 'Mr Burgess, I want you . . . to be me, from now on! I have lived long and I must now pass on my illustrious baton to someone younger and ready.'

I was staying in a hotel in Dublin when I received a text from Kevin Rowland. It said, 'Tim, please call me – Kevin.'

I called as soon as I got out of the minibus taking me and the rest of the band to the hotel from the venue. He answered.

'Tim, thanks for calling. Listen, I have an idea. When we released *One Day I Will Soar*, I always thought of it as a theatre piece as much as a pop record, so we want to do a run at the Old Vic. Problem is, I doubt I would be able to do seven nights a week. It's too intense.

'For a couple of nights a week, I want you to be me.'

The strange thing is, I'm sure I dreamt the dream before the real one actually happened.

Clifford T. Ward, *Mantle Pieces*

Recommended by Pete Paphides and Nathan

May contain ABBA

Much of the time vinyl shopping is a lone endeavour. Maybe it's just me, but there's a level of concentration that makes you forget who you're with, how long you've been looking and what you went in there for in the first place. There's a kind of glare that non-record shoppers have that they save for someone who's been looking through albums for more than twenty minutes.

It's rarely that exciting for whoever's with you, unless they're into records as much as you are, and if that's the case, they're probably oblivious to the fact that you're there too. Added to that, it's a kind of distraction when you see them pick out a sleeve and you just know it's a record you'd want to get. It's a lone-wolf occupation, and what I'm saying is, if I'm with you and we see a record shop, it's better that we just meet back up in an hour.

Some people have a list of the records they want that only exists in their head. Some have a pocketbook that's always updated with wants and needs. I find those notes pages on your phone are handy for not forgetting a recommendation and they're always to hand. It's a similar feeling to when I used to collect Panini football stickers at school – your eye was trained to spot the gems missing from your collection, and an adrenalin rush would hit you if you came across anything on your needs list.

So, much of the time purchases are planned ahead. Often a trusted record-shop owner or member of staff can let you know of something you simply have to buy. Beatin' Rhythm in Manchester even kept a box with records they thought I might like, and I'd listen to them whenever I went in. They had a surprisingly high hit rate.

Then sometimes someone in a shop will find a record they own and insist that you get a copy.

At the Isle of Wight Festival, as part of Tim Peaks, we invited Oxfam to set up a record shop alongside the coffee. For weeks, generous folks sent in their donations, and our strict rule of 'No James Last' stood firm – none of the flotsam and jetsam with musty sleeves that usually sulk at the back of the shop. We had original Who, Beatles and Rolling Stones 7-inches in pristine label sleeves, a John Cooper Clarke plectrum-shaped coloured vinyl, and as many other gems as you'd hope to find in a top-quality second-hand record shop.

I'd put together a day of bands, DJs and talks in the tent, and first up was an onstage interview with Pete Paphides. Riding the Low were playing. The View stopped by for a few songs, and Mark King made his DJing debut that day. They all left with a bundle of records. It's what links us all.

I was first in line for the Oxfam stall and made a fatal error: a record caught my eye, a combination of album title and artist I had not come across before and a feeling that this was something I needed to hear. I even took a photo of it, read the sleevenotes and placed it back in the rack, convinced that within the next hour it would not find a new owner. I was wrong. On my return, Nathan, Pete's friend, was holding the album, while Pete was enthusing about not only that record but the entire Clifford T. Ward back catalogue.

'I was looking at that record before,' I said quietly, but possession being nine-tenths of the law, things weren't going my way.

To make it worse, the stage manager, Paul, happened to be walking past. He stopped, put his hand on Nathan's shoulder, closed his eyes and slowly shook his head. 'Such a beautiful record,' he said.

Nathan took out the lyric sheet and beckoned me over. 'To an Air Hostess,' he said, and pointed to the words. 'Such a beautiful song,' he added, gesturing that I should read them. I knew I had lost my chance, as Nathan wouldn't undo his grip.

I have since forgiven Nathan, as he wasn't to know.

Paul removed his hand from Nathan's shoulder, shook his head and said, 'Clifford T. Ward died a few years ago. MS, I believe. Tragic.'

Those couple of minutes, along with watching Mark King DJ, meditating with Paddy Considine in a transit van and videoing Shaun Keaveny blowing out his birthday candles – they were all beautiful moments that made the festival for me.

There's a small sense of the unknown with a record like Clifford T. Ward's, the thought that it could leap into your top ten favourites and open up another branch of your vinyl family tree. *Mantle Pieces* is such a great title – a kind of English whimsy that reminds me of Anthony Newley, Gilbert O'Sullivan and even an element of David Essex. I got it home and went through the songs. Sadly, Clifford T. Ward died in 2001, but he scored himself a No. 8 hit single in the UK in 1973, a song called 'Gaye', which had passed me by.

And that was that. I'd found me a new singer to keep an eye out for, like a new seam in a gold mine. That can happen at any time. So, yes, much of the time record shopping is a lonesome kind of pastime, but it's sometimes good to buddy up and see what other people make of what's in the racks – just as long as Nathan doesn't end up buying the LP you were after.

King Curtis, *Live at the Fillmore West*
Recommended by Bill Bailey

Missing persons

I heard about a record shop I had never come across before, and its name intrigued me possibly more than any other shop name ever: the Record Detective Agency. It conjured up ideas of film noir and some kind of hard-boiled owner with his feet on the desk chewing a cocktail stick in the stifling heat.

'This dame you're after, she's going to take some finding. Sibylle Baier hasn't been seen on vinyl for some time. Nobody knows what happened to her. But don't worry, Mr Burgess, we'll get to the bottom of this case.'

Most of that didn't happen, but it was the hottest day of the year as I headed to Parsons Green and got my first experience of the Record Detective Agency.

I'd been told about Derek, the proprietor – I'd even spoken to him on the phone. A record-shop legend, he was always happy to spend time discussing otherwise long-forgotten bands. When I arrived, it wasn't Derek but a guy who looked after the shop while he was away. I asked about a couple of the LPs on my list, but the holiday-cover bloke metaphorically threw up his hands – it was too hot to actually throw up his real hands, plus there was so little room he'd have definitely knocked something flying. There was something of the pulp novel about the place, with organisation definitely not top of their list of concerns.

'There's a kind of order to things, but I'm not that sure what it is,' he said, in more of a welcoming than dismissive way, suggesting that you have to put the time in to get the rewards – a vinyl equivalent of 'No pain, no gain.' I was in for the long haul, so I headed out for a coffee and asked the guy if he'd like one too. He ordered a black Americano and told me with a wink that my generosity would guarantee a discount if I was to end up buying something. It was definitely morphing into a Philip Marlowe film.

The shop is laid out with just enough room for anyone under XL to move through the boxes of records nimbly, although there's not quite enough space to do it with your hands by your sides, so there's a kind of ballroom dance, hula-hoop-stance thing going on. I looked among the racks and we chatted from time to time, with him gently nudging the conversation towards Frank Zappa from whichever point it had started. Maybe three or four people came in while I was there, and with three customers at the same time we subliminally moved to a one-way system, with everyone's eyes going over to any record that held another potential buyer's interest for more than a couple of seconds.

It turned out that the guy looking after the shop was a record-dealer acquaintance of Derek's. He sells to other dealers, and while he's manning the till at the Record Detective Agency his reward is the pick of anything anyone brings in to sell. We talked about Clifford T. Ward – 'an amazing artist but somehow people just don't buy his records' – and how the previous day he'd sold Bob Marley's debut single for £1,500. Classic browsing talk.

After Isle of Wight-gate, I was on the lookout for *Mantle Pieces*. I'd made this known to Bob Stanley, and he informed me that he was a Clifford T. Ward fan too, perfectly describing him as 'potting-shed music'. Bob is like the patron saint of record-collecting. I recently saw a feature he wrote about some of the lesser-known elements of Bucks Fizz's back catalogue. His knowledge and enthusiasm is vast. The first time I met him was when he interviewed me for the *Melody Maker* in 1989. It was our first interview in any of the three major music weeklies, so it was a big moment for the band. He said he liked The Charlatans, but that his favourite new band from Manchester was Paris Angels.

A few months later my girlfriend brought home two 12-inches of 'Only Love Can Break Your Heart' by St Etienne – the original and a remix by Andy Weatherall. Both versions blew me away, more so when I was told it was a Neil Young cover. And I was totally knocked out when I realised my *Melody Maker* interviewer was one of the two protagonists. I went to see St Etienne play, and it was almost like a glimpse into Bob's record collection – nobody else would have chosen to cover Candlewick Green, who'd won *Opportunity Knocks* eight weeks on the trot.

I met Sarah Cracknell in Manchester – she had been singing for St Etienne, joining shortly after 'Only Love Can Break Your Heart'. We went out clubbing. We became friends and thought it would be a great idea to sing together. Back in London, walking back from the pub one night, Bob and I spoke briefly about it. A day in the studio was booked. Bob met me off the bus near to where St Etienne's studio was – a house near South Wimbledon, home of engineer Ian Catt and his parents. Bob, the lover of ace pop music, decided we should do a Christmas song. And thanks to him, I usually get to hear it a few times every December before it fades away again with the tinsel and fairy lights.

Bob is a regular visitor to the shop in Parsons Green, and if there was a real Record Detective Agency, Bob would be their version of Columbo, or maybe Jim Rockford.

I left the shop with a stone-cold banger from King Curtis. The album is *Live at the Fillmore West*, as chosen by Bill Bailey. It's apt that Bill chose a live album. There's a spark with a live recording – it's a one-off and could go wrong at any second. There are probably more parallels with stand-up comedy and playing in a band than you might imagine. Both involve having your mind partly in the present and partly reviewing what happened a second ago, with some of your brain occupied with what's about to happen. 'Memphis Soul Stew' begins with a deconstruction and introduction of the whole band and the ingredients that make up the album that follows. I've seen Bill hilariously deconstruct music, from Billy Bragg to a full orchestra, all done with insider knowledge and the love of what creates a great song, stripping music back to the basic building blocks from which anything can then be built. We took elements of the Memphis sound for The Charlatans – we were all huge Booker T. fans, and it was something that united us at the start.

So a case got solved at the Record Detective Agency, but still no word on that missing dame or that elusive Clifford T.

*

After the Isle of Wight, we decided to contact the nearest specialist Oxfam to each festival and invite them to bring a record shop. We asked for suitable donations to be sent, and in due course parcels began to arrive. In one, a rare Beatles release in mono – Clarke, why did you write your name on the front in biro, dropping the value from around £2,000 to about £150? Ah well, that's the thing about records – they're living, breathing things.

*

It's always when you least expect it that the good shit happens – the good shit being Tim Peaks Diner at Kendal Calling, two months after the Clifford T. Ward debacle, with Paddy Considine on a fake radio broadcast with Chris Hawkins from 6 Music, and Professor Tim O'Brien's scale model of the solar system using blueberries, grapes, balloons, £1.00 footballs and humans. Oxfam were setting up their stall. This time I wasn't going to miss out, and loitered while they brought the boxes out of the van.

My initial search revealed nothing, but like a prisoner in one of those Second World War escape movies, I realised the benefit of befriending the guards, or in this case the record-shop volunteers.

I brought a steady stream of coffee and signed the records they gave me by The Charlatans, my solo singles and a couple I had done with The Chemical Brothers. I put in the legwork so as not to feel guilty about sharing my wants list with Dave, a hippie volunteer who loved regaling everyone with his exploits on the live-music scene from the very dawn of time. A couple of further searches proved fruitless, but then Dave approached in his festival poncho and cowboy hat clutching a record. 'If I'm not very much mistaken, young man, I think this is one of the ones you were telling me about.'

He was holding *Mantle Pieces* by Clifford T. Ward – my victory in the non-existent battle with Nathan made all the sweeter by this one being in much better condition than the one that got away. £2.00 later and the record was mine. I'll not go on about the fact that it was all done in the name of charity.

The Shadows, *The Very Best of The Shadows*
Recommended by Paul Cook

Nothing like each other. Completely different styles

At some moments, there was a feeling of the project resembling a time machine – records that had lain undisturbed for a while ending up in collections and finally hitting second-hand shops for me to scoop them up in the present day. The recommendations had come from people who at one time stared down from posters on my bedroom wall. I like a thread that joins things, and there's a chaotic kind of jumbled order here, especially if you like your links a little obtuse. Boy George had been in an early incarnation of Bow Wow Wow, who later became Chiefs of Relief with Paul Cook on drums; Paul drummed in Edwyn Collins's band; George is Paul's daughter's godfather; Chris and Cosey are my son's godparents – and they're all in here somewhere.

I'd sent my messages, texts and emails out. It was like a fisherman launching lobster pots into the sea. I'd forget about them and every so often I'd get a buzz from a text or an email and there it'd be – my next mission set out for me. We were on our way to a festival near Oxford when an email came through from Paul Cook. I'd grown up worshipping the Sex Pistols, in some ways Paul and Steve Jones even more than the others. Paul had sung lead vocals on 'Silly Thing', one of my favourite Sex Pistols songs. His choice of record was *The Very Best of The Shadows*. I would try to find a link between the person recommending a record and their choice, but I wasn't sure I'd find one between the Sex Pistols' drummer and mum-friendly guitar-led 1960s instrumentals. In particular Paul loved a song called 'Wonderful Land'. I'm no expert on drumming, so I watched a recording of it with

Pete Salisbury and asked if there was any connection between the way Paul drummed and the style of Tony Meehan, the drummer from The Shadows. Pete was the drummer in The Verve from the start until the end, and has been The Charlatans' drummer since Jon Brookes became ill. He's taught drumming to a high standard and owned a drum shop. There was nobody I knew that was better qualified. After very careful consideration Pete declared, 'Nothing like each other. Completely different styles.' At least I found out, though.

I'd tracked down a record shop in Oxford that had three of my favourite things: new records, second-hand records and coffee. Truck shared the name of the festival we were headlining, and at one time they were run by the same people. Coffee in hand, I looked through the racks. Paul's Shadows album was top of my hit list. The second-hand racks were looking promising, with lots of Rod Stewart and *The Visitors* by ABBA, but zero Shadows. I asked at the counter, and it turned out that the guys who owned the shop had packed up and taken hundreds of records to the festival with them. We phoned ahead to check if they had a copy with them. An hour before we were due to play, I headed over to the Truck Records marquee to be greeted by a pristine copy of an original German pressing of The Shadows' bestsellers from 1963.

You're very much shaped by the music you buy. *The Great Rock 'n' Roll Swindle* was mine after blowing my holiday money on it, and it made a huge impression on me. My mate Cadge brought Paul to see The Charlatans, and I really wanted to meet him, but it all fell apart at the end like it so often does after a gig. Being a dad meant I had the responsibility of getting a tired Littlest B back to the hotel, so we headed back to Camden.

As we got out of the van, I heard a voice – 'Hey, Tim' – and there he was, the unmistakable figure of Paul Cook. We hugged and talked about my son, who was sleeping in his pushchair, and

Paul's daughter, who I had played a gig with in Liverpool. He told me he had loved the show, and the meet-up in the car park turned one of the best nights into *the* best night.

Hüsker Dü, *Metal Circus*

Recommended by Chan Marshall aka Cat Power

The healing powers of Cat Power

Festivals are a rite of passage.

Glastonbury is the Earth mother and year zero of all festivals. Woodstock was more of an event, but Glastonbury has continued and evolved and is as relevant now as it has ever been.

I went there for the first time in 1987. It was my first festival. New Order were headlining the Saturday night, and for the rest of the time I just wanted to have a wander and take it all in. It was never shown on TV, and what I knew about Glastonbury was hearsay and legend from friends and friends of friends that had been before.

I drove my yellow Vauxhall to London and picked up my friend Adrian. We had an orange tent that had been retired to the loft since the days of camping by the River Weaver with my friends from Moulton when I was fourteen. We packed a full loaf of cheese sandwiches and six bottles of Strongbow. With directions marked out in my dad's *A–Z*, we made a compilation tape each and brought enough cigarettes for three days.

On arrival, we set up camp, made arrangements over how to meet if we got lost and prepared ourselves for a big weekend. I remember glorious sunshine, techno crusties and guys on the bridges hissing, 'Hash, speed, acid, whizz, 'shrooms' – heavy manners and heavy overtones.

We headed for the Pyramid Stage. We heard music – excitement grew. As we got closer, I could make out Bob Mould's Flying V guitar and Greg Norton's pre-Shoreditch, post-1920s waxed moustache. I knew people who liked Hüsker Dü but

I'd not heard anything that had grabbed me – not until that moment.

New Order debuted 'True Faith' and ended their set with 'Sister Ray', with Bernard smashing his guitar through his amp. Julian Cope played directly beforehand and ended up naked, clambering on his iconic mic stand – 'World Shut Your Mouth' was the hit of the festival for me – and Barrence Whitfield and the Savages were instantly my favourite band for the next six months.

I headed back in 1994 and watched Oasis play in mid-afternoon, and they were brilliant. Johnny Cash, in his own words, played one of the top ten gigs of his life – June duetted with him for an astonishing version of 'Jackson'. The Beastie Boys had not long since released 'Sabotage' and were at the top of their game. I watched the whole show with Ione Skye in the rain, the only bit of rain that I remember at the festival.

In 1995 The Charlatans played. The Stone Roses had pulled out due to John Squire injuring his shoulder, and Pulp stepped in and became part of Glastonbury history. The Verve played just before us. Pete Salisbury told us that their gear packed up, so he and bassist Si Jones performed an impromptu bass-and-drums jam. It would become their song 'The Rolling People'.

In 2002 The Charlatans played the Pyramid Stage again. It was in crazier times, but that's not to suggest I don't remember what happened – looking back that far, the details have disappeared but the headlines remain. I remember a huge hug from Ian Brown and a *Sun* journalist following us around hoping for a story, but most of all I remember The White Stripes' set. I watched, mesmerised, from the side of the stage. Jack, like a master puppeteer, doing so much all at the same time, and Meg – she was so tiny but made a massive sound. At the end of the set she headed for the ramp at the back of the stage. As she went past, she looked at me. I said 'amazing' or 'brilliant' or some such superlative. She replied, 'Why thank you, sir,' with a slow nod of her head. No matter how many bands you see live, defining performances like that stay with you for ever.

In 2007 I sang 'The Only One I Know' with Mark Ronson and his band. Mark had done a cover version of the song with Robbie Williams, reinterpreting it as a 1970s US cop-show theme. It was a song we always thought was untouchable, but he did a pretty good job. He asked if I fancied jumping in with them on that song in Paris and at Coachella. I went to both and we had a ball.

The Chavs played an impromptu set on the Joe Strummer Stage. This was our side project of all side projects, involving Carl Barât from The Libertines and Dirty Pretty Things, Martin Duffy from Felt and Primal Scream, Razorlight's Andy Burrows, and Jamie and Steffan from The Klaxons. When we unveiled the band to the press we said that Christopher Lee and Paris Hilton were members, and they seemed to believe us.

In 2013 I played a solo set on the Park Stage in glorious sunshine. I bumped into Gregg Foreman, Cat Power's keyboard player, outside his tour bus. We had DJ'd together in Miami around 2003, and I'd been a fan of Cat since I first heard her cover of The Rolling Stones' 'Satisfaction'.

Around that same time I was in the Viper Room in LA, and only two other customers were in the entire place. One was Har Mar Superstar. He called me over and introduced me to the other person: 'Tim, this is Chan – she's my favourite singer in the whole world.' At the time I thought it was Har Mar's usual hyperbole, but within a few months I messaged him to say that I agreed. I don't know how it officially works, but Chan Marshall is Cat Power and Cat Power seems to sometimes be the person and sometimes the band – but yeah, she is/they are awesome.

In 2015 The Charlatans were invited by Emily Eavis to play the 'secret' unannounced opening slot to kick off the whole festival – I say secret, but obviously we knew and were allowed to drop some hints. It was a huge crowd, and to some of them we would have been a complete surprise.

From the first time I went in 1987 to the last note we played in 2015, Glastonbury has always been at the top of the festival tree. People say it's changed, got too big, become too commercial, or they go into a rant about who should and who shouldn't play, but it was the best back then and it's stayed the best.

*

I was making plans to record my second solo album and life had changed for me. Giving up drinking and drugs had left a vacuum that was first filled by amplified excitement, but followed by huge come-downs and then quick climbs back to a point where I could function. It might seem dramatic condensed like that, but ironically the ups and downs echoed my life during my more hedonistic years. Spookily, not taking drugs provides similar feelings to when you're taking them, but involves less money and fewer frantic phone calls.

I needed to rebuild myself and felt fragile and exposed. After a gig, I'd sit on my own at the front of the bus and look for some solace in music. I'd put on my headphones and listen to anything I thought could help.

There was one album I went back to every time. Not only did it see me through, it became the blueprint for the album I wanted to record. Not the same songs, or even the style of music, but the feel of the album and the idea that a record can have such an effect on someone. That album was *The Greatest* by Cat Power – it all resonated while looking at the night scenes of Cologne and Hamburg and the tracer lights of the autobahn. It was the way her voice was exposed, which left the songs needing little help to get through. Completely modern, but with a heart and soul that could just as well be from any point in the previous century.

It was written in whatever key I was in at the time, and slowly but surely the more I listened, the more fixed I felt. Songs like 'Lived in Bars', 'Living Proof', 'Empty Shell' and the title track spoke directly to me. The album had been recorded in Memphis at Ardent Studios and had the atmosphere of both the studio and the city. I wanted my upcoming solo album to have the feel of the studio and the city where it was recorded too. I chose Nashville for my backdrop, but it was listening to *The Greatest* so much that gave me the drive to record the album that would be released as *Oh No I Love You*.

I asked Chan to recommend a record. Her reply read:

Hüsker Dü

Ready . . . :)

Metal Circus – Hüsker Dü.

It was my 13th birthday & my sister and I were at the mall.

We went into Camelot Records like we always did to look at records on sale.

My sister told me to pick out any record and she'd buy it for me and I chose *Metal Circus*.

I still feel the same way when I hear the entrance of 'Diane', soothingly electrified, an immediate 'high' when I hear that riff . . .

So good.

So I got me a copy of *Metal Circus* from Rough Trade East – a record shop that to me has been at the forefront of the renaissance of vinyl, helped by the resurgence of east London and not hindered by the fact that they serve great coffee.

Bruce Springsteen, *Born in the USA*
Recommended by Gary Neville

Better the Neville you know

Touring life is not always rock 'n' roll excess. It can sometimes be launderettes, motorway services and airport check-ins. Don't get me wrong, I am not complaining, but for every television that goes out of a window there's also hours spent watching, but not understanding, foreign daytime TV. If you don't find some kind of routine, you can waste weeks convincing yourself you're 'recovering' from the two-hour gig the night before. I know people in bands who will go to the museum or galleries in an attempt to learn a little about where they are. As I may have mentioned, my routine involves record shops.

Because of this, on a rainy Saturday in Dublin I discovered Freebird Records. It's a bit like if God made record shops. The floor space is split with a bookseller, but Freebird Records has been quietly doing its thing since 1978, with new and second-hand vinyl, CDs, T-shirts, tote bags . . . After I'd had a few minutes to settle in, the owner, Phil, came over and introduced himself. I told him of my quest and we got talking about music. That pretty much explains why I seek out these places: someone I had never met before connecting over something we both love. Talk was of The Brian Jonestown Massacre, The Circle Jerks, Exploding Hearts, The Dark, the Washington hardcore scene, how Hanoi Rocks hadn't aged too well and forgotten Belfast pop punkers The Starjets.

And it's not just me who decided to call in after a show in Dublin. Phil took a picture and said he would add me to the hall of fame, which included Ryan Adams, Robert Plant and a veritable who's who and what's what in music. We discovered mutual friends, from old label bosses to long-lost bass players, and discussed young bands being led to the dark side by older bands who should have known better.

The record I was there to buy was part of a reissue series for Record Store Day. It was Bruce Springsteen's blue-collar meisterwerk *Born in the USA*, recommended by Gary Neville. I am a Manchester United fan, Gary is a Charlatans fan, and our paths crossed at gigs, so I knew he had decent taste in music. I decided to ask him for a recommendation. *Born in the USA* was the first album Gary bought with his own money – an important landmark in anyone's collection. The first few records may be begged, stolen or borrowed, but then the spending starts. I knew of it, as Springsteen fever hit a peak in 1985, when he came over to play at Roundhay Park, Wembley and Slane Castle. Springsteen and Prince had been worshipped in the States for years, but until then their status hadn't translated fully in the UK. But for both, resistance was futile and soon enough they were filling stadiums here too.

Springsteen spoke to the beating heart of America. His lyrics read like the pages of a high-school yearbook, bringing to mind wood-panelled station wagons parked outside clapboard houses almost anywhere in America. Jocks and right-wing US politicians mistook the title track to be a fist-pumping celebration of the Stars and Stripes, but Bruce is cleverer than that. This was a state-of-the-nation address regarding where they'd been going wrong, like an updated version of John Steinbeck, with abandoned Vietnam vets replacing the tenant farmers from *The Grapes of Wrath*.

There'd been a kind of parallel between football and music at the time that Manchester United came back to prominence. There always had been, but the *Loaded* lad culture seemed to drive them headlong into each other in a blur of spilt Carlsberg and terrace chants. A couple of years after The Charlatans made it big, Manchester United won their first league title for twenty-five years. Some young squad members had broken through and were about to usher in a dominance last seen with Liverpool in the 1970s. The Class of '92, as they would become known, often name-checked The Charlatans when they were asked about music. Ryan Giggs, David Beckham, Nicky Butt and Phil and Gary Neville were bucking the trend of appalling taste that footballers are usually credited with. Our songs would be played during goal round-ups on TV, and there was a link between terrace fashion and how our fans dressed. The Haçienda was at its most vibrant and all eyes were on Manchester.

My dad, Allan, started watching Manchester United in 1956. Growing up in our house, you were either a Man U or Bolton Wanderers fan, like my grandad, Albert. He was a plumber at Bolton's ground – it was a claim to fame that often got him a free half of mild if he happened to be in a pub within a stone's throw of Burnden Park. When I first became aware of football, the United team included Stuart Pearson, Martin Buchan, the Greenhoffs and Gordon Hill. Although most trophies eluded them, there was an excitement about them that was hard to resist.

The Charlatans were booked to play a big Manchester show at Castlefield Bowl, only a few months after we'd played the Albert Hall there. Gary was at the Albert Hall show and had invited us down to check out a hotel that he'd opened right next to the United ground. On the roof was a five-a-side football pitch, complete with astroturf and sliding glass cover. We joked about playing a gig up there, but the joking became serious when Gary said he'd happily hire a PA and let us stay over the weekend when we were playing at Castlefield. There's a good tradition of rooftop gigs, with The Beatles and U2 both on the list – we thought we'd add The Charlatans.

Big gigs and tours are always great fun, but most of the details are looked after by the promoter. This was something we worked on directly with Gary, from how to get the PA up to the roof to who to invite. The capacity was only 150 people – half were friends and family and the rest were competition winners, so there was a real sense of excitement.

We had one final surprise for Gary, as we'd heard he'd played guitar but had had to give up thanks to the demands of work, being a dad and maybe realising his chance of hitting the big time in a band might have passed him by. We'd had guest guitarists join us before – Johnny Marr, Ronnie Wood and Kevin Shields – but none of them had won the Champions League. Mark asked Gary if he was up for learning the extra guitar part to 'Just When You're Thinking Things Over', and Gary accepted the challenge. He left with hastily filmed footage of Mark playing the required parts, and the next time we saw him was at the gig. He'd learnt it and did a brilliant job – his only request was that we played the song third in the set to save him from not enjoying the songs and wandering on nervously for the encore. Gary was definitely out of his comfort zone, but it's good to shake things up once in a while – I'm still waiting for my invitation to play for United.

Lou Christie Sacco, *Paint America Love*
Recommended by Bob Stanley

Hey, it's paper all the way

Anyone who collects records has people around them that they listen to a bit more intently when it comes to tips on what to buy. I am often getting told, 'Oh, I think you'd love this,' only to find out that it's a slab of sludge, but some people can have a high hit rate and become an oracle of where to go for new finds. At one time, my chief tipster was *Melody Maker* photographer Tom Sheehan. The first time he recommended anything, it was *Bringing It All Back Home* by Bob Dylan. He then helped me navigate the order in which to listen to Bob, after a couple of failed attempts of my own.

So, like a squirrel that an old lady feeds nuts to in the park, I became a bit more trusting of Tom. Soon I would be eating out of his hand (still using the squirrel/old lady thing) the likes of Stoneground, Bobby Charles, New Riders of the Purple Sage and Howard Tate, alongside classics like The Beach Boys' *Surf's Up* and *No Other* by Gene Clark. I am hoping it was a two-way street, but you never know. I think I introduced Tom to The Mad Lads, Junior Parker and Jackie Mittoo.

We discovered Cat Power at the same time.

Enthusing about a record can be a bit like bearing your soul to someone, even though you may not realise you are at the time. Tash, who used to work at Heavenly Records, once told me, 'Never walk out on a record, because a record will never walk out on you.' She said it as she was putting on *Breathe on Me* by Ronnie Wood, and it's a maxim I have stood by ever since.

Jim, who works with us as security on tours and has the

demeanour of a traditional Scottish hard man, and I got talking about music and he told me he was a lifelong Willie Nelson fan. He said that those songs could floor him, unlike anyone he'd come across in his work. I always saw him differently after that.

The records we love reveal layers about us that people may not pick up on through how we act, the job we do or the public face we show. A recommendation from someone you don't know can cause trepidation – but when it comes from Bob Stanley, it only generates excitement.

I had never heard of Lou Christie Sacco before, and at first the album title seemed to mean nothing. But now the words *Paint America Love* light up a little something inside me that, until you hear it, doesn't make much sense at all. Bob described it as a gently philosophical manifesto album.

Sometimes when you're searching for a record my rules say that if you stumble across the CD, you're allowed to snap it up, while biding your time for the vinyl, like snorting a line of speed while you're waiting for the coke dealer to come round. Maybe the CD is like buying a print, but the vinyl is like having the original.

Aficionados always want to have the original pressing of a record, even if it means paying far more – that's exactly the way it's meant to be heard. The artist would have had a direct hand in what you're holding – their fingerprints would be on it. Reissues can be like a videotape that's been recorded over loads of times. Extra tracks are sometimes chucked on and confuse the authenticity. Also, the original is far more romantic.

Second-hand records seduce all the senses. The copy of *Paint America Love* I found has a gatefold sleeve that emanates a musty 1970s vibe. The shape of the vinyl has made its presence felt on the cover like the Turin Shroud. And with titles like 'Chucky Wagon', 'Campus Rest' and 'Waco' it reaches out from another time. In the top left-hand corner a hole is drilled where the circular vinyl has missed the square cover. When I'd first seen this in my teens, I'd been puzzled by what it meant, and – as with explanations for most things – the answer had come from a record-shop guy . . .

Marshall's Records in Piccadilly Plaza was always a stop-off and potential home for my Christmas money. I'd noticed that many of the albums in there had had a corner unceremoniously snipped off, and others a hole punched in the same spot as my copy of Lou Christie Sacco. I asked one of the guys.

'It's a code between record shops that means it's a brilliant record but that regular people don't know. It's like a Freemason's handshake that only record-shop workers understand.'

The fourteen-year-old me felt I had been let into the inner circle of the record-shop illuminati. Not long after I got a slightly more convincing explanation from a much more trustworthy source – it was indeed a sign to record-shop owners and workers, but it was a sign that the records were remaindered and were to be sold discounted in any which way they could. The only thing linking them was that the label and the distributor never wanted to see them again.

On its release Lou Christie Sacco's *Paint America Love* wasn't the success it deserved to be.

Pearls Before Swine, *One Nation Underground*
Junior Wells, *Hoodoo Man Blues*
White Zombie, *Soul-Crusher*

All recommended by Iggy Pop

You just name it, and we're playing it

This may have never been said before, as I am not sure anyone has ever cared enough to ask, but Iggy Pop was the biggest influence on The Electric Crayon Set (who became The Electric Crayons, after the designer of our debut and final single sleeve decided our name was just that bit too long).

I was late to the game when it came to Iggy. My entry-point album was *New Values*, released in 1979 – mine was bought in 1987. I had set my sights on being a rock star and wanted some of Jim Morrison's carefree, flipped-finger attitude. But what he had he only had for a short time. Iggy Pop was still feral from his days in The Stooges, and – although I wasn't to know it then – he would lose none of that in the thirty years that followed.

I first heard *New Values* at Nick Clare's house. Nick was the bass player for The Electric Crayon Set/Electric Crayons. At that time, the triumvirate of albums that ruled my Northwich environs was:

1. Iggy Pop, *New Values*
2. The Prisoners, *In from the Cold*
3. The Cult, *Love*

Bubbling under were:

The Cramps, *A Date with Elvis*
Beastie Boys, *Licensed to Ill*

B.A.D., *No. 10 Upping Street*

The Cure, *Head on the Door*

Pop Will Eat Itself, *This Is the Day . . . This Is the Hour . . . This Is This!* – from the masters of throwaway, goofball cut-and-paste, who were harbouring in Clint Mansell one of the most talented and brilliant film-score writers and composers of the next twenty years.

Anyway, back to Iggy. He was on my wish list from the start, but we'd met only briefly, which resulted in him giving me a friendly headlock. To me, there is a rock-star food chain in which the toppermost levels need no introduction – I am not sure of the rules, but Bowie, Jagger, Iggy, Madonna and Lemmy all got there. Maybe it's a one-name thing – the world just knows who they are.

I am from a few steps down, where I say both my name and that of my band – usually to be met with, 'Aww, c'mon, I know who you are.' But I am often not convinced they would have known without a push in the right direction.

The Charlatans were on the same bill as Iggy Pop at a festival in Belgium. European festivals can sometimes be strange fish. Nicki Minaj was top of the bill, with a fair smattering of Europop DJs I'd not had the pleasure of hearing/remembering. I was having a coffee in the catering tent with Iggy's guitarist, Kevin Armstrong. When he walked in, I recognised him, but we didn't know each other. I did my introduction and he did the 'I know who you are' thing.

Backstage at a festival can be an odd but brilliant place – similar to an airport lounge, but the payoff is not a flight but the performance in front of thousands of people, so it can be a mixture of edginess, apprehension and excitement. I've had chats with David Bowie, Wu Tang Clan, and Stills and Nash, but not Crosby, and for some reason it's more enjoyable the more mundane the conversation is – from where to walk your dog in

LA, to the problems of humidity and hair frizz onstage in the Far East. Like the subject matter of an in-flight magazine.

As we talked I inevitably mentioned Iggy. I asked Kevin what was in the set. He said, 'We've slowed the whole thing down. Time's catching up with Iggy, but it's working out brilliantly. The Berlin-era sleazy slowed-down gear is where we're at.'

As much as I felt a pang of sadness that Iggy was having to leave the exuberance behind, the Berlin-era songs like 'Nightclubbing', 'Sister Midnight' and 'The Passenger' were what I consider the high-water mark of the Ig.

It was Kevin that had played guitar on *Blah Blah Blah*, so he lent a sense of authenticity to the gig. He could sense my excitement about what I would be watching later, so I giddily said, 'What else, what else?'

'Man, whatever you want to hear – you just name it, and we're playing it.'

'Really? Wow. In that case, "Shades", my favourite track from *Blah Blah Blah*.'

'Ah. Not sure whether the drummer knows that one.' It went quiet for a bit and we both stared at our coffees.

'How is Iggy before a show?' I asked.

I am aware that those from high up the festival food chain prefer some solitude before they perform. Backstage can sometimes be a bit of a misnomer – rather than Jon Bon Jovi high-fiving Mick Fleetwood, you're more likely to catch Franz Ferdinand's accountant enquiring about Wi-Fi codes.

Most tour managers and crew know most of the bands, so it becomes a hotbed of small talk about old friends and good times, but some performers need a ritual – there's a required headspace when someone walks onstage to 100,000 people that can't be found discussing potential school places with your band's former guitar tech.

I was curious as to what Iggy did before a gig. I told Kevin about this book, and we discussed a few of the recommenders and recommendations.

'You know, I think Iggy would be up for that – but he won't see aaaanybody before a gig. Like, absolutely nobody,' he said, before gesturing over to Nina, Iggy's wife, who was sitting reading outside the dressing-room door. 'But if you write him a note, we'll get it to him.'

Somewhere in the dressing room, Jim was becoming Iggy. Jim is polite, caring and charming, whereas Iggy in less than two hours would begin one of his songs by imploring the crowd to 'come up here and fuck me', with the crowd roaring back as one primal animal. So I got myself a piece of paper and wrote a note to the Ig.

I watched the set from the front, where every gig is best appreciated. Some people like to get backstage or watch from the side of the stage, but nothing enlivens your senses like being front and centre, where all the speakers are pointing. I was standing and as eager as anyone for the entrance of the one and only Mr Osterberg. Whatever his pre-gig ritual was, it worked – he sidled on and seemed to magnify the adoration of the audience, reflecting it back in gigantic proportions, the likes of which only a handful of performers can achieve. Like any sixty-odd-year-old, Iggy's mind, I imagine, is willing but his body may want to resist. His performance was beautiful – totally given over to the audience, with the moves of a leather-trousered garbage-glam Richard III.

The showman really put on a show. Two days later I received an email sent from the rooftop of his hotel in the south of France: 'Hey Tim, I am getting back to you – I will get back to you in a couple of days.'

A few hours later his recommendations were in. When it comes to the Ig, I will give it to you how he sent it:

Hey Tim,
    I couldn't stop, so here . . . you got three:

One Nation Underground by Pearls Before Swine, with the Hieronymus Bosch cover.

I bought this record in 1967 at Discount Records in Ann Arbor, Michigan. I played it a lot while getting high and coming down, at the first Stooge house on the U of M campus, in the Summer of Love. The cover is a depiction of Hell. It's the weirdest record I've ever heard. It was on ESP.

Soul-Crusher by White Zombie, their first full-length album.

I saw this record in a store window on Carmine Street in NYC, 1988, and bought it because the band members looked fresh and cool. It was an unrelenting, screaming mess of strange, ugly noises – mostly without even a beat. I really liked it. I got to know them and do appear on one of their later, more 'professional' records . . . but this was the best one. It was on Caroline.

Hoodoo Man Blues by Junior Wells, on Delmark Records. Delmark was a small label run out of Chicago by Bob Koester, owner of the Jazz Record Mart, on Grand Avenue. It's an amazing record, very masculine, and tight as a drum. Buddy Guy is on guitar, credited as 'friendly chap'.

I got the record from Michael Erlewine of the Prime Movers Blues Band in Ann Arbor, Michigan, 1966 – I think.

He signed off as 'Ig'.

Rage Against the Machine, *Rage Against the Machine*

Recommended by Carl Barât

Hot Turkey

I was with Carl, or more accurately, it was just after I was with Carl that I took it upon myself to quit drinking and taking drugs. Now, I'm not saying it was anything to do with Mr Barât's hedonistic ways, but it was more like the epiphany was going to hit me and he happened to be around when it did.

We're from different generations and nobody does elegantly wasted quite as well as Carl. I had started to lose what little elegance remained, so I needed to start a new chapter. We'd formed a band together – me, him, Andy Burrows, sometime member Martin Duffy and a Klaxon and a Libertine or two. We were called The Chavs (Martin Duffy's suggestion, The Chilblains, was overruled but, on reflection, might have been better), and our live shows were as ramshackle as our lifestyles.

But it's how we loved to do it.

Carl always had a sense of poetry, and we saw ourselves as a gang. We lived under the constraints of management and labels and felt like outlaws, but in truth we were more like badly behaved children.

He moved into Sarm East studios, where The Charlatans were recording *Simpatico*. We spent our time recommending films to each other – we must have watched *Once Upon a Time in America* a dozen times. We would argue about who out of us was Max and who was Noodles, like Mark Collins and I had done a decade before. He introduced me to Shane Meadows's latest film, *Dead Man's Shoes*.

We would write songs for The Chavs, record them and forget about them – we were much more about the process than the results. Like some kind of gonzo conceptual-art piece, the *raison d'être* of The Chavs was to play five shows, the fifth of which would be at the Carnegie Hall in New York.

Some would say we failed. Others, including me, would say that we haven't played either the fourth or fifth show yet. The original some who would say we failed would then maybe say, 'So, are you going to play the fourth or fifth show then?' To which I would reply, 'No – I don't think so.'

The three shows were:

The Tap and Tin, a pub in Chatham
A short-lived TV show
Glastonbury

Our time together could only be considered as halcyon days. There was a freedom to explore all things wild and crazy. We might not have been good for each other, but it definitely felt like we were. Playing together was all about the camaraderie and the immediacy of the performances.

It was a kind of end of days for me – a sense that the hedonism had to stop, but while in the company of those who were outstanding in the field of taking things a bit further than they really should go.

There's something hugely romantic about the way a second-hand record arrives in someone's hands – the person and the record may have been roaming the Earth for decades until their paths cross, the record having a previous owner who's fallen out of love with what it has to offer or who's lost their turntable in some kind of format rejig. Like in a film, both entities take different turns and live different lives until that moment when the album in front is flicked forward and the strings spark up in the soundtrack of your life. You're never sure when that might happen, so hopes are always high when crossing the threshold of somewhere selling vinyl.

*

Istanbul is somewhere I've never spent much time record shopping, and to be fair, much time doing anything else at all really. A few hours before a gig there I asked the promoter about any decent record shops, and he scribbled down some names – Lale Plak, Kontra Plak and DeForm Müzik – and a rudimentary map.

In my other hand, I had the current list of records I was looking for, including Carl's choice, *Rage Against the Machine*. I'm not sure if it was the weather mixed with the sounds and smells of Istanbul – all beeping horns and bustling streets – but there was a kind of undercover-agent feel to what I was doing. I was thinking a cross between Indiana Jones and *Casablanca*, as I made my way through the bustling, tightly packed streets.

I got the feeling I was getting near to the first shop and thought I'd check with someone. It's at times like this that I realise there are a few giveaway signs to someone who might know where a record shop is. Statistically it's more likely to be a bloke – a bloke already listening to music; someone who just has an air of being a record-buyer. Button badges help, and a bag containing an album is a dead giveaway.

I chose well, as the guy popped out his earbud headphones and let me know I was two streets away.

As I turned to continue on my mission, he said, 'English? Which team?'

The promoter had already pointed at the local flags and said, 'This is Galatasaray.' I didn't know if that was a district or just the name of the football team – the team that had signs saying 'Welcome to Hell' when Manchester United played them and whose fans had long had a beef with any English team they came across.

I nervously said, 'Manchester United?' but made it sound like a question, just in case that was the wrong answer. Direction Guy laughed, but it seemed a friendly laugh so I took it that I was OK.

'You had a player in UK. He came here to manage Beşiktaş,' he said. 'Name of John Toshack.' As he said it, his rattling smoker's cough went into overdrive.

I couldn't really get a handle on what he was getting at. I knew of John Toshack, Kevin Keegan's sidekick in the all-conquering Liverpool side of the 1970s. 'He came here but something he didn't know. In Turkish, "Toshack" means "bollocks".' The laugh got even louder and rattlier, and he thrust out his hand for me to shake and set off down a side street. I checked later, and it was true.

It just shows that maybe when you least expect it, something you've never given any thought to can end up causing you grief somewhere else – seems like the coughing guy took great pleasure telling any English person he came across that 'Toshack' means 'bollocks'. (I'm aware John Toshack is Welsh, but I'm not sure the guy was.)

I entered the first shop and headed for the counter. I asked if they had Junior Wells's *Hoodoo Man Blues*. 'No. Finish,' was the reply.

Lale Plak was the shop, specialising in blues and jazz but having an impressive collection of new and second-hand vinyl in dozens of categories. There was a copy of *Rubber Soul* and *Twins* by Ornette Coleman in the window . . . the striking and simply unforgettably stark sleeve of *Tutu* by Miles Davis on the wall at the back behind the counter.

Next stop was Kontra Plak, a fantastic little shop five minutes' walk from the first. Okan, the owner, displayed his signed vinyl behind the counter. I asked about the copy of Ariel Pink's *Mature*

Themes that I spotted there, and we hit a spot of mutual appreciation – always a good start when striking up a conversation in a record shop. Not for sale! But then again, I am not sure how many people would want a record that said 'To Okan' on the sleeve.

He asked if I'd ever tried Turkish coffee and disappeared into the back. He came out a few minutes later with two drinks and, under his arm, a copy of 'Then' by The Charlatans on 12-inch. He handed me the coffee, the 12-inch and a pen.

I went through my list and he said no to everything, except for Edwyn Collins's recommendation. He excitedly pointed me to a section that seemed to feature New Age and ambient records – definitely a category I knew little about, outside of *Music for Airports*, *Tree Line* by Michael Trommer, The Orb and a couple of others.

Tomita, *Snowflakes Are Dancing*

Recommended by Edwyn Collins

Hot Turkey II

I found three records by Tomita, and the last one was the one I was looking for. I took it over to the shop's two turntables, unwrapped it with Okan's permission and dropped the needle at the start. In a second I was taken out of the crowded Istanbul streets and transported to an anime world of soft colours and cartoon bubbles.

The music was hypnotic, and a picture of Edwyn's smiling face came into my mind as it played – a fantastic example of how music can take you somewhere else. I wasn't aware of having previously listened to Tomita, but his music had a familiar feel and had been used everywhere, from Olympic gymnastics to Hollywood movies.

As the music played through the headphones it acted as the soundtrack to what I was seeing, replacing car horns, the sound of construction and a busy city.

I took the headphones off and crash-landed back in the real world. I downed the coffee, excitedly scooped up a couple of other records I had my eye on, and headed to the next record shop.

DeForm Müzik was next on the list. In the window display were The Associates' 'Kitchen Person' 12-inch and Riechmann's *Wunderbar*. It gave me a good feeling about what I might find. The owner was sitting behind a desk eating olives, and he casually let me know with a quiet tut that I was disturbing his lunch. I was undeterred by his frostiness and asked him if he was aware of whether there was a copy of *Hoodoo Man Blues* or White Zombie's *Soul-Crusher*. He became much more interested – so much so that he put his olives to one side and dabbed the corners of his mouth with a napkin. He started nodding slowly and ushered me over to the other side of the shop.

'With Junior Wells, I might be able to help.'

We walked over to a rack. He flipped through a dozen albums and said, 'We don't have.' He explained that they had a warehouse out of town where he could take me the following day – thousands of records, he said, sweeping his arm to demonstrate some kind of endless field of vinyl. I told him I was leaving at 7 a.m., so I continued browsing.

'Which others?' he asked, and we spent some time discovering that they didn't have them. He asked me if I'd ever come across a singer by the name of Ajda Pekkan, as he took a 7-inch out of the racks. The limited amount of Turkish pop I had heard had all been recommended by Andy Votel. He's not necessarily an advocate of Turkish music especially – it's more that Andy has records from every conceivable genre: psychedelic Welsh-language 1960s bangers, eastern European cartoon soundtracks, vampire-movie themes and my favourite compilation of his, *B-Music – Cross Continental Record Raid Road Trip*.

But back to Ajda Pekkan.

The sleeve was classic early 1970s – Ajda looked a little like Dusty Springfield. I nodded, smiled and said I'd buy it, before gesturing that I'd take a look around. He went back to his olives.

It was Mark's birthday and I was looking to get him something. I noticed a copy of *Back to the World* by Curtis Mayfield. It was a record that reminded me of Mark, as Curtis was the biggest influence on our album *Wonderland*. It was a perfect present, but it was a second-hand copy so I thought I'd better check the vinyl for any damage. The record was in perfect condition but was actually a copy of *Diamond Dogs* by David Bowie – a brilliant record but not such a good present. 'Hey, Mark, what did Tim get you for your fiftieth?' 'Yeah, it was a real memorable gift – a David

Bowie record in a Curtis Mayfield sleeve.' I didn't buy it. But I was on a roll – I saw and grabbed the first album by little-known 1980s LA outfit Indoor Life. My copy had succumbed to some serious rain damage on the runway at LAX, and the chances of finding it again in a record shop were slim.

Ornette and Miles Davis were calling me back to Lale Plak, where I promised myself I would return to buy something. I had a spare fifteen minutes before I had to leave, so I bagged them both, plus another Ornette album. With only minutes to go, I had one last look around. There was a box in the window that was mainly rock and metal. Halfway through, I found a picture disc of the twentieth-anniversary edition of Rage Against the Machine's debut – the record that Carl Barât had recommended.

*

And so it was in the narrow streets of Istanbul – like a character out of a Graham Greene novel, with a slight sheen of sweat in a tumbly-down quarter of town – that I bagged Carl's choice. It's kind of fitting that it was *Rage Against the Machine* – it's as uncompromising as Carl and flew in the face of just about everything that got in its way.

I first saw Rage Against the Machine on *The Word* in around 1993. This coincided with the birth of my voracious teenage angst, provid-ing the perfect conduit through which to express it. I got the album from a mate who nicked it from HMV, and it was all I listened to day in, day out, for months, either pogoing around the room or quietly (and with a sense of anger and righteousness) poring over the lyrics. I then got to see them live at Reading Festival, where I went into my first mosh pit. I felt a sense of (abrasive) love and belonging. And this was with a band who, unlike my previous musical heroes, were still together/alive. They may not be now, but that album sounds as fresh to me as it ever did.

The next communication from Carl was shortly after I'd bought the record. The Libertines were releasing a new album and they didn't want to do things in the regular 'band releases record' kind of way – they'd taken over a shop next door to Dublin Castle, where they played an unannounced gig before packing up and heading off on tour. The shop was the base for exhibitions and happenings, and Carl was a fan of Tim Peaks Coffee, so he asked if we could supply the shop and send a few people to help out – a far cry from nights making our way through bottles of red wine with repeated phone calls to those guys who deliver late at night. That's where we'd ended up. My coffee in their pop-up shop – much more civilised and with a greater chance of me surviving to see another day.

Pink Floyd, *Relics*

Recommended by Noel Fielding

Captain Whizzo's light fantastic

The first time I met Noel Fielding was like tumbling down the rabbit hole to Wonderland. It was on the set of a TV show, and I asked him if I could interview him for a Charlatans blog I was doing. His brother Mike came along and it was like opening a door to a psychedelic world with different laws of physics.

I'd not come across The Mighty Boosh as I was living in America, although eventually I saw them on billboards above Sunset Boulevard. The timing was comical – I'd given up drink and drugs, but conversations and nights out with Noel were trippier than any hallucinogen I'd ever taken. The Mighty Boosh had come over to Hollywood to launch their series on BBC America. They stayed at the Chateau Marmont, partied round at Courtney Love's – under the biggest chandelier I've ever seen – and Rich Fulcher dived into my Christmas tree when they came to visit.

The first time I got into Pink Floyd was after spending time with Martin Blunt and Jon Baker. It was in a club in Walsall called Punch and Judy's. There was something about Syd Barrett that drew me in. I always felt their music was trippy enough to forgo the need for mind-altering drugs – it already possessed qualities that helped you detach from the regular world. Post-Syd albums lost some of the appeal that he brought but were undeniable masterpieces in so many other ways.

We covered their song 'Lucifer Sam' and we got ourselves Captain Whizzo to work our lights like we were Pink Floyd. Our songs got longer and our trousers a little wider.

King Bee Records is in Chorlton. It's been there as long as I have been going there. Mark used to live round the corner, so I'd go and browse as often as possible. It has all the classic traits of the best kind of shop – not in the centre of town, more gig posters than two eyes can take in, and rack upon rack of decently priced vinyl. Bill Brewster and Pete Paphides both mentioned King Bee when running through their favourite record shops in the north-west, and Johnny Marr is a regular customer.

It makes perfect sense that Noel loves *Relics*, from the Heath Robinson-style artwork to the absurdist lyrics of 'Bike' – 'I've got a cloak, it's a bit of a joke. There's a tear up the front. It's red and black. I've had it for months.' Sounds like something straight out of The Mighty Boosh – and at any given moment Noel looks like 'Arnold Layne' might be playing in his head while he's talking to you.

Barry Ryan, *The Very Best of Barry Ryan*
Recommended by Neil Tennant

A trip down Brick Lane

I'd written a list of who I would like to recommend the records that make up this book – heroes, friends and people I have met along the way. For most, I had a phone number or an email address; some were friends of friends, but there was one for whom I didn't have any contact details. I had met Neil Tennant before, and I was going to ask Bernard Sumner if he was still in touch with him from his Electronic days. However, fate, the London sunshine and the pop-music gods were smiling on me one Thursday when I went to Rough Trade East for some interviews, record shopping and record-label business. Somewhere on Brick Lane, just by Cheshire Street, a familiar, well-dressed figure saun- tered towards me, smiling. As we drew level I realised it was him. 'Neil,' I said, and the figure spun round. He moved his sunglasses down to the end of his nose and peered over the top of them. 'Tim Burgess,' I said.

'So it is.'

We talked music, records and the ungodly hours of LA dog-walkers. I told him about this book and my mission – that I was looking for a recommendation from the heart and nothing necessarily too super-hip. He put his hand up to his chin, rest- ing his first finger on his lips, and tapped gently while looking up slightly. Neil has the speaking voice of a matinee idol.

'Well, I was doing some record shopping in Rome, and I found an amazing album – *The Very Best of Barry Ryan*. He's the guy who did "Eloise" with his brother, Paul. I think he got fed up working with his brother and struck out on his own. There's a song on there called "Kitsch", and it's the album I would highly recommend.'

We took a photograph together and went our separate ways in the afternoon sunshine.

*

I remember seeing someone on TV in around 1985 talking about how we'd get our news in the next century. They said we'd pretty much choose it ourselves – different people would send in news stories each day, and we'd all have a different configuration that was governed by whether we liked politics, music, sport or whatever. They said it would all land in front of us, complete with videos and footage. It seemed as far-fetched as hoverboards and silver-foil outfits. On reflection, it was a fairly accurate description of Twitter. We choose who we follow and they hit us up with their news – or if you follow me, regular updates about what songs I'm listening to and bands I think you should know about, with the odd bit of information about coffee or music festivals.

Recently I tweeted James Corden, who had just taken over *The Late Late Show* in the US. I said we were heading there and we should play on the show – within half an hour, he'd tweeted back and said it was all sorted. That's pretty mind-blowing, if you consider the number of people involved in an appearance on *TFI Friday* midway through the 1990s.

Loudon Wainwright III, *Album III*

Recommended by Sharon Horgan

Muse blues

I'd seen an astonishing TV show called *Catastrophe* – bizarrely enough, the writers, Sharon Horgan and Rob Delaney, had met on Twitter. I recommended that people watch the show, and Sharon let me know she was a fan of The Charlatans. She was heading to Manchester the weekend we were playing at Castlefield Bowl, so she brought her family to that show and the one the night before at Hotel Football, where Gary Neville played guitar for us – something else that was facilitated by Twitter. There was a feeling we had around *Modern Nature* that there was a freshness about the band. Much of it came from the freedom to communicate with fans and other people involved in TV, music or whatever. So much in the past was done by committee – very much our people talking to someone else's people, with us rarely involved. But now, with social media, it clicked much more with how I loved to do things.

With an album, you get a 3D film of where someone was at a certain time. Like points of longitude and latitude giving a geographical position, a story and an album can come together, allowing you to take a direct look into the past. If I hear and think of the characters from my time in Hollywood, it's like I'm there again – revisiting the anxieties, narcotics and the summer smells of Laurel Canyon, while celebrating recording *Wonderland* and looking out from Griffith Observatory.

There's a source of the folk/blues river somewhere near the crossroads where Robert Johnson stood, but it flows and rises in Chicago, Glasgow and Dublin and lives on through Neil Young,

Buddy Guy and a thousand characters in Tin Pan Alley, Grafton Street and the Latin Quarter of New Orleans. I'd first come across Loudon Wainwright III sometime in the 1980s, when he'd pop up on Jasper Carrott's TV show. Loudon is a troubadour, a folkie and, at times, a comedian. He also weighs in as the acoustic-guitar-wielding don of one of the most prolific musical families of modern times – father to Rufus and Martha, and one-time husband of Kate McGarrigle.

I'd never owned an album of his – he'd mostly passed me by, although I knew who he was. I'm sure I'd even heard a fair few songs, but nothing had stuck. When Sharon Horgan sent me her choice, it came with her story of where she was and the characters in her life at the time, giving clues as to how she maybe found the confidence to harness the skills for writing comedy that shows a deep-seated understanding of life's more absurd moments.

The ABBA song 'The Day Before You Came' charts the mundane existence of the protagonist before their life was changed twenty-four hours later. I look back to my time before joining the band – cycling round the chemical works, whistling songs that were playing on my Walkman, with no real fear about the future but no proper idea of what it would bring. Then, when life moves on a little, it becomes less carefree and with a whole load more responsibilities that make you look wistfully back at the kid on the bike, whistling.

I remember September 1985, listening endlessly to *Steve McQueen* by Prefab Sprout. It was the thirtieth anniversary of James Dean's death – cinemas were showing his films and his image was everywhere. I was eighteen years old, and I'm still transported back to that time if I hear that record or see photos of James Dean.

I'd looked up some songs from Loudon Wainwright's *Album III* and sent Sharon a message saying how much I'd enjoyed them. I played them again when she sent some notes on what the album meant to her. The clarity of her story mixed with the music, and the combination was about as emotional as anything I'd ever read:

I love that you've been listening to this. It was the first kind of acoustic-y folk record that I fell in love with.

I got it in 1991, I think.

Definitely in a record shop off Grafton Street in Dublin, but I can't remember which one.

I was introduced to Loudon Wainwright by my boyfriend at the time, and subsequent close friend, Mic Christopher, an amazing musician and singer.

Mic was part of the busking scene on Grafton Street with Glen Hansard (remember I was telling you – from the Swell Season and The Frames) and a trad band called Kila and a tribe of other troubadours.

All these incredible musicians who beat their guitars to splinters when they played and sang their voices hoarse. They would perform together and sometimes alone and I think I must have stopped and just listened one night and got talking.

I was in art college in Dublin, Mount Joy Square, but I'd have to walk down Grafton to get to my flat in Ranelagh. So I'd see them all there of an evening.

Also, I worked in a fairly famous late-night eating and drinking spot just off Grafton Street called the Coffee Inn. Famous because it stayed open late and if you were prepared to buy the ropey chilli or spaghetti you could sit around for hours and sink a ton of cheap red wine out of the cold. All the buskers would end up in there and I'd serve them. Happily. Anyway, they had this huge impact on me. I'd never been part of a significant scene before. I'd tried to hang round with the punks a bit but I think they could see how clean and convent school-y I actually was so it never really happened. I preferred these hippies anyway.

All the Grafton Street buskers listened to Bob Dylan, Neil Young, Van Morrison, The Waterboys, Scullion, John Martyn. Like I said, I'd never really listened to any kind of folk before. But I really fell for the

173

whole telling a story, just a singer and his/her guitar. But it was *Album III* by Loudon that just seemed to encapsulate that time the best for me. Little bit angry, little bit drunk, messy and in love.

Mic, the boyfriend who introduced me to that world, used to do this incredible raw version of 'Muse Blues'. It was beautiful. He very sadly died fourteen years ago when he was touring with The Waterboys. He fell down some steps in Groningen one night after a gig and hit his head and never woke up. So it's kind of hard to listen to now or to even think about that time really, although it was a hugely important part of my growing up.

Being part of that scene sort of began the formation of me. If you know what I mean.

So, not only did I go and find Loudon Wainwright III, but I looked up Mic Christopher too – there's footage of him singing 'Suspicious Minds' with Glen Hansard on Grafton Street.

Tragic stories happen all around us, but we're often not aware they've taken place. Mic had just supported The Waterboys on the night he died. There are a couple of albums available – one was finished and put out by his family after his death.

Photek, *Modus Operandi*
Recommended by Jason Williamson

Stockholm Syndrome

I was in the land of ABBA and heading for a shop named after one of the albums I was looking for. The signs were promising. We'd arrived at Debaser, the venue we were playing, and I was looking for Pet Sounds – it's my kind of place, where they name record shops after great records.

I'd phoned ahead to check if the shop had any copies of its namesake Beach Boys album – it was Kevin Shields's recommendation, so I thought, like an MBV album, it might be more complicated than it seemed on the surface.

They had sold out of copies of *Pet Sounds* the day before, but I was assured by Steffan, who ran the shop, that if I brought along a list of what I needed, they'd definitely have something.

As I walked through the door, Steffan greeted me. 'All of this is yours,' he said. The most enticing welcome I've ever had in a record shop, or perhaps in any kind of shop for that matter. He said we'd start by looking for *Pet Sounds*, just in case one had slipped through the net and was waiting for us in the racks. 'Nope,' was the answer after a couple of minutes of searching, proving it to be another tricky fella who's a bit tougher to find than I thought he would be. I had now asked for, and failed to find, The Beach Boys in more places than was healthy. At one time, you were able to buy it in almost every record shop. It was then that Juhani, who runs the shop with Steffan, appeared – they looked similar, slightly greying beards and very Swedish glasses. I complimented Juhani on his Tommy Boy sweatshirt, and the three of us set about the task.

I passed him my list. Juhani thought there might be a reissue of *Pet Sounds* . . . somewhere.

'Is a reissue a problem?'

'No, not at all – I will take whatever you have.'

He went off to find it and came back empty-handed.

'No?'

He shook his head.

By now, I was in browsing mode, looking for Roxy Music's debut for Kevin Rowland, when my friend Tive suggested he call his friend, Jens, at Bengans Records. He went through the list, dotting the i's and crossing the t's.

'Jens has *Roxy Music*. He will bring it to the venue.'

Wow! Is this allowed? Yeah, course it is. I am making up the rules, and deliveries count.

Back to the browsing, and I saw a familiar old friend, a record I have grown to love, a recommendation from Peter Gordon – *First Blues* by Allen Ginsberg.

Did I need a second copy? Steffan and Juhani watched me and gestured an 'is he or isn't he?' with their hands. Kind of gentle t'ai chi moves.

Maybe . . . I will come back to it. I think they know what the outcome is going to be.

Do I want it? Of course I do.

Juhani studied the list and said, 'Loudon Wainwright we have – it's old traditional!' – yep, sounds about right. 'Over here, but only on CD.'

Agh!!! Hmmmmm – an age-old conundrum, but I've often bought an album on CD and used it as a stopgap until I find the record, which can take years. So I bought it. Little did I know I'd find a copy on vinyl less than twenty-four hours later. Them's the breaks, though.

Next stop was just around the corner. Record Mania, a fantastic shop. I was served by Martin. He enthusiastically took the list and proclaimed, 'We have this one.' The front of the shop looked like any unassuming record shop, though an original of *Organic Music Society* by Don Cherry, father of Eagle Eye and Neneh, in the window gave me high hopes of finding one of the more elusive characters on my list. But out the back was different – there were maybe five people wearing headphones with mouthpieces, like some kind of vinyl stock-market/air-traffic-control thing. They seemed pretty busy.

'It's Australian,' he said. I was assuming he was talking about the record on the list, but he could have easily had a pet koala. He reached behind the counter – I'm not an expert on counters but this one was definitely Swedish, all minimal and functional, while looking like something from an art gallery – and there it was. Pristine and perfect – *One Nation Underground* by Pearls Before Swine, as recommended by Iggy Pop, the Hieronymus Bosch cover a depiction of Hell, looking just as cool as Iggy's description in his message. It was an amazing feeling. I felt I had done justice to Iggy's recommendation. I was beaming.

Thank you, thank you.

So I have one of the three Iggy recommendations – a brilliant day's work. Now where the fuck am I going to find White Zombie and Junior Wells?

Sound Station in Copenhagen went from being somewhere I'd never come across before to my favourite shop in the world in the space of about an hour.

My affection for shops like Rough Trade, Monorail and Piccadilly Records is pretty solid. I try not to compare them as I love them all equally and they're my favourite spots if I'm in London, Glasgow or Manchester, but I felt I was kind of cheating on them with the speed at which I grew to love Sound Station. Stacked high like the slightly jumbled but ordered mind of a brilliant scientist, its best feature didn't seem to be open to all – a basement where you undertook an unspoken test, and only those that passed gained access. It was home to the rarest records in Scandinavia, according to Nikolai, who ran the shop. Now, this might've been some sort of sales trick, but it hooked me in pretty easily. I felt that a privilege had been bestowed upon me and I had to remind myself I was out buying records. Nikolai had an air of Joe Pesci about him, but only the good points – I never felt like he was going to kill me with a ballpoint pen, not even once. He had a panda tattoo on one arm and a squid on the other. While he was helping me, he was also serving up to three other people.

He glanced at the list and said, 'Yes. We have. Uh huh,' and, 'Got it.' He also said 'YES!!!' out of total and utter excitement at seemingly every opportunity. Surely he didn't have everything on there? And how could he know for sure what they had?

He said, 'Mmmmm,' and jumped from one wall of vinyl over to the next, running down steps and climbing ladders like a character in a video game – one arm reaching out to grab a record, his other arm held out as a counterbalance.

I found a beautiful copy of Joe Byrd and the Field Hippies' *American Metaphysical Circus* to replace the water-damaged copy I have at the Charlatans' studio (if it was in good condition it would be in all its pride and glory in my house). It was mostly the As that got damaged on the LAX runway – good news for Bob Geldof, Pete Murphy and Mick Jones.

Also found was a reissue of the very elusive Beach Boys album, a double fortieth-anniversary edition of *Pet Sounds* – one record in mono and one in stereo. It seemed perfect to find a version where the audio difference meant everything. Just as Kevin Shields's 200 cassettes sent to journalists in 1991 were individually checked by him to see if they came up to scratch, so Brian Wilson's attention to detail made him appear eccentric. He began to write with his feet in a sandpit and wearing a fireman's hat for the perfect compositional ambience.

I told Nikolai about Sharon Horgan and the importance of

finding her recommendation. He looked at the computer as I pointed out *Album III*. 'Yes!' he shouted. I followed him as he ran towards the back of the shop, feeling like Anneka Rice about to jump in a helicopter in the search for treasure . . . but it wasn't there! 'I have it,' Nikolai reassured me. We went to the basement, and at the bottom of the vertically organised section of folk and pop not yet put out for the rest of the world there was Loudon looking at me with a beautiful beardy grin.

In the space of fifteen minutes I'd crossed three off the list. They may not have had the records the next customer was looking for, but the records I was after were there. The others were in record shops scattered around Europe, but I had me an app and a ten-day tour to find the rest.

Nikolai even brought me his own personal copy of *Modus Operandi* by Photek, one of Sleaford Mod Jason Williamson's recommendations. He cycled to the show and gave me the leather and canvas record bag he brought it in – it was about the most Scandinavian thing that's ever happened to me.

*

Berlin was where many of the roads seemed to lead. Glen Hansard was playing a couple of nights before we arrived. Two days after we left, Sleaford Mods were due to arrive for a show. I'd first come across them early in 2014, and they stopped me in my tracks. Within a couple of days of hearing them, I sent them a message asking them to come and play at Tim Peaks at the Isle of Wight Festival. I'd not heard anything that pulled the rug so effectively from under the self-satisfied middle-management types since I was obsessed with Crass sometime around 1982. It was a kind of music that had all but disappeared but, as it stood out on its own, seemed to have even more power. The message came back that Jason was getting married and had cleared the whole of June of any gigs. However, the offer was for the romantic hotspot of the Isle of Wight, and the band had started to really pick up some coverage in the *NME*, *Q* and other magazines that had ignored anything Jason and Andrew had released in various guises over the previous few years. With some light persuasion, they joined the line-up and put in the performance of the festival, according to Swim Deep, who told everyone during their set later that day.

I got my recommendation from Jason before we set off for Europe:

Hi mate.

If you've got it, I'll throw something else over sharpish.

J x

My recommendation is *Truth* by The Jeff Beck Group.

It's a slab of horribleness to be honest, and the cutting production is so close to your ears you feel like the fucking netting on the unfortunate valve amps he most probably used. It's got this weird Tudor-style cover of 'Greensleeves' on it, a half-decent cover of Tim Rose's 'Morning Dew' (or did he cover it?) and a cheeky stab at 'You Shook Me', a blues cover that arguably faired better in Jimmy Page's hands a year or so later. In fact, folklore murmurs that back in the day Beck broke down on hearing early Zep demos claiming they'd ripped him off. You can see why. I would say at this point in history, Beck fucking nails it, as it was recorded from '66 onwards. You have to remember that not a lot of people were coming up with this noise at that time, although it was released in '68. It also features an egoless Ron Wood and Rod Stewart, obviously. Stand out tracks are 1 and 2. Track 2's intro ('Let Me Love You') fucks you up properly. It's absolute sleaze. A masterclass in proto rock/metal.

'I do have it,' I replied, 'but that's not a problem at all. I bought it in NYC at Bleecker Bob's. But . . . if you wanna send another then feel free – x – this is ace, though.'

Then this came through:

Modus Operandi by Photek, released in 1997, is my recommendation. It's the business – a peerless monotony of cuts attached to a drum and bass formula that was way more refined than a lot of its contemporaries, although it does contain that double bass which is familiar to a lot of music of this ilk towards the end of the nineties. Standout tracks are 'Hidden Camera', 'Modus Operandi' (the title track) and 'Minotaur'. It hasn't aged really – a slab of concrete to match a society hurtling towards the later stages of its implosion.

Around the corner from the venue was Anton Newcombe's studio, where, a couple of years earlier, he and I had recorded a cover of Hank Williams's 'The Battle of Armageddon'. I sent Anton a message, and within a couple of hours he had joined us at the venue. We ran through a version of 'Sproston Green' with Anton on guitar – complete with his Princeton amp and a Vox 12-string Starstream. As when Kevin Shields had joined us, Anton pointed out that our sound engineer, Di Barton, who works for us and New Order, was one of the best he'd ever heard.

I eventually found Neil Tennant's recommendation, *The Very Best of Barry Ryan*, in Soultrade during a break, which was kind of poetic – to me, The Pet Shop Boys have perfected the Europop sound, without losing any of their coolness.

The Allman Brothers Band, *The Allman Brothers Band at Fillmore East*

Recommended by Kurt Wagner

Oh No I Love You

Returning to somewhere you used to live but haven't been back to in a while is a little like switching on a soap opera that you stopped watching some time ago. The places are kind of the same, but most of the cast are different and the connection from one thing to another can seem hazy. Add in a healthy dose of jet lag and it all gets a bit like a Charlie Kaufman film.

So it was that we landed in LA ahead of our US tour. The time difference and the sensory deprivation of the flight added to the feeling of a waking dream – mix it all up with the kind of sunlight that's like a permanent camera flash, and the scene is complete. And it was made even more surreal by the fact that our first stop was James Corden's *The Late Late Show*.

Our LA trips were a game of two halves bookending our tour. We had nine shows, taking in Sacramento and Washington, with a festival in Austin, and lots of record shops in between. They were our first shows in America since Jon had collapsed. Five years had passed, but travelling and tours were always a reminder of his absence. He'd always come bowling into the airport full of high spirits, and quite often a few measures of spirits too.

As soon as we arrived, I walked to the local supermarket on Franklin Boulevard, a place I went to every day when I lived in LA. I'm not sure if it was out of habit or boredom, but it was always worth it as the food there is the best I have tasted in the world, ever (pretty expensive too, but hey . . .). It has a tractor beam that draws me in whenever I'm in town. Next door is Counterpoint Records and Books, which makes the pulling power ten times stronger and always managed to get me out of the house when I lived on La Punta Drive ten years before, in a soap opera I wasn't watching any more. Dust hitting your lips as soon as you walk through the door. It was reassuring to see Throbbing Gristle's *Greatest Hits* – the second most self-deprecating album title ever, after their own *20 Jazz Funk Greats* – sitting proudly at the front of the rack as I walked into the building for the first time in five years. With Cosey Fanni Tutti's face looking down on me, I imagined her saying, 'Hiya, luv,' in her beautiful Humberside tones.

In the window, a copy of the Moondog biography, *The Viking of 6th Avenue*, began to talk to me.

'Hey, Tim, are you going to buy me or what? Nyah, take a look around. You'll be back to buy me before you go.' And so I was.

Five years ago, along with Amoeba, I would visit Counterpoint at least once a week, given its locality and it being just a brilliant place to spend time. However, since leaving LA I had been told of a new place.

We hear of record shops closing all the time, but there seems to be a healthy abundance of new places opening up. Whether it's good business or just enthusiasts giving it a shot and having somewhere to call work and spend their days – who knows? There's just something about vinyl. It feels good, and we all need a new place to visit when we reacquaint ourselves with an old friend – in this case, an old friend called Hollywood.

Record Emporium opened sometime around 2013 and has been flourishing ever since, helped along by the annual frenzy of Record Store Day and a resurgent enthusiasm for vinyl. I always have a quick walk around the racks before I allow myself to start looking through the records. I like to think of it like a lion circling its prey, but I think it looks mostly like a guy walking round a record shop. A quick recce of the place – I'm not sure why, but it takes a minute or two to acclimatise.

The first record in the Allman Brothers section of the shop was the one Kurt Wagner had recommended – sometimes it's just that easy. I picked it up. The notes on the plastic sleeve read, 'Pink label original, a bit worn – $12.98 plus tax'. OK. It's in the bag.

'Records don't come any more American than that one,' Clifton said from behind the counter as I handed him Kurt's recommendation. It seemed appropriate that Kurt had chosen one of the best examples of southern rock.

I first came across The Allman Brothers when The Charlatans played on the same stage as them at Roskilde Festival. We were the new kids on the block, and we were playing with all these legends. 'One of them was married to Cher, you know,' I heard Jon Baker say in his soft West Midlands accent. Jon didn't say much, but when he did, I listened. I mean, who doesn't love Cher? *Look at Us*, the first LP she did with Sonny, was one of my favourite records of the 1990s. Even though it came out in 1965.

I first came across Kurt via a compilation TDK my friend made for me in 1998, and I have been a fan ever since.

*

Jet lag comes in waves. We had been to *The Late Late Show* for an 11 a.m. soundcheck and after we'd finished, at around 12.30, we were free to go back to the hotel till our arranged pick-up time of 3.45.

Record Emporium is only a block away from Amoeba. Some might say it's a little brave, or foolhardy, to compete with the behemoth that is Amoeba, but I say record shops aren't like that. Maybe they're like one of those symbiotic relationships in nature – those birds that clean a crocodile's teeth.

Record shops don't have to compete – they are too cool for that. They can all exist in harmony; they're there for everyone. In a dreamy reality, record shops would all stick in the same vicinity.

They should call it Record District or the Vinyl Quarter or something. Throw in a coffee shop and I'd never leave.

I put the record on in my hotel, a place on Franklin and Cahuenga. I love it here, its smell and style – kinda dusty and old, but clean, without pretension. I like also that it's exactly where I wanted to be, within walking distance of the venue we were going to play later. Even though we'd be travelling east before heading back, well . . . it's nice to get your bearings.

US tours remind me of Westerns a little – you arrive in town, nobody cares too much where you've been, and you're heading on the next day. Perhaps someone's seen you on a poster outside the venue. There's a kind of buzz and there's definitely a sense of feeling out of place, not so much in New York or LA but definitely in Milwaukee and Sacramento. We play the show and then saddle up and head off.

So, yeah, back to The Allman Brothers. 'Stormy Monday', a T-Bone Walker song, has the feeling of Lambchop until the shredding begins. I told Kurt, and he said, 'There you go. Try having a listen to "In Memory of Elizabeth Reed"' – a Lambchop title if ever I heard one.

'In Memory of Elizabeth Reed' live from Fillmore East begins like a Steely Dan song, right down to the timings and the standard of the chops. It sounds like a song I already know, all finger clicks and jazzy chords. It's brilliant.

I have heard people say there will never be another Duane Allman, especially people in the south, and I subscribe to that. The organ-playing is pretty sweet too – so instinctive. It's Duane's brother Gregg, and if I was being a little less modest I might say there was a hint of what I had with Rob Collins around the time of *Some Friendly*.

Clifton was right. It was an American soundtrack – a shared DNA with so much of the music I loved when I lived here. And I am sure I could hear the distant sound of Kurt Wagner whistling along.

Paul Simon, *Graceland*

Recommended by James Corden

From Hollywood to Graceland

I've mentioned that we were asked a few years ago if we'd allow 'North Country Boy' to be used in an independent film by Shane Meadows – I've always been keen on sharing songs for use in films or other interesting projects, from when we had to ask Robert De Niro's permission to use a sample of his voice on '109 Pt. 2'. When we saw the final version of *Twenty Four Seven*, we were knocked out to have one of our songs in such a fantastic film. It was the first time I'd seen James Corden too. Via Broadway roles, films like *The History Boys* and stints hosting The Brits, James was the new darling of late-night US chat shows. When we played 'Let the Good Times Be Never Ending' on *The Late Late Show*, I could see him dancing all the way through it, off-camera. He's definitely got the moves. After we'd recorded the show, he asked us to play another song just for him and the studio audience – he told us he'd been a huge fan of 'North Country Boy' ever since it had been used in the soundtrack to *Twenty Four Seven*. James danced all the way through, looking at us, smiling. I smiled and looked back. It was such a great start to our trip. We sat together after the show, some Hollywood high fives were exchanged, and I asked James to recommend a record.

'Just one? The pressure is on,' he said. 'There's a big album that I always go back to: *Graceland*.'

I've always been a fan of Paul Simon. My first memory of him is '50 Ways to Leave Your Lover', when I was eight or nine years old – it has a kind of nursery-rhyme quality that I liked. Most kids of my generation had some mainstays in parental record collections. Simon and Garfunkel were high on the list of mine.

The Simon and Garfunkel songbook has had a major influence on The Charlatans – in particular, 'North Country Boy' borrows subtly from the melody of 'April Come She Will' from *Sounds of Silence*.

Paul Simon's cultural influence on a kid growing up in the 1970s was spread across various formats, from the *Graduate* soundtrack and *Simon and Garfunkel Live in Central Park* to him popping up in *Annie Hall* and on *The Muppets*.

Graceland was one of the most controversial albums of its time. Simon had worked with South African musicians, breaking the cultural boycott that was in place over apartheid. Unlike Queen or Rod Stewart, who were trousering big cheques to entertain at the whites-only resort of Sun City, Simon wanted people to hear musicians who had no way of sharing their music with the outside world. He said at the time that 'when there are radical transfers of power on either the left or the right, the artists always get screwed'.

John Peel and Andy Kershaw had championed bands like The Bhundu Boys from Zimbabwe. They went on to support Madonna at Wembley before line-up changes and more than their fair share of tragedy saw the end of the band.

Lizzy Mercier Descloux recorded 'Zulu Rock' in Johannesburg in 1983, which was her French disco take on the jit sound. Songs like 'Don't Go Lose It Baby' by Hugh Masekela were getting played in clubs. Maybe the catch-all label of 'world music' was too general, but African music was moving towards the mainstream. Then came *Graceland*, bringing together Masekela and the voices and style of Ladysmith Black Mambazo to sell just under two million copies in the UK alone.

2011's *So Beautiful or So What* is up there with Simon's best. It's a beautiful, textured record with songs about spirituality and mortality, lots of bells and a song about Christmas.

If I was asked by myself to recommend a Paul Simon-related record, I'd choose *Bookends*. It captures the 1960s, the seasons, passing time and the sounds of the city beautifully – songs like 'Old Friends', 'Overs', the electric percussive version of 'Mrs Robinson', and the classic 'Hazy Shade of Winter'. It is a thrillingly well-written moment in time that documents New York City as well as *The Freewheelin' Bob Dylan*.

*

Austin, Texas. Famous for the bats under Congress Avenue Bridge, which I can see out of my window. I am staying at the Hyatt Regency Hotel, which evidently backs right up to the Fun Fun Fun Festival, where we're playing alongside Ride, Wu-Tang Clan and Grimes. Every evening by the bridge just about sunset up to 1.5 million bats emerge into the sky. It's a huge tourist attraction, but Austin's major claim to fame is South by Southwest – the biggest new music platform for the best bands in the world. Maybe CMJ comes close, but everyone loves South by Southwest.

And it doesn't stop there. It has the Austin City Limits and Fun Fun Fun festivals too. Music is a huge part of the culture in Austin. It's not surprising that it has more than its fair share of record shops – my phone app lights up when it realises I'm here.

First stop is Waterloo Records. With a neon mod target as its logo, it looks like it's straight out of Camden. Only it would look cheesy in London – it gained coolness by being as far away as possible, and ended up with an extra helping. Before I go in, I head over the road for some watermelon.

Queuing up in an American supermarket is pretty fun. There is back and forth conversation between customers. Some are happier to chat than others. Some have very little on the conveyor belt, and you get the feeling that they're just there for the hell of it – perhaps a little bit lonely and this is the only time in the day they'll get the chance to talk to another human being. The man in front of me is telling lots of jokes and genuinely making the cashier laugh.

'Do you want your meat wrapped in plastic sir?'

'No-oh . . .' comes the growly Texan drawl. 'I'll have mine wrapped in stain . . . less steel' – drawn out for effect, but pretty funny. Much polite laughter, then it's my turn and on to Waterloo Records.

John Coltrane's *A Love Supreme* and Junior Wells's *Hoodoo Man Blues* are on my list of hopefuls to get at Waterloo. The Junior Wells LP especially has become something of an enigma for me – I have never heard it, haven't even sneaked a listen on YouTube, but I have to say I think its my favourite record of this adventure. Maybe it's the mystery and the fact that it seems impossible to find.

Both the Coltrane and Wells albums were recently mentioned in the same sentence in a David Toop article I read on the train from London to Norwich. It named them as two of the most important records of their era, which makes 1965 seem like a very exciting time for musical explosions. So much happened between 1963 and 1966; it's hard to think of another three years that produced even half the number of groundbreaking albums.

Lying on top of a pile of other records, looking like it needed a place to live – maybe it just hadn't been filed yet – was a copy of *David Toop and Max Eastley's New and Rediscovered Musical Instruments*. I didn't have it. It felt like a sign. I thought I'd better bag it.

Beneath it was a copy of *Graceland* in its protective see-through wrapper. 'The Original *Graceland* LP. Anniversary edition of Grammy-winning album. High-quality 180-gram vinyl. Includes collectable poster PLUS download MP3s of full album + 3 bonus songs. $25.99.'

Bingo.

Elliott Smith, *XO*

Recommended by Tom Sheehan

A bag for those slices

Tom Sheehan is probably the photographer with the closest link to The Charlatans. When we met he was working for the *Melody Maker* and, alongside Kevin Cummins at the *NME*, they were the two photographers who best documented the times. We asked Tom to do the cover for 'Crashin' In', which came out on Boxing Day 1994. It was a homage to the Beastie Boys' *Check Your Head* album cover. On our version a Hammond organ replaced the ghetto blaster that was on theirs.

We worked with him on all the singles and albums until *Wonderland*. No fall-out or anything, we just always put a time frame on anyone we collaborated with, whether it was with producers or video directors and photographers.

I was in touch with Tom recently and asked him for a recommendation. His reply was instant:

XO, Elliott Smith.

Then he reminded me why:

It has to be *XO* because it was the record I remember telling you about way back that became one of your favourites. You came round to our place one summer's evening. My daughter, who is now twenty-one, was only a year old – I put on 'Waltz #2' and it had an immediate effect – you couldn't stop moving. It really captured a moment.

After the reminder, I could see the day clearly in my mind. I had come back off tour, which always left me in kind of a daze, but a daze that I really loved being in. We danced in the garden and that album stuck in my head and has never left.

I've travelled a lot, being in a band. Not only does that mean seeing lots of places but so much of the time you're in transit. Sometimes in transit on a luxury tour bus or a flight somewhere exciting. But sometimes literally in a transit – converted to take merch and gear in the back, driver and tour manager up front, and the band sat around a table like players in a long-since abandoned poker game. Half-finished drinks from the rider rolling round at the turn of each corner. And if you were heading to a gig, whatever you could find to try and shift the hangover from the night before.

The sense of limbo that travel brings is the ideal gap to be filled with music – the anaesthetic that takes you away while the miles are being eaten up. For me, there are no better songs to listen to on a journey than those of Elliott Smith – it's possibly the fragile quality of his voice that captures the precariousness of travel. The will we/won't we nature of whether you'll make it or not. Not necessarily whether you'll make it in one piece, but more without whatever mode of transport giving up or weather closing in to put an end to getting anywhere for a while. Touring often seems like a board game, where the draw of a card has a dramatic affect on what happens next. 'Chicago O'Hare is closed due to snow, tonight's show is postponed – stay in and drink the minibar dry, followed by a cocktail from an Easter Island head in a tiki bar downtown.' 'The head gasket on your shaky splitter van has gone – sit by the side of the motorway in the rain until fifteen minutes after you are due onstage.' It leads to a strange state of mind where, although the shows are your reason for living at the time, there are so many things that can get in the way. You and the band end up like some ancient tribe, with a slew of superstitions and offerings to the travel gods in order to keep you on the move.

The best travel soundtracks for me are those with a sense of longing, not having made it from one place to the next – the lyrics of Cat Power, the voice and pace of Bill Callahan. Somewhere you can immerse yourself and stick around for a while.

So yes, Elliott Smith. I first went to see him at the Roxy on Sunset Boulevard with Anton, Charles and Frankie from The Brian Jonestown Massacre. There was a bleak beauty to his music that really struck me. In the dressing room, Michael Stipe and Courtney Love were holding court, but Elliott seemed distant – his demons never seemed far away. They had provided him with the songs that had brought him success, but everything remained so raw for him as he sang through his pain each night.

I met him again when he played a surprise show at the Three Clubs on Vine St. in LA, where I knew the bartender, Tammy. Elliott and I spoke about music and life and his plans for the future. Things had started to move pretty fast for him but it didn't seem that he was built robustly enough for the times or for the life he was headed for. He was the name on everybody's lips, and he seemed a little overwhelmed, lost in a crowd backstage at his own event.

I saw him play a few more times in Manchester and LA, and his music was my travel companion for much of the time. He always seemed to hover between this world and the next – there's the feeling that his songs were from a place not many people would want to spend time, either voluntarily or otherwise. I remember hearing that he had tried to take his own life by running off a cliff. A tree had broken his fall, but he injured himself so that he couldn't play guitar and had to cancel some gigs. There was a sense of inevitability when I heard that he had died in October 2003.

'Waltz #2' is a modern masterpiece, and there has to be a place in every record collection for *XO*. *Either/Or* isn't far behind. It set the template – 'Between the Bars' was a song for the crazy girls of LA, girls who wanted or thought they should have more but who never fulfilled their dreams and aspirations.

'Drink up with me now / And forget all about / The pressure

of days'. It made so much sense to me when I was still boozing. To hear it now takes me back to those times and those places. Listening to Elliott's words while you're travelling allows you into his deeply personal, cinematic worldview.

When you're travelling, there's a sense of adventure, tempered by wanting the comfort of what you know. With me, I was always leaving someone I loved to go somewhere, or leaving somewhere I recently fell in love with. Listen to 'Bottle Up and Explode' and look out of the window or across an airport lounge. Love, beauty and loneliness have never been better expressed in song. It was just that the person those qualities were given to was unable to function with the weight of what he knew.

My haul from Waterloo was completed by the last copy in the shop of a reissue on heavyweight, 180-gram vinyl – *XO* by Elliott Smith.

I thought of Tom Sheehan, days in LA, Anton, Charles and Frankie Teardrop – our lives now and our lives back then, and the loss to the world of an amazing talent.

'Do you want a bag for those slices?' one of the staff asked.

I just thought that was the best thing to say about records ever. I was out the door and went back to the hotel to look at my finds and eat my food.

Later that afternoon, it was raining. I headed out in the opposite direction to End of an Ear. It was a two-mile walk but I needed the exercise after being on a plane for all that time. It's good to get out – good for jet lag too.

I walked past the Texas School for the Deaf, and then shacks and restaurants, houses and Airstreams, and general good-time, fun people on the street. Austin people really are kind and smiley. It's something to do with the amount of festivals they have and how much vinyl is in their city, I'm sure of it.

A young girl, maybe ten years old, rode up to me on her bike and said, 'I like your hair.'

'Thanks – I like your bike. Hey, there's a record shop around here. Do you know where it is?'

She didn't know.

Why would she?

She is ten years old.

But this is not just an old man's game, this record-shopping lark. It's something that begins in our teens, takes a hold, then steers you on a path, with no looking back. My mum said to me, 'Buying all these records isn't going to help you in your future, Tim.' Little did she know I would one day be writing a book about record shops while playing in a band in America.

'Blue building,' said a guy, pointing in the direction I was heading. He looked like he might be into vinyl. And there it was – End of an Ear Records. It's my favourite kind of play on words, one that doesn't quite seem to work. It lacks the smugness of the ones that work perfectly. Like a crackle on a record, it adds to it rather than taking anything away.

I spoke to the guy behind the counter and mentioned the Coltrane album that Paul Weller had recommended I pick up.

'*A Love Supreme* is between pressings,' Dan said. Dan is the owner and had seen my tweet about going into the shop a couple of hours earlier. He talked of his love of record shops around the world, mentioning his two favourites. One was in Oxford, Mississippi, a very small campus town. The shop had three rooms of 7-inch blues, country and soul.

'What's it called?' I asked. 'It sounds incredible.'

'Ah well, it's similar in name to ours,' said Dan. 'It's called The End of All Music. And Drift in Cornwall – do you know that place?'

'By name and reputation. The owner reached out to me through a friend of a friend.'

'Both beautiful places,' Dan said.

Peering over at the blues section, I thought I may as well have a look and see if *Hoodoo Man Blues* was there, but there was some-one else flicking through the racks, so I left it and carried on talking to Dan. I was beginning to resign myself to the fact that I wouldn't be finding the album I was looking for. I had looked it up on Discogs. It's expensive. But I was still drawn over to the blues once the coast had cleared, and there was a Junior Wells section – I was beginning to think he didn't exist outside of Discogs. And without so much as a drum roll or big build-up or a punch in the face, there it was – a brand-new version of a record I had been looking for in every record shop I had been in since July. One of Iggy Pop's three recommendations: *Hoodoo Man Blues* by Junior Wells.

It was a moment in time for me, like Stanley meeting Living-stone, Hercules and whatever he was looking for. I'd found it. I took a photo and sent it to my friend at home. He sent back a snap of his own incredulous face. I understand that the world may not find this amazing, but there was a crate-digging minute of celebration.

I asked Dan where it came from. 'Delmark records re-press every now and then. I guess you just got lucky.'

I had no idea it had been reissued. I told Dan about what I was doing, and he was thrilled to be a part of my adventure. I had to go and do the show at the Fun Fun Fun Festival. We were play-ing late afternoon, and I needed to get myself together. Dan gave me a discount on a $13 record – my total came to $9. What a man. What a day. Austin, I love ya.

The show was packed and we had a great time. As we walked off, Andy Bell and the rest of Ride were standing at the side of the stage. We had a little bit of food together, then it was their turn to play. I stood at the side of the stage. 'Leave Them All Behind' and 'Taste' were both brilliant, and 'Cool Your Boots' even more so, with Andy dedicating it to The Charlatans. It's like they never went away, but at the same time they seem even better than they were the first time round.

We played the Daytripper gigs together. Brighton and Black-pool, 1992. Them on first in the north, and us on first in the south – an idea that Andy had come up with during our time hanging around together in the early 1990s. He would come up to Salford, where I was living, and I would go down to Oxford. We shared ideas and a lot of music, and went out to clubs together. Daytripper was a moment of clarity during a big night out.

We always seemed to release our records at the same time. It must have been youthful energy. We knew all the same people. They were our friends, and as we were all eating in the festival catering tent it felt like we were all slightly older and quite a bit wiser. Someone did ask out loud what year it was and what had happened to the twenty-three in between. It was so good that so much had changed, but brilliant that a lot had stayed the same.

John Grant, *Grey Tickles, Black Pressure*

Recommended by Dennis and Lois

Everybody these days thinks they're a badass

It's Monday 9 November at 6 a.m. NBC are outside the hotel because the holiday season is about to kick in with the unveiling of the 2015 Christmas lights.

Maybe I am a bit early, as the camera crew are quite a way from setting up and the tree and small Santa in the park are yet to be lit. Anyway, I need coffee, and it's the first time in 2015 that I have worn gloves.

Coffee got, I return to the room. I tune in to Lauren Laverne, who is a few hours into her show. Curtis Lee's 'Pretty Little Angel Eyes' is playing and her guest, Howard Marks, is introduced to talk about his new book, death, the joys of Ecstasy and jail.

Howard has put five Dylan Thomas poems to music and has asked me to release them on Record Store Day 2016. The first track, 'And Death Shall Have No Dominion', was debuted on Lauren's show for National Poetry Day.

Today turns out to be the anniversary of Dylan's – can I call him Dylan? – death in the Chelsea Hotel in New York City, a place I will be visiting tomorrow (I go there whenever I am in New York) when we play Webster Hall.

Bob Dylan took his name from Dylan Thomas, and Marc Bolan took the first two letters of Bob and the last two letters from Dylan to make his new surname.

Dennis and Lois have been transplanted out of New Jersey and are on their way back home via Milwaukee after doing the merchandise for John Grant's tour.

Happy Mondays, indeed.

Dennis and Lois are legendary gig-goers in the extreme. Lois is now in a wheelchair but that doesn't stop them travelling thousands of miles to see bands. There is almost nobody they didn't meet from the 1970s New York music scene. Well, almost nobody. While driving around the city one day, Lois spotted Andy Warhol and gestured to Dennis that they should stop and give him a lift – it had caused some jovial friction between them ever since, as Dennis didn't pull over and they didn't get another chance to meet him. I inadvertently brought it back to Lois's mind, as her first words to me were, 'Tim, you look like Andy Warhol. Did I tell you the story of when Dennis wouldn't give him a lift?'

In the world of music, Dennis and Lois are one-offs, having dedicated their lives to rock 'n' roll. They've been patrons of the NYC music scene since the heyday of CBGBs and hosts to visiting UK bands since 1977. Starting as fans but making themselves an integral part of the story, they kept it up, rather than being caught in a moment in time – from The Clash and the Sex Pistols through becoming friends of ours and the Happy Mondays to The Vaccines and Elbow more recently.

Anyway, I agreed to meet them at The Exclusive Company Record Shop. They were outside in their car. I asked them if they had a recommendation for me, and they began to talk, not saying whether they had or hadn't. They told me about Mark E. Smith and how they'd booked the Fall tour where a fight broke out onstage. Mark got arrested, and they were left with a $20k bill – it bankrupted them.

'We didn't mind being bankrupt,' Dennis said.

Their first date was at CBGBs watching Television and Talking Heads. 'Lou Reed was shooting pool wearing a white T-shirt, cigarettes tucked into his sleeve – short hair, shades.'

'Was he watching?' I asked.

'He was shooting pool,' Dennis said, with that Long Island shrug of his.

'So he was listening . . .'

Lois stayed in the car – she can barely walk. Dennis and I went inside. We flicked through the reggae/dub section.

'Bob Marley . . . Bob Marley,' he said, in an almost dreamlike state. Dennis pulled the record forward in the rack. 'Now when we saw Bob Marley it was at the Manhattan Center, which is now the Hammerstein Ballroom. We watched from the balcony, were the only two white people in the audience – I tell you, man, in front of his people, phew! We saw him levitate.'

'Was he playing guitar?'

'A little bit, but he was mostly just moving. Then we saw him at the Beacon Theater – mostly white kids there, a completely different feeling.'

The Exclusive Company uses the term 'pre-owned' as opposed to 'second-hand'. Dennis and I agreed that it's a really nice way of describing once-loved records.

'So it's the new John Grant record, Dennis? Is that your and Lois's recommendation?'

Dennis said, 'Sorry to keep going on about him but we're so in love with him right now.'

'It's absolutely fine,' I replied. 'I love it. Living in the moment is a wonderful thing.'

'We went on tour with him selling his merchandise. We told him we were coming, so John said if you are, you may as well sell the merch. We are directly in contact with his fans – so much better than having someone who doesn't know anything about him selling it.'

'Here it is. Let me get it,' I said.

'We have some in the car. You don't have to buy it.' After a little persuasion, I agreed to let them give me one out of the boot of the car. I'm making the rules up as I go along. After all, they were running the merchandise stall on the tour. I've bought some amazing limited-run vinyl from gigs – they are kind of like a record shop. And it's Dennis and Lois, so rules must be shifted slightly to accommodate them. As Dennis pointed out, 'At this time we are a record shop, so it still counts. John is such an important writer – he will be thrilled that I have given you a copy, Tim. Please take it.'

Back outside, Lois had been patient. 'I just told Dennis off,' she said. 'He just went into that shop and didn't buy that Ork Records box set.'

'I know. I wanted that too.'

'You know, he always goes into a shop and sees something and never buys it. We're going back tomorrow. We can send you one, if you want us to. It would be our privilege.'

And such is the generosity of two of the most amazing people in pop history.

We talked about Milwaukee, home of the Bronze Fonz, and my new catchphrase: 'You might be able to talk the talk but can you Milwaukee the Milwaukee?'

I'm not sure what constitutes being worthy of a statue, but Milwaukee's Bronze Fonz might just make you wonder if someone slightly more deserving had ever spent time there, bearing in mind it wasn't a statue of Henry Winkler, who played The Fonz, but an actual homage to the fictional Arthur Fonzarelli, the shark-jumping motorbike mechanic. Having said that, some of the conversation with Dennis and Lois was about a fictional mutual friend who'd been immortalised in bronze in his adoptive home town of Timperley. After Chris Sievey's death, his many friends and fans clubbed together and put on events around the country, and now beside the two pillar boxes in the middle of Timperley stands a life-size statue of Frank Sidebottom, complete with his papier-mâché head rendered in bronze.

Chris was friends with Dennis and Lois and wrote to them often. He had a tour planned later that year, but had told them he was 'frightened of America'. So he decided the solution would be to go on a practice mission and visit New York for the day, arriving early in the morning and leaving at 11 p.m.

After landing, Chris was beckoned by a stern immigration officer.

Immigration guy: 'What is the purpose of your visit?'

Chris: 'A day trip.'

Immigration guy: 'How long are you here for?'

'Just the day.'

'One day? All the way from the UK? Where is your luggage?'

'Here!' Chris said, holding up a carrier bag in which he had some fruit and a jumper.

'Where are you staying?'

'Dennis and Lois's.' Chris was starting to believe that he and the immigration guy were getting on well after a difficult introduction.

'Dennis and Lois?'

'Yes, that's them. Do you know them then? Lots of people do. There's a song about them.'

'I meant which city, not the names of the people,' immigration guy continued.

'New York. I think it's somewhere near the Empire State Building. I think it's near a park.'

'This Dennis and Lois – what are their surnames?'

'I've never asked. They don't really use them, you know? A bit like Madonna. Do you know Madonna's surname? I know I don't. Anyway, that's them.'

Chris pointed at Dennis and Lois waving frantically through the glass at arrivals. The immigration guy figured that his ordeal was over and that Chris posed no kind of threat and was just visiting for the day. Possibly the only thing that could have made it any more ridiculous would have been if Chris had had Frank's papier-mâché head with him to further explain his visit. It's maybe better he didn't.

A tour used to be like setting sail with a gang of pirates. The Jolly Roger would be raised above the tour bus and adventures and high times would be sought. Times have changed for us now, but the band and crew love to share stories about our generation's musical Big Bang, sometime around the Sex Pistols gig at the Lesser Free Trade Hall.

Perhaps even more than some piratical set-up, a band's crew is like one of those heist-movie crack teams – not safe-breakers or getaway drivers but a band of road-hardened sound engineers, tour managers and roadies. For our US dates we were joined by Davo, our tech. There's nothing about any instrument he doesn't know and he's always cheerful of disposition. His potential had been spotted by Mick Jones in his Big Audio Dynamite days, and Mick instructed his legendary roadie Flea to 'train him up'. The best roadies are like Jedis, and Mick saw that the Force was strong in Davo. He has toured with The Stone Roses, Paul Weller, Primal Scream and The Verve. But often roadies are like icebergs too. So much is unseen: when we filmed *Later* with Jools Holland, James Taylor was on the same show, as in 'Sweet Baby James' Taylor; he greeted Davo like an old friend, and they chatted before James went to soundcheck. I think I must have looked stunned to see them shooting the breeze, as Davo laughed and said, 'Did I not say I knew him? Yeah, he's a good lad James,' before going back to tuning the guitar he was holding.

Dian Barton is our sound engineer; more famously, Di is New Order's sound engineer too. A legend in the Manchester live-music world, Di, her partner, Ed, and her brother, Ian, used to do not only the sound at gigs but also had PAs that they would supply too. It was their PA at the Haçienda, and having all the gear meant they could do gigs outside of regular venues. They worked for The Fall, New Order, The Smiths and Cabaret Voltaire all over – as local as Liverpool and Leeds and as distant as Holland and Italy.

According to legend, once you've done the sound satisfactorily for Morrissey and Mark E. Smith, there's not much that can faze you.

Women sound engineers are a rarity now, but in 1982 they were unheard of – the live-music scene was as blokey as Hai Karate aftershave. Di would spend the first ten minutes after arriving at a gig convincing the venue that she was more than capable of working their mixing desk, then during the show she'd blow their minds with how good she was. Di is always the first person I chat with after a gig. We run through the good, not so good, our favourite songs, and go through anything we might need to change or whatever.

Warren is our tour manager. His CV includes being guitarist with Eddie and the Hot Rods and stints on the road guitar-teching for Sinéad O'Connor and The Libertines, in the heady pre-Gary days, when the drum stool was occupied by the fifty-year-old, fantastically monickered Mr Razzcocks. Cutting your teeth touring with The Libertines kind of means there's probably not much that could crop up that you've not seen before when you then head out with other bands.

The Modern Lovers, *The Modern Lovers*
Recommended by Nik Void

Everything can change in a moment

I first heard Factory Floor at the Underage Festival in Victoria Park, a brilliant concept for kids from fourteen to seventeen at a time when bands like The Horrors, Larrikin Love, Florence and the Machine, and Mystery Jets had many fans that couldn't get into over-eighteen gigs.

I was DJing with Dan, the singer from punk band Flats. He asked me if I'd heard of Factory Floor, and had in his hand a copy of 'Bipolar', their first single, on orange vinyl. I told him I hadn't and he played it next. Some of the kids looked terrified. There was lots of screaming and feedback, like a nuclear Joy Division meets The Fall – it was the best thing I'd heard in ages.

I bought the record for myself and looked the band up. They weren't so social-media friendly, which suited the band. I saw that they were supporting The Horrors at the Electric Ballroom in London. I was mesmerised by the updated techno, with visuals that involved just one light shining on the front person. Their music had me transfixed, and there was an anti-band aesthetic that I loved. They became my favourite band and I went to see them as often as I could.

I first spoke to the lit-up front person, Nik, after they played at the Deaf Institute in Manchester. If truth be told, I had been angling for that to happen for a while. So we talked as the other band members packed their gear away. We got on pretty well – so much so that we wrote some songs together, recorded some tracks, started a record label, and we now have a son.

Nik, along with Chris Carter and Cosey Fanni Tutti, made one of the most remarkable albums of 2015, $f(x)$, an intense, swamped-out electronic record inspired by nature in Norfolk. In 2012 Carter Tutti Void released my favourite album of that year: a live recording from the Mute Short Circuit Festival at the Roundhouse. They called it *Transverse*. Factory Floor are, as we speak, working on the follow-up to their brilliant debut.

I asked Nik for a recommendation, and *The Modern Lovers* was her choice. She was moved by the simple beauty and how raw it was. I felt I should try to buy it in New York – it just seemed the thing to do.

New York has a magnetic quality for artists. The number of venues and labels means scenes can be supported, bringing in designers and fanzines in an upward spiral for creativity. Often, venues become a place for band members to work.

Jonathan Richman upped sticks from Massachusetts to try his hand in the Big Apple because of his love for The Velvet Underground. Nothing came easily, but eventually his lo-fi approach caught on. Bandmates included future members of The Cars, Talking Heads and Arthur Russell's band.

When The Charlatans played in New York, former Modern Lover and Arthur Russell cohort Ernie Brooks came along to watch. We had played together in Paris, Barcelona and London with Peter Gordon, so I had got to know him a little. At Webster Hall in Manhattan we talked Modern Lovers, Gram Parsons and Kim Fowley. And, of course, Arthur Russell.

I got fully immersed in their New York scene when we met up at Peter's place, instruments in hand, to run through some ideas. It was a thrill to know those same instruments had gone through ideas with Jonathan Richman and Arthur Russell.

The final day in New York was set aside for record shopping. Sharon Horgan had been at our show the night before. A few blocks away, she was filming a new HBO series that she'd written.

I had a guided tour of the set and we headed out to Rough Trade in Brooklyn.

Sharon had met Ernie at the gig and told me that although she'd heard of The Modern Lovers, she didn't really know too much about them. I took that as a cue to grab two copies of their eponymous debut – one for me and one for Sharon. That's record-buying adventures at their best, if you ask me.

It's one of my favourite records of all time – I love its simplicity. But when I talked to Ernie about this he explained there was a more pragmatic reason than simply Jonathan's wistfulness. He said that the final version was pretty much their demos. In the time after recording, but before the planned release, the band had visited Bermuda and moved to LA, but all attempts to re-record the songs had only highlighted how good the original versions were.

The Modern Lovers was recorded in 1972 but did not come out until 1976 – just in time to fit snugly with the DIY ethic of punk.

Pick-a-Dub Featuring King Tubby and the Barrett Bros, arranged by Keith Hudson

Recommended by Richard H. Kirk

Call a Cab

I was twenty-two years old when The Charlatans went on tour for the first time, in January 1990. We had hopes that our dreams would be fulfilled and beyond. We didn't set out with any kind of manifesto, just to make music that meant everything to us, to be cool and maybe to get high once in a while. At least they were achievable.

We had our 100 per cent authentic psychedelic oil-wheel visuals supplied by Captain Whizzo. We had our intro tape – Fifth Dimension's 'Age of Aquarius' and The Beatles' 'Across the Universe' – and a tour DJ. I can't remember his name but he was a Manchester United fan who would keep us up to date with the latest releases. His day job was working for Pinnacle Distribution, and he had access to some of the best records, as well as a proper income to buy all the vinyl he wanted – Guru Josh's 'Infinity', 808 State's 'Pacific State' and 'Real Wild House' by Raul Orellana. But it was Sweet Exorcist's 'Testone' that sent me crazy and gave me the shivers, whether high or straight. The flip-side featured 'Testtwo' and 'Testthree'. There was a second 12-inch with 'Testfour' and, yep, you guessed it – 'Testfive' and 'Testsix'.

Looking at the sleevenotes I noticed that the image was a still from a video made by Jarvis Cocker, and Sweet Exorcist was actually Richard H. Kirk of Cabaret Voltaire.

When travelling around the world with the band and crew you get comfortable with your mates. I always end up hanging with our sound person, Di. I love Di's stories, and when she talks about the Cabs her eyes light up.

'Richard brought about twenty-two TV screens and had them all set up onstage. He liked the white noise. Once the gig was over he took them home and set them up all over his house – he even had one in the toilet. He can't sleep without the TV on.'

There is an extensive dub section in Rough Trade. I looked, and although the sleeve wasn't quite how I remember seeing it, Richard H. Kirk's recommendation, *Pick-a-Dub*, was there in the Keith Hudson section.

Richard said, 'It's the first proper dub album I heard – on John Peel – and I bought it circa 1975.'

Featuring King Tubby and Augustus Pablo, it's an incredible record – rough and sexy and, as you can probably imagine, dreamy and totally spaced out.

Duane Eddy and the Rebels, *Have 'Twangy' Guitar Will Travel*

Recommended by Howard Marks

Do not go gentle

It is Friday the 13th in Chicago, and I am looking for John Coltrane. The world's biggest specialist jazz and blues record shop is called . . . Jazz Record Mart. According to my Vinyl District app, it is just around the corner on East Illinois St.

In the window is a Junior Wells *Hoodoo Man Blues* T-shirt. It's weird – Junior Wells is cropping up all over the place.

I am looking for *A Love Supreme*. It's mentioned on the website that they have it. I decide to ask one of the guys behind the counter.

'*A Love Supreme*? No, we don't. We have it on CD.'

He points as if to get rid of me. Part of me doesn't believe him, but I think that's because of the info on the website that 100 per cent stated I could 'add it to basket'.

It is a fantastic shop. There was a lot of Ornette and Coltrane memorabilia and posters – traces of what might have been on in days gone by, maybe. I mentioned on Twitter I was there, and Ian Rankin and Tim O'Brien showed me respect.

I was to find a record on my list, but it wouldn't be *A Love Supreme*, which is turning out to be a slippery beggar.

I noticed a new section of 1950s music and remembered one of the recent recommendations, not from the list on my phone but from the new scribbled list that exists only in my head – the new arrivals. Howard Marks recommended Duane Eddy's *Have 'Twangy' Guitar Will Travel*:

Purchased in 1958 from Victor Freed's record shop in Cardiff. On the train back to Kenfig Hill, a guy sitting opposite me said he'd never heard of 'Will Travel'. Hence I've never forgotten the incident.

As I bought the record, I asked the other guy behind the counter, not because he looked more knowledgeable or, indeed, more trustworthy, but because I wanted to be absolutely sure: 'If a record was advertised on the website but isn't in the shop, would it be likely to be in a secret part of the shop or is it more likely to be a mistake?'

The two men looked at each other and smiled. It seemed like they got asked that all the time. 'It takes our website a little bit of time to catch up, maybe a few months. We decided we're more analogue – face to face.'

Being on tour is always such a celebratory element of being in a band. Packing a bag, joining your friends and hitting the road, playing songs for people who have gathered to hear them. Regular life is put on hold and in a whirl of hotels, meeting fans, running through songs at soundchecks and catching up with friends in each city the real world is often held at arm's length for a couple of weeks for the band and, hopefully, for a couple of hours each night for everyone who has a ticket. You become a family – with all that entails, good and not so good – with support bands, sound engineers, tour managers, representatives of the promoter, merchandise people, lighting technicians and a travelling circus of folk that work together to put on the show. Much is made of the rock-star life on the road, and I have played my part in contributing to those stories over the years. I'm not sure someone who works a more regular nine-to-five job with less excitement and more stress would be sympathetic to any of us talking about missing our families or feeling alone in a big city, with few remnants of normality to hang on to. Heck, isn't that why they invented Jack Daniel's and cocaine?

In November 2015 I was in a record shop in Chicago when I heard about what was happening in Paris. Le Bataclan, a venue we had played in, had been attacked. Eagles of Death Metal, a band we had friends in, were onstage at the time. The idea that a gig was some kind of escape from the seriousness of the real world was broken in seconds. I can only imagine the hell that followed.

More than any other place, a gig by a band like EODM would have had an audience who shared the idea that everyone is entitled to their own beliefs, that world events that encroached on innocent people were the most abhorrent incidents – that our fellow human is our equal.

I saw an appeal on Twitter by the girlfriend of the guy who sold the T-shirts for them. She'd not heard from him. Nick was his name. It was hours after the event but he could have been injured and unable to contact her. He'd have been somewhere at the back of the gig – even in the foyer. The merch has to be where people will go past on the way in or out of the venue. The same place the gunmen came in. Eventually it came through that Nick hadn't made it. He had died inside the venue. So did Guillaume Decherf from *Les Inrockuptibles*, a French music magazine that had helped bands like Eagles of Death Metal, The Charlatans and countless others for as long as I can remember. And so many more people, music fans and friends on a night out. I started to see the Paris coverage on my phone and thought of the band, the audience, the people working at the concert and the fact that at that moment the bubble of detachment from the real world that gigs offered had maybe been burst for ever.

*

Dusty Groove in Chicago is a special place.

It opens at 10 a.m. and there are already a few people waiting outside at 9.55. There are no special offers, no new releases. This is just the norm – this is an exciting shop all year round. It used to be mail order only and open one day a week, but now because of its popularity it opens every day.

Looking for Paul Weller's recommendation, I head straight over to the left-hand side of the room. It's the jazz section. I go to the Cs. There is no 'Coltrane section', just 'C', but there it is – a few Coltranes behind *Ascension* and *My Favourite Things* and just in front of Ornette Coleman's *Original Quartet* and *Prime Time* – sitting there unassumingly: *A Love Supreme* on 180-gram vinyl, price $16.99. Finally!

Talking about Coltrane's masterpiece with Peter Gordon in B&H Restaurant in the East Village over a bowl of mushroom and barley soup, he said:

'It is my scripture, my liturgy. It is my teaching and meditation. I bought it as a teenager, when it was first released. I had it on the automatic record changer as I would go to sleep. I would drift off, then wake up to the chanting, with the soloing that followed indelibly imprinted in my soul. I still have my original vinyl. If I had one record to listen to on the proverbial desert isle, it would be *A Love Supreme*. It is the only music I have never gotten tired of.'

I wanted to know if there was a link between Ornette Coleman, Pharoah Sanders and Alice Coltrane.

'They were all of an era when jazz was being freed of certain harmonic constraints – melodies became farther reaching; beyond the chords, a variety of sounds and textures were used, pushing boundaries of tone texture. Chord changes became unnecessary. There was a heavy influence of eastern music – Indian music in particular – sometimes directly, sometimes indirectly. Sometimes this extended to personal practice and spirituality. And there were a lot of psychedelic substances around as well.'

I asked, 'What about Miles?'

'Miles was a consummate artist who changed the course of jazz many times over.'

In Dusty Groove, Dr John, the Night Tripper's 'Croker Courtbullion' is playing, and I feel like staying for the full hour. Ace photographer and Emmy-winning video director Casey Mitchell is my guide this morning. He is also the person who promised Warren, our tour manager, that he would have me back before eleven.

Feeling like a recommendation, I fall into the trap of the very cool and enthusiastic members of staff, who put my way:

Marcos Valle, *Garra*
Azimüth 1975
Jorge Ben, *A Tábua de Esmeralda*
Novos Baianos, *Acabou Chorare*

I can't wait to hear them.

George Jones and Tammy Wynette, *Golden Ring*

Recommended by John Cooper Clarke

Recommendations in a hotel foyer

For bands, hotel foyers and motorway services are meeting places that offer the chance to hang out. Late at night, early in the morning, you're always on the move – just arriving or just leaving. After midnight, when gigs have finished, dozens of transits full of amps and bands head back from where they've played, fuelled by adrenalin and beer. The luckier ones head for a hotel – no Riot House to smash up, more like a budget hotel with a vending machine and no minibar.

One such night I'd been doing an in-conversation event with Paddy Considine in Sheffield. I was checking in late when I heard a familiar nasal twang waiting in line to check in after me. John Cooper Clarke had been playing a show at Sheffield City Hall – our paths had crossed a few times, and we were seasoned professionals at foyer chat.

I asked him for an album recommendation.

'Well, I'm on tour with Squeeze – they've got a pedal-steel player. I love country music – it's the roots of Middle America. George Jones and Tammy Wynette are the story of country music. It has to be Tammy and George. They couldn't live without each other, as hard as they tried. Big hats, big hair and big emotions.'

To a kid who had grown up at the fag end of punk, in Northwich, country music didn't say too much. In my world, when bands had a problem with something they'd write about their frustration with it. In country music, if the songwriter didn't like something, they'd slap it first – and if that didn't work, they'd shoot it. That's how I used to see it, anyway. It was music listened to by my grandparents more than even my parents. It was different music from a different world in a different time. That view changed as I got older, and then even more when I heard Gram Parsons for the first time in Camden in 1993.

When I recorded *Oh No I Love You* in Nashville, Tammy Wynette was the featured artist at the Country Music Hall of Fame.

'Look up a producer called Billy Sherrill,' says John. 'The best music Tammy and George made was with him. He wrote with Roy Orbison and came up with the theme tune to *The Incredible Hulk*. That's some body of work.'

I had been trying to avoid the behemoth Amoeba, but at midday on the day of our show at the Fonda Theater in Hollywood temptation got the better of me, like some kind of vinyl waxy drug thing – like something I can't live without. I visited so many times when I lived there that I was on first-name terms with most of the staff.

Duets in country music have been around for a long time, and, like co-hosts on a TV breakfast show, if the couple are actually a real couple, the authenticity really cuts through.

Golden Ring is a beautiful album. 'I've Seen Better Days' is one of the most incredible Tammy vocal performances ever – so hurt, touchingly fragile and powerful, and the Billy Sherrill production is just flawless. This isn't a happy affair, though. With songs like 'Even the Bad Times Are Good' it eventually turned out that the bad times were bad and maybe the good times were non-existent. While it contains lyrical gems such as 'I wouldn't want to live without you / I love everything about you' and 'Your middle name should be perfection / 'cos that's what you are to me', Tammy and George divorced even before the record came out.

Life imitating a country-and-western song.

Q magazine asked me to present an award to John Cooper

Clarke a couple of years ago, and I wrote a bit of a speech on the train on the way to the ceremony.

I first came across John on a Granada TV show called *So It Goes* in 1977 – I was ten years old. My knowledge of poetry was limited and my interest in it was minimal. Poems we'd been forced to read at school were from another time, by other people from a different world. But here was a guy from the same city where I was born, caretaker by day but some kind of sweary, hilarious revolutionary in his spare time. Part beat poet, part social commentator, all hero. They called him the 'Bard of Salford'. He called himself 'Johnny Clarke, the name behind the hairstyle'. He hung around with some of my heroes: the Sex Pistols, New Order, the Honey Monster. One of the best things about John's poetry is that it doesn't really exist without him. He is the only person who can deliver it properly. If you read it out loud, you lose so much of the urgency, gusto and impeccable timing. If you read it yourself, it is John's voice in your head. Try it if you've never thought about it before – the poems and the man come as a package, wrapped in the tightest suit money can buy and topped off with a hairstyle that defies gravity as much as it defies the passage of time.

Old-style poetry was something that would haunt my schooldays. Some dusty verse read by a teacher on the verge of a nervous breakdown to a bunch of disenfranchised teenagers was always going to give it a bad reputation, but John Cooper Clarke showed the possibilities of what could be done with words. Added to this, his delivery and demeanour meant we had someone to look up to who spoke back to us. Unafraid of telling it how it is, John was our very own sweary punk superhero. I had a cassette recording of 'TWAT' that would get an extra-loud airing when the teenage me had slammed the door to my room after my regular fall-outs with my parents. He represented celebrating what you had rather than aspirations to some kind of higher material world that we spent our teenage years rejecting.

John's work has been variously adored, overlooked, under-appreciated, celebrated, dismissed and lauded, but he was always there – doing his thing, regardless of how interested the world currently was in what he was doing. He would go quiet, disappear for a while, but his words were always relevant.

An updated 'Beasley Street' became 'Beasley Boulevard', saying in a couple of minutes more about our homogenised, identikit, teeth-whitened, latte-guzzling world than any book or documentary.

John's influence on songwriting is now being mentioned more and more, and his skills as a radio DJ have lead to a whole new audience for his work.

So, we've established he's a hero, a genius – he's also one of the best orators and funniest people in the history of everything, so you'd be better off listening to him rather than me . . .

Ladies and gentlemen, please stand for Mr John Cooper Clarke.

David Bowie, *The Rise and Fall of Ziggy Stardust and the Spiders from Mars*

Recommended by Holly Johnson

Luv 'n' Haight

San Francisco is very hilly and quite a contrast to LA. We have a day off. Some of our gonzo touring party head off to the Bay Area to take a boat to Alcatraz. Davo, Dian and Pete end up in San Quentin – not because of any wrongdoing, just for a tour. Bands always take a bit of an alternative expedition when they're away. Maybe they're more morbid than regular tourists, but cemeteries, prisons and notorious murder spots seem to figure highly on the map.

Alone, I make a pilgrimage to what Hunter S. Thompson called Hashbury, but what almost everybody else calls Haight-Ashbury, home of the 1960s San Francisco sound of Jefferson Airplane, Janis Joplin, The Grateful Dead and even my band's pioneering namesakes, The Charlatans. There are still people living the dream – sockless, slightly battered, red-faced sixty- and seventy-year-olds smoking that cannabis bar that only old dudes seem to be able to track down and wearing tie dye.

I head to Amoeba on Haight St. Maybe I'll pick up a copy of *The Amazing Charlatans* – it's an incredible record, everyone should own it. 'We're Not on the Same Trip' and 'Alabama Bound' are brilliant songs that capture the times, perhaps even pre-empting them. They were part of the counterculture, always a little underground – so much so that we hadn't heard of them when we ended up choosing the same name. There was never really any kind of wrangling over it – we stuck 'UK' at the end of ours and little more was said. They kept the kind of coolness you'd expect from a band with the sound they had.

While going through the letter 'B' I hit a plastic divider marked up as 'David Bowie'. I was hoping to find Holly Johnson's recommendation, *The Rise and Fall of Ziggy Stardust*. Even the biggest records ever recorded are sometimes not in print and can be pretty hard to find, depending on whether the labels have the appetite to keep making them while knowing that demand might be met by the number available on the second-hand market. One of the classic misunderstandings about the value of a record is that it is increased by its popularity when it came out, as opposed to its rarity. My uncle Barry has a pile of Queen singles, including 'Bohemian Rhapsody'. Everybody knows it's one of the biggest-selling singles of all time, but there is a huge supply of them, often in charity shops, so it's unlikely to gain too much in value, though who's to say that in a few years a beat-up copy won't cost a fortune. It's the rare stuff that's worth more and fires up the interest of vinyl geeks.

For one reason or another, entire runs of singles and albums were destroyed. Darrell Banks's 'Open the Door to Your Heart' was released in America to a fairly lukewarm reception, but the London label in the UK saw it as perfect for the northern soul scene, a movement that involved records that had already been released in one continent but were then claimed by a scene sweeping across an entirely different part of the world. But that's a whole other story. So yeah, London wanted Banks's song to be rush-released, as they thought it was perfect for that exact moment on UK dancefloors. They thought too that they'd done enough to make this happen. Only they hadn't. Every copy they'd hastily pressed up was ordered to be destroyed because the licence had never been granted, and the rights were then sold to a rival label. Supposedly no copies existed, but, like some kind of fantastical creature, stories abounded that maybe one had survived.

Then, in December 2014, it appeared – the one that had been

apparently smuggled out of the pressing plant the day before the run was destroyed. It eventually sold for over £14,000.

As well as anomalies, there are also records that are overlooked but later find their way into musical history. The Winstons released a single in 1969 called 'Color Him Father'. On the B-side was a song called 'Amen, Brother', which, although a great track, mostly passed people by until it took up its place as one of the most important segments of music ever recorded by anyone. Nobody knows who was the first, but somewhere in the dawn of hip-hop time someone sampled a small break of the drums, and it became one of the building blocks for hip hop, jungle, garage, speed garage and any number of styles and genres you can think of. N.W.A., The Prodigy, Mantronix, Skrillex and innumerable others have all used the 'Amen' break, so who knows? – a record overlooked and forgotten from way back could still end up claiming a place at the top table of music history.

'Amen, Brother' and 'Open the Door to Your Heart' are now legendary in the story of record collecting. And maybe somewhere in a charity shop or long-forgotten collection lie other albums or singles that'll one day change the course of vinyl history. It's one of the reasons I was bitten by the bug – no different from people who go metal detecting or trainspotting, or any other hobby that outsiders don't understand.

Looking through the Bowie albums available on vinyl, I flick through *The Lodger*, *Pin Ups* and *Scary Monsters (and Super Creeps)*. Next I find the one I've been searching for, wrapped tightly in cellophane and see-through tape: *Ziggy Stardust*, so ahead of its time that Bowie still looks like he is from the future. And in the hotel sign there is the premonition of rap's superego, or that's probably how Kanye West would see it.

I'd played a few of the same shows as Holly, and we always enjoyed spending time talking about music. His band, Frankie Goes to Hollywood, blew up like no other – overtly sexual and political, ruffling the feathers and quivering the stiff upper lips of the Establishment. And not just retired colonels and Mary Whitehouse – Radio 1 DJ Mike Read found 'Relax' a little too hot to handle and thought he'd do the country the Stalinist-style favour of banning it. Around thirty years later, Read's racist calypso proved he'd lost none of his power for making dumb decisions.

Read's refusal to play 'Relax' did nothing but bolster Frankie's image and increase their fanbase. Broadsheets talked about the record with regard to freedom of speech, but most importantly kids loved it. Watching 'Relax' climb back up the charts after dropping down to No. 31, then hitting No. 1, before landing at No. 2, below Frankie's following release, 'Two Tribes', was just about the biggest music-related two fingers since the Sex Pistols.

The curveball of 'The Power of Love', an absolute beauty of a song, confounded even further, and Holly won the hearts of the nation. Well, those in the nation that were cool with a bit of leather and the occasional reference to ejaculation.

It doesn't take a genius to figure out that Holly is probably a Bowie fan. He was born in 1960 and has been in bands from the 1970s onwards. I'll let him tell you the story:

As far as records go, there's a few that have had a profound effect on me. T. Rex's *Electric Warrior* was given to me by my sister. Then there was a record shop in Lodge Lane in Liverpool 8 which had a record club. My mum would send me there to do errands each Saturday from Penny Lane bus terminus, near to where we lived. Kids could put part of their pocket money in each week and save up to buy an album.

I bought *The Rise and Fall of Ziggy Stardust and the Spiders from Mars* by David Bowie.

Other records – *Slider* by T. Rex, *Transformer* by Lou Reed and *Trans-Europe Express* by Kraftwerk – came later. *My Life in the Bush of Ghosts* by Byrne/Eno and *Remain in Light* by Talking Heads when I had left home to live in town; *Scary Monsters* by Bowie, *Rickie Lee*

221

Jones, *Kuku* by Debbie Harry, *Diana* by Diana Ross produced by Chic, *Dare* by The Human League – they all played a huge part in my musical education before Frankie Goes to Hollywood, but the one that had the most profound effect on me was *Ziggy Stardust*.

I was already aware of 'Space Oddity' and that the title was a play on the film title *2001: A Space Odyssey*. I'd heard the song on the radio getting ready for school in 1969. Like many people I discovered Bowie via *Top of the Pops* while waiting to see if T. Rex were on – the 'Starman' moment that people talk about when Bowie put his arm around Mick Ronson and pointed at the camera for the word 'You-oooh-ooh'; the metallic blue EKO 12-string guitar slung about his side, the custom-made outfit and make-up, like an exotic bird of paradise.

He came to Liverpool and played licensed venues, The Stadium and the Top Rank. A schoolboy couldn't attend the Ziggy shows due to age restrictions . . . until 1973, when the *Aladdin Sane* tour came to the Liverpool Empire a week or so before the final Hammersmith Odeon show. It was the first concert I ever attended. He had five albums in the Top 30, all re-released to cash in on the sudden runaway success of this incredible and ambitious talent.

I first sat up and really paid attention to David Bowie in 1980. I had just bought 'My Girl' by Madness and 'Crazy Little Thing Called Love' by Queen in Northwich, and had stopped in at Ann's Cake Shop on the high street when 'Ashes to Ashes' came on the radio.

It's like it had a laser beam that targeted the records I'd just bought, rendering them slightly more regular than before the song came on. That Thursday, I saw the video and started to look through Bowie's back catalogue – music that had previously belonged to older mates' sisters and the kid who used to hang out in the shopping centre with no eyebrows and an orange Ziggy feather cut.

I didn't own an actual official copy of *Ziggy Stardust* until about 2006, but I was familiar with the songs, and somehow a home-taped C90 made it into the glove compartment of my dad's Austin Ambassador sometime around 1988 (although extensive Internet searches and questioning of my dad have failed to confirm an exact date).

Tchaikovsky, Symphony No. 6, 'Pathétique'
Recommended by Vini Reilly

One dollar, no tax

Portland, Oregon, in recent times has become something of a UK expat musical oasis and hotbed of some of the best sounds coming from America, sometime home to Johnny Marr, a Crib or two, and more than a handful of session musicians I've worked with.

When in Portland, visit record shops. I have my guide, Chris Slusarenko, a local musician, formerly of Guided by Voices and currently in Eyelids, who are opening for The Charlatans on the final night of our US tour. A true advocate of this marvellous city, Chris assures me that it's small enough to take in five or six of the best of the roughly twenty record shops in the hour or so before I have to go to the soundcheck. Time is marked by the things I have to do and the gaps are filled by buying records.

The first stop is Crossroads Records. It's like a record fair inside a record shop. In fact, that's exactly what it is. There are pitches, and someone in charge knows which pitch is most likely to have what you're looking for, and it's his job to minimise the amount of haggling and maximise sales. The payment goes into the till, and I figure (though I don't know why I am even thinking about this) about 80 per cent then goes to the guy whose record it was and the rest is for overheads.

We're directed to the classical section. I'm looking for a record recommended by Vini Reilly, the closest to a classical composer of anyone who features heavily in my own record collection. I'm not sure why I say 'the closest' – his music is pure classical.

A Paean to Wilson, which Vini performed as The Durutti Column after Tony Wilson's death, is as beautiful a piece of music as you could hear. Wilson understood Vini and stuck by him when the landscape was about as tough a place as could be for the music he was making.

I'd asked Vini what album he'd send me out to find, and this was his reply:

Tchaikovsky's 'Pathétique', the Greatest piece of Music!! Nothing even comes close to this. PERFECTION! PACKED WITH EMOTIONAL PAIN, HOPELESSNESS and UTTER DESPAIR UNTIL THE ENDING. THE SOUND OF A Gay Man WITH Absolutely No hope left for Love, between Himself and a minor Aristocrat – To Quite simply Love each other. Shortly After THIS IMPOSSIBLY PERFECT and THE GREATEST EVER PIECE OF MUSIC IN THIS WORLD which NOTHING EVER WILL SURPASS, it's widely believed That Pieter Deliberately allowed A Deadly plague (by consistently Drinking Water Full of That contamination), which ensured His own Death, a form of 'Passive-Suicide'. All that man wanted to do Was To be allowed To Share his Love with Another Human being Who loved him in the same way. There is no greater sadness.

It's not the first occasion that I have been looking for what Vini describes as the greatest-ever piece of music – two shops in Sacramento to no avail, shops in San Francisco and Amsterdam, but it was off the beaten track of the music that I usually buy. Finding it in Crossroads made my heart go giddy up. And it was only $1.00 with no tax, so a total of $1.00.

I listened to the record at the hotel. It took me back to being at my uncle Norman's house, one of the few places that constantly played classical music when I was growing up. He was an organist, and I once proudly asked him what he thought of The Charlatans' music, since we featured his chosen instrument heavily.

'Not that keen,' was his reply.

Not the answer I was hoping for, but I definitely knew he was being honest.

Some recommendations have been harder to find than others. It's kind of a frustration and a seed for determination all in one.

Chris and I moved on to the next shop on the street. I asked for Daniel Miller's recommendation, *Fireside Favourites* by Fad Gadget, and I was pointed to a few spots where it might be. There was a 12-inch copy of 'One Man's Meat' in one section, but it wasn't what I was looking for.

White Zombie was a name I got really into asking for, partly due to the fact that no shops had them. It made me smile – one of those things that just feels good when you say it. Everybody seemed to know them and like them, but like a long-lost friend, no one seemed to know where to find them any more.

The guy at Crossroads said, 'If we had a copy we'd have it up on the wall with the other prize items.' Nikolai at Sound Station in Copenhagen pulled out a copy of *Make Them Die Slowly*. It wasn't the album I wanted – *Soul-Crusher*, Iggy Pop's third recommendation – but I bought it all the same because of the effort he'd made in finding it for me.

I even located a copy through Discogs as a last resort, just in case I couldn't track it down. And I wrote to Rob Zombie via social media to see if he had a spare copy in his vaults. Yes, I am supposed to be finding records in record shops, but as I've said before, the rules are mine to break – an original first pressing sent in the post by Rob Zombie himself would have made for good reading.

But after asking, in my smiley-asking voice, for about the 387th time, the guy behind the counter in Exiled Records pointed to the wall and there, in all its trashy glory in a see-through bag, in a smallish space at the edge of a parking lot off Hawthorne Boulevard in Portland, was *Soul-Crusher*.

In Portland the music community is tight-knit. Musicians

shake hands with shop-owners and jog each other's memories of how they know each other.

'I met you at a party. We were introduced by our mutual friend Xany' – 'Ahh, that's right. You're in a band with John Moen.'

$1.00 for Pieter Tchaikovsky.

$69.99 for White Zombie – an average price of $35.00 each, which, using my record collector's financial-justification-outlay theory, counts as a bargain.

Still no Fad Gadget, though.

*

The last time I was in Mexico City was as a DJ playing before Carl Barât's post-Libertines outfit The Dirty Pretty Things. It was early 2006 and I was making my final stand as a fully committed drug addict. I had never had banana-flavoured cocaine before.

We were there for a week. We had two shows – I flew in from LA and they flew in from the UK. The first show was in an expanse of rubble and concrete. The record decks were on an angle, and you could see the arm of the record player fighting to move upwards along the grooves. The records skipped and popped but nobody appeared too bothered. Everyone danced and seemed really pleased to see us.

Once The Dirty Pretty Things finished their set, the decks were lifted up by two burly bouncers. They put me and Carl into the back of a cab, destination unknown.

I was given a bag of cocaine. I offered money.

'No, no, no, it's fine,' came the response.

We pulled up in a narrow bustling street – dogs barking, babies crying, cars honking. It was 2 a.m.

'Out!'

These men were in a rush. Were we being kidnapped?

We'd seen films about drug cartels and we weren't sure whether we'd just become part of a bigger game. We were pushed into an underground tunnel with a broken wooden door and hurried down the corridor.

Could this be it?

We were pretty scared, but one of the guys pushing us aggressively did have a turntable under each arm.

'Here.'

All of a sudden the lights go up. It's a massive hangar with a makeshift bar. Let's go. Phew, I guess it was time to party.

*

There is a big difference being in Mexico and not hooking up with anyone in the drugs trade. It was only after shaking the addiction that I could see clearly the damage that it did to places like this. It shouldn't have taken long to figure it out, but that's the nature of being in thrall to coke. One more line and I'd think, 'Ah well, I'm sure they'll be alright. If they get any of this stuff for free, they'll be fine.'

A friend of David Claxton, who plays in my solo band, was living in Mexico City but couldn't get a ticket for the gig. She got in touch and asked if I could help out, and I swapped a tour of record shops for two backstage passes.

We headed to the Roma district of Mexico City to find Retroactive. It's a brilliant shop, just a shutter that pulls down in front of three walls, with as much vinyl and as many CDs as the racks can hold. I wondered what the chances were of finding Fad Gadget. Not in Retroactive.

There is another shop opposite, Musica En Vinyl.

'I am looking for Fad Gadget. It's on Mute Records.'

'I know, I know – Depeche Mode, Erasure. But unless it is big hit we don't get in Mexico. You should get in England.'

'OK, I will. At least I tried.'

It's a great shop, with such varied releases. I decided on Miles Davis's *Sorcerer*, recalling my conversations with Peter Gordon in B&H in the East Village. Also thoughts of Jon Brookes sprang to mind. The only record Jon ever gave me was *Bitches Brew* by Miles Davis. He loved Miles and thought I would really get something from it.

Here's thinking of you, Jon.

Sibylle Baier, *Colour Green*

Recommended by Kim Gordon

Tonight, when I came home from work

OK, so this book is about buying records in shops – the personal touch, crate-digging, sharing stories, feeling at home, looking for that elusive vinyl.

But like some mythical place that isn't even mythical, there exists a place where almost every record you've ever heard of is listed. It'd be the biggest shop in the world, and even just looking through the letter 'A' would take you all day. 'What is this place you speak of?' you might ask, if you spent your time with fictional pirates. ''Tis Discogs,' I might reply if the pirate thing was catching on.

Now, this is not some online monster that threatens to rampage through Recordville eating all the shops. Far from it – Discogs is a place that I believe helps real-world vinyl outlets survive.

My name is Tim Burgess and I'm a Discogs addict. It started sometime around 2006. My habit isn't getting any better but it's a comforting addiction – less thrilling than finding a record needle in a vinyl haystack, but the Internet appeals to the 'I want it now' part of our brain, and Discogs can help with that.

As I may have mentioned, I have been buying records very enthusiastically since the age of eleven, only briefly taking a break when my interest in drinking replaced most other things. My wants list is both way too extensive and way too expensive for me to ever get everything I'd like. However, here are some of its current incumbents:

A Su Tissue record I am desperately seeking, *Salon de Musique* – it's a beauty, so if anyone is reading and they have a spare, send it over my way.

I always like to see if I can get pristine copies of *The Lion Sleeps Tonight* by Brian Eno. Don't ask me why, it's just part of my addiction. Every time it comes up I buy it.

Elodie Lauten, 'No Man's Land'/'Sunrise' 7-inch. A hard one to get, it's been on my wants list for a couple of years now and I haven't even seen one for sale.

Chris Britton, *As I Am*. Again, three years, no sign.

One such elusive beauty is Sybille Baier's album *Colour Green*. I tried every record shop I knew after Kim Gordon sent it as her recommendation. I looked in the racks and asked in all the shops I could, and phoned all the shops I couldn't get to. All the copies out there seemed to be taken and the only information I could find was that a label was planning a re-release but no date was set. I received this description from Kim:

The back story is that her son found a cassette in a drawer a few years back and gave it to a friend of a relative of a friend of mine who sent it to a label.

It was written after her relationship with Wim Wenders ended and she was suicidal. Her friend took her on a road trip and she came back and wrote this record. I think it's her only one. I simply love the beauty and stillness of it. I can feel her pain but mostly I find it beautiful and so simple and brave in its music and lyrics.

Kim x

So rather than face defeat I turned to Discogs, and within three days I was holding it in my hands, ready to play on my turntable for the first time. It was a record I had not come across before and I'd resisted the temptation to listen to it on YouTube or have any kind of sneak preview.

The bigger the love the greater the heartache, and sadly one often leads to the other. A broken heart, unfortunately, makes great records, just as sweeping, all-encompassing, overwhelming love does. Course it does – if you can write about one, you can write about the other, holding back the tears while laying the vocals down, contemplating the happy songs that were written before love left town. Songs from someone you have never met can have a profound insight into your life and speak to you in times of heartbreak. And when you're at a loss to put the chaos in order, music has such a healing power that sometimes it doesn't have to be heard or shared for it to take effect – the process of writing can start the healing. One such album is *Colour Green* by Sibylle Baier.

I had sent a message to Kim Gordon telling her about my project and asking if she would send a recommendation. What came back is in some ways the best example of what I set out to discover when I started thinking about this book. What could be expected from a bass-guitar hero from a cooler-than-uber-cool American noise band?

Kim's recommendation was an album that has remained unheard for decades but has a beauty as well defined in its melancholy as any set of songs you could hope to hear. They were songs that had existed only on tape and were a document of heartbreak. It took thirty years for the album to be released but the subject is timeless. Who knows what other relics might be lying in a drawer and one day see the light of day, chiming with an audience who would otherwise never have got to hear them? Here was a folk record, but unlike anything I'd heard before, and it had a power that very few albums possess. I was listening to it at that moment in my life, but I was also listening knowing the pain that Kim had gone through in hers. Being in a band gives you so many positive things, but being put in the public eye when you're going through tough times is a downside. Ironically, it's the songs of others that can get you through those times.

*

Nottingham was the first stop-off on our UK tour in December 2015, and where we played was one of those places with an important chapter in the Charlatans story.

Great venues come and go – The International and International 2 in Manchester, The Powerhouse in Islington, JB's in Dudley, the Duchess of York in Leeds. But some have been around since the dawn of time, or at least the dawn of when I started watching and being in bands. One of the venues that has resisted closure, being moved up the road and all the other woes that befall anywhere putting on gigs is Rock City in Nottingham. We first played there on a rainy Monday back in 1990, and we were back to play at their thirty-fifth birthday celebrations.

Rough Trade opened a branch there in 2014. It was a progressive kind of record shop, with a cafe, bar and gig space. A double-album version of *Modern Nature* was released on see-through vinyl just as we went on tour, so we sorted out a signing session and asked our support band, Frankie and the Heartstrings, to play an acoustic set. I've always enjoyed a signing session, partly for being able to chat to our fans but also for the chance to check out some records while I'm there. My list was down to the final few recommendations and John Grant was on display on the wall. His album was Dennis and Lois's choice, but they'd given me a copy as a gift. I wasn't sure how that affected my rules, as I'd sort of said the selections would be from record shops – but you can't knock back a gift, especially not from such lovely folk as Dennis and Lois. So I found my way round it. I grabbed the record and thought that I would keep the good feelings moving, so it's now wrapped in Christmas paper until I can work out who it's going to.

Captain Beefheart, *Trout Mask Replica*
Recommended by David Lynch

The Lynch Foundation

There's no disputing the oldest record shop in the world, as it is older than records themselves. Spillers first opened its doors in Cardiff in 1894. It's moved a few times around town but it's now settled in a cutesy home in a Victorian arcade.

The search for the last few records had been in vain but the great thing about record shops is that they look after each other, and I was told there was a place where I might find what I was after.

Five short minutes later, after following some directions I walked into Cardiff market – or Marchnad Caerdydd, if you speak Welsh – another beautiful Victorian structure which took me back to the 1970s in a sensory time machine: a fresh fish stall, a pet stall with guinea pigs and rabbits. It reminded me in an instant of markets I'd been to as a kid. Up the stairs and past a hardware stall I found what I'd been looking for: Kelly's Records, established 1969. It too had moved, from the far corner of the market when it was started by Mr and Mrs Kelly – it was now being run by Allan Parkins, ex-Cardiff City footballer and vinyl enthusiast – the latest incarnation of Kelly's took up maybe four stalls, with a barber's in the middle of the run. As I walked up I saw 'Tomorrow's Girls' by UK Subs at the front of a box of singles, and album covers were stuck on every surface of wall and ceiling. Boxes and boxes and rows and rows – from jazz to blues to you name it. The place was a real hive of activity. Callum, who was serving, passed me a card and said that 90 per cent of what was in the shop could be found online. Record shops have often pointed the finger at websites for being able to sell without expensive overheads, but they could even up the fight by having a website and selling all over the world from their Cardiff market base.

Everything was neatly in order, with just enough room for one person to fit between the rows of boxes. I headed to the Captain Beefheart section and bagged myself the only copy of *Trout Mask Replica*. It's an album that confounds as much as it elicits praise – almost like there's a code that needs to be cracked for the listener to fully enjoy it, and some people just don't have the combination. It's not a snobby thing or a muso thing, just that it's not easy on the ears for some people, while others think it is without equal. Who chose it? Well, someone whose work confounds as much as it elicits praise, someone whose work maybe seems like a code that not everyone can crack, but for those who love him he has no equal. If Don Van Vliet's Captain Beefheart has an equivalent in the world of film, then I'm putting forward the name of David Lynch, because, dear reader, *Trout Mask Replica* was his choice. Now I didn't have his number on speed dial (does anyone have anyone's number on speed dial? What even is it?) but I did have a way of getting in touch.

The first David Lynch film I saw was *The Elephant Man*. It's probably the least Lynchian film of them all. It was at the Gate Cinema in Notting Hill that I knowingly went to have my first proper Lynch experience, watching *Blue Velvet*. It was at a time when art-house cinemas were thriving. I count myself as a *Twin Peaks* fanatic and, in the unlikely event that I was to go on *Mastermind*, Agent Cooper, Ghostwood and the Black Lodge would be my specialist subject.

I loved *Mulholland Drive*. I saw it the day it came out, at the cinema closest to the actual Mulholland Drive. And I worshipped *Lost Highway*, *Inland Empire* and his tales of film-noir otherworldliness, doppelgängers, girls in trouble and dreams.

*

It's Monday and we are heading to Edinburgh, the list of recommendations slowly but surely being whittled down. I had asked Ian Rankin to meet me at a shop called Unknown Pleasures on Canongate, near the Royal Mile. I was allowing myself to go off road with some selections and was buying a copy of Judee Sill's album *Heart Food* on the reissue label 4 Men with Beards.

Judee was a singer from Laurel Canyon who never received the acclaim that she deserved. As I was buying the record I saw Ian and wanted to greet him with a classic detective-novel line like, 'You must be wondering why I asked you to meet me here?'

He'd emailed me the Foreword, which I am guessing you have already read. I knew my mission was coming to an end and I wanted to thank him. Not sure if you remember, but Ian's selection was the record *Unknown Pleasures* and we were standing in the shop Unknown Pleasures. In my bag I had a copy of *Unknown Pleasures*.

I'd had the idea of bringing Ian a gift, and I'd asked Stephen and Bernard if they would sign it when I DJ'd at New Order's Warehouse Project gig earlier in the year. I had bought Ian's recommendation nearly a year before from Monorail in Glasgow. Warners had released a reissue but I wanted a first edition on Factory, which I sourced on Discogs. I took the record out of the bag, all signed up. There was a symmetry that I loved about this – a friend, a beautiful slab of vinyl, a great record shop and the involvement of our favourite group. We left some tickets to be found in the shop, and I asked Ian to leave a clue in Rebus fashion. We then went to one of Rebus's favourite Edinburgh pubs and talked about Mike Love, Dennis Wilson, Charles Manson, Hawkwind, Peter Hamill, Rick Wakeman, Genesis P. Orridge, Ian Anderson, Arthur Lee, Joe Strummer, Coil and Can. We made our way to the Usher Hall, where Ian thought he would be DJing in the wings, but the decks were front and centre on the stage. Suicide, 'Cheree', Depeche Mode, 'Personal Jesus', Dr Feelgood, 'Roxette', some Orange Juice, Booker T, Velvets and a few more were spun before we bid the adoring crowd farewell.

Alexander 'Skip' Spence, *Oar*
Joe Gibbs and the Professionals, *African Dub Chapter 3*

Recommended by Bobby Gillespie

The fever I was faking

I first heard Primal Scream's 'It Happens' on John Peel's Radio 1 show in 1985. The song had a huge impact on me. I pretended to be ill the following day and called in sick at work so I could go and get it. I cycled to Winsford and back, a round trip of eight miles, just in the nick of time before my mum got home. I think my bicycling exertions had the same side effect as the fever I was faking, so it all worked out pretty well.

In 1987 I went to see them at ULU with my friend Adrian. I bought their debut LP, *Sonic Flower Groove*, and named two songs from *Some Friendly* after the first two-thirds of the title.

I saw them at the Haçienda during *Screamadelica* sometime in '91, but it might have been '92. Bobby Gillespie handed my girlfriend a Gram Parsons CD to give to me. We had never met so there was something extra-sweet about the gesture. A few months later, in The Ship on Wardour Street just before *Give Out But Don't Give Up*, we finally did meet. We talked all evening. I told him about my love of 'Velocity Girl', the B-side of 'Crystal Crescent', their second single. He sang 'Tumbling Dice' to me.

Bobby was hugely supportive when Martin Duffy stepped forward and helped us finish off *Tellin' Stories*. We bump into each other now and again, and it's always a pleasure to see him and swap stories. When I told Bobby about the idea behind the book, he was keen to know who else was involved. I went through the names. David Lynch. Iggy Pop. Cat Power.

'What did Chan choose?'

'Hüsker Dü – *Metal Circus*.'

'Ah, that's a good choice. She raised the bar high.'

I told him what Iggy had chosen. The reaction to Junior Wells's *Hoodoo Man Blues* was, 'Aye, brilliant!' Pearls Before Swine got a 'Wow'. And White Zombie . . .

'Ouch!! Are you sure he's off the drugs?'

He couldn't pick between two albums: *Oar* by Alexander 'Skip' Spence and his first thought, *African Dub Chapter 3* by Joe Gibbs and the Professionals. I told Bob that both Richard H. Kirk and Andy Weatherall had chosen dub.

'I'm in good company then.'

It's funny that I should find *African Dub Chapter 3* in Flashback, the same place as Andy Weatherall's choice and also the place I bumped into Bobby a few years ago, before we went for a smoothie. No sign of Bob this time, but Joe Gibbs and the Professionals jumped out at me, like he'd left it there himself.

The Groundhogs, *Split*

Recommended by Mark Radcliffe and Stuart Maconie

Secret code to a new universe

After a couple of shows in Edinburgh and Dundee, and before the Newcastle gig, I took a detour to Salford and headed to Media City to talk to Stuart Maconie and Mark Radcliffe – just a bit of an end-of-year catch-up, but also the chance to ask them for a recommendation. Stuart brought up the subject of the book while we were on air, so I thought I'd ask them during the interview. They had a bit of time to think and they had to confer as it was to be a joint suggestion. After a quick meeting, they came up with The Groundhogs' *Split*.

The journey started at Beatdown Records in Newcastle – a labyrinth that connected what seemed to be two shops, and although they didn't have what I was looking for, they directed me to RPM Music, round a few corners, past a cat cafe, Mog on the Tyne, and up some stairs. I had a vague recollection of having been there before and felt at home as soon as I got through the door. There were boxes and boxes of records and some beautifully restored turntables, amplifiers and even radiograms. Marek and Richard introduced themselves as they were working away. I asked in vain for Skip Spence and Fad Gadget, but one mention of Groundhogs and it was like I'd found the secret code to unlocking a new universe. As well as record-shop workers, there's also often a kind of record-shop counter-hanger guy too, like a vinyl version of a barfly. No sooner had I said 'Skip Spence' than Peter was part of our gang. A sweet guy who was back in Newcastle spending time in his favourite shop after being away, his way into the conversation was a brief precis of Skip's biography, taking in many of the other Moby Grape members and what they had done previously and since. It's only in a record shop that this kind of conversation can happen. Your workmates or spouse or kids are unlikely to have the necessary interest in long-forgotten bass players from early incarnations of Quicksilver Messenger Service, but in a record shop this kind of info is a badge of honour – as long as you can judge how long the rest of the customers and staff want to hear your potted history of music and the gigs you've attended. Richard, Marek and Peter were all Groundhogs fans but had conflicting views on their best work. According to Marek, '*Hogwash* is the greatest unheard album of the century.'

'Really?' I replied.

'Well, one of them,' he said to counter his grand claim – possibly after three more great unheard albums of the century landed in his brain.

He put the vinyl copy of *Hogwash* on a 1979 turntable and we all fell silent in appreciation. Marek was in raptures. 'Listen to that production. It's like he could be next door.'

Rich didn't crack a smile but said, 'He probably is, mate. I think he's still gigging in pubs. I'll go and have a look.'

He grabbed me a copy of *Split* and we all spoke some more about our favourite albums before I left, some twenty minutes after arriving. I'm not one for sitting in a pub chatting about the football but I tick those blokey boxes when among the sew-on patches and reconditioned stereo gear, talking 1960s prog vinyl with people like Marek, Peter and Rich.

Love, *Forever Changes*

Recommended by Cosey Fanni Tutti

Hot on the heels of . . .

I've known Cosey Fanni Tutti for five years, known her music for thirty-five and known of her art for twenty-five. She was a founding member of Throbbing Gristle, half of Chris and Cosey – now Carter Tutti – and one-third of Carter Tutti Void. And now she can add keen gardener and rock 'n' roll godmother to her CV.

In 1976 Throbbing Gristle – Cosey, Chris Carter, Peter 'Sleazy' Christopherson and Genesis P. Orridge – became the first purveyors of a sound that was a new genre and would later be labelled in record shops as 'industrial', with the emergence of Clock DVA, Cabaret Voltaire and SPK. It was a hybrid of krautrock, punk and left-field audio experimentation informed by a non-music and high-art aesthetic.

Not hemmed in by music alone, they had extracurricular activities. Sleazy was part of Hipgnosis, working with Storm Thorgerson, most notably on the Pink Floyd album sleeves but also on artwork for Peter Gabriel and Wings, among others. At the time, Cosey was doing her art actions, as well as modelling, performing striptease and working with filmmakers such as Peter Greenaway and Steve Dwoskin. Chris Carter, meanwhile, was building his own electronic instruments and working at ABC News, refitting and upgrading their London studio.

As a collective, they were influenced by the tumbledown bohemia of their surroundings in Beck Road, Hackney, during the 1970s. Throbbing Gristle broke down boundaries and changed the rules of what being in a band entailed. I'm not sure they even realised how much their music and art would shape the future for over thirty years and still be relevant today.

Cosey's choice for me to track down was a record I'd owned, given away and been influenced by, and the subject of one of the most heartbreaking live performances I've ever seen. In 2004 The Charlatans were booked to play one of our favourite festivals, Benicàssim in Spain. We'd played the first one and took the opportunity to go back whenever we could. I always look at the rest of the line-up at a festival and make a mental checklist of who I'll be seeing – over the three days at Benicàssim, Lou Reed, The Chemical Brothers, Lambchop, Brian Wilson, and Arthur Lee and Love were also playing.

I made my way to the stage where Arthur Lee was due to play – *Forever Changes*, track by track, complete with a string section, all taking place in the glorious Spanish early-evening sunshine. I noticed that Brian Wilson's band were standing next to me as we watched from about halfway back in the crowd.

Everyone in the band took to the stage as per schedule, but there was no Arthur. There was a sense of mild peril within the band, and all did not seem well.

As friendly and as accommodating as festivals might seem, there's one golden rule for the bands – get on on time and don't overrun. Or is that two rules? The peril increased from mild and moved through the crowd.

We then noticed the familiar figure of Arthur Lee appear in the wings, but he seemed unsteady on his feet. He looked like a boxer in his corner between rounds, his corner men checking whether he was OK to take to the ring.

His struggles with drugs and alcohol are well documented. He had done time in prison for firearms offences – sentenced to twelve years, serving five and a half. While he was inside, Arthur refused interviews and visitors, and two members of Love died. His life had seen more tragedy than triumph but his legacy was beginning to be more appreciated than ever.

He remained off stage and, if anything, appeared even more unsteady.

A chair was placed centre stage.

And with little choice, the band struck up 'Alone Again Or'. The classic Spanish-guitar intro struck up a communal sigh of relief, but where there should have been a 'Yeah' there was no 'Yeah' and still no Arthur. Finally, he set off towards the microphone but went the long way. The intro was repeated. Band eyebrows became more raised and glances were exchanged. The intro was repeated again, then again, and possibly once more, but this time they carried on. Arthur was on the stage but wasn't singing. The band didn't know what to do, and even the backing vocals came in where they were meant to be.

Arthur arrived at the microphone stand, which he seemed to need for support. He stopped the band and the crowd began to realise that, for everybody's sake, there would be no performance. Arthur began to explain what had happened: two days before his good friend and fellow troubled singer Rick James had died, and it had knocked Arthur for six. Whatever demons he had managed to keep under control had overwhelmed him, and the last time I saw him he was being led off the stage, bewildered.

It was so sad to watch. Super-fans were in tears, while the less forgiving people in the crowd booed and threw plastic cups. None of it was good to see, so we left. A couple of years later, Arthur died, leaving behind a legacy that included one of the greatest albums ever made.

Forever Changes was a classic from its release in 1967. It guaranteed its enduring status not from radio plays but from older siblings who would pass it down through what they saw as their responsibility for the musical education of their brothers and sisters. It has been cited as a major influence on The La's, Shack, The Stone Roses and The Brian Jonestown Massacre.

As complicated as Arthur's life was, the record demonstrated what was possible, more than being a straight-up inspiration. Almost impossible to emulate, it stood alongside *Sgt Pepper* and *Pet Sounds* as the stone tablets of what could be achieved with an album.

The West Coast sound of America and the west coast sound of Liverpool have always gone hand in hand – a shared love of jangle meant Love could be heard echoed in The Coral forty years later.

I'd first heard of Probe Records as the place that Pete Burns worked in before Dead or Alive hit big. It had opened in 1971 and was a hugely important part of not only the Liverpool music scene but the whole of the independent-label set-up for the entire UK. Julian Cope worked in the shop. It was a hub where they eventually set up their own label, with Half Man Half Biscuit calling it home since the days of 'Trumpton Riots'. A few relocations around Liverpool meant that when we headed to the city for a Charlatans gig I didn't know where to find it. The city centre looked so new, I didn't know where to find anything, but once I tracked Probe down it was love at first sight. It was possibly the busiest shop I've been in on my travels – record sleeves on every wall and racks of CDs and vinyl with handwritten notes on rarity, whether it was a reissue and any other info tucked between the inner sleeve and the cover. A father and daughter were talking about Pink Floyd and The Velvet Underground, and the two guys behind the counter were kept busy retrieving the vinyl for the covers they were handed by the customers.

I started looking for what remained on my list, and I left with two recommendations. To buy *Forever Changes* on vinyl in Liverpool felt like capturing it in its natural habitat. Then I saw one of the more elusive LPs I was after. Bobby Gillespie's request was for me to find *Oar* by Alexander 'Skip' Spence. I'd felt a little like that guy in the *Yellow Pages* advert looking for the fly-fishing book – every time I asked for *Oar* I was met with plenty of information about what a great album it was, but nobody seemed to have it. I took my double win to the counter, and one of the other customers recognised me. He tapped me on the shoulder and said, 'We're playing with you tomorrow night.'

Mostly when I get recognised someone will talk about a concert of ours that they went to perhaps, or a song that means something to them. As I turned, I realised that the band we were playing with the following night was Echo & the Bunnymen, and the shoulder-tapper was one of the faces that had been on posters on my wall as a kid. Will Sergeant was the dad who was in the shop with his daughter, Alice. He was clutching a Velvet Underground banana T-shirt that he was just about to buy, and there was me with my copy of *Forever Changes* – magical moments happen in record shops, and this was definitely one of those.

OUTRO

Willie Nelson, *Stardust*
Recommended by Mick Jones

I never saw the sun shinin' so bright

The final record on the list – the one that had eluded me at every turn – was Daniel Miller's choice, *Fireside Favourites* by Fad Gadget. Our UK tour was coming to an end and I'd not seen a copy in the dozens of shops I'd been in, so I sent out a plea asking if anyone knew of the whereabouts of a copy. A copy that was for sale. While we were on our way to our Liverpool Academy gig, word came through from South Record Shop in Southend-on-Sea – a slight, 100-mile detour on the trip from Liverpool to our final show of the tour at Brixton Academy.

A 5 a.m. start was the only way to make sure we made it to the shop and then the soundcheck. I'd spent some time in Southend-on-Sea, and for a few years I ended up DJing on Boxing Day in The Railway for an annual party put together by The Horrors – a celebration of psyche and northern soul 7-inches.

The road trip took in several coffee stops before we landed amid the brutalist splendour of Southend town centre. I'd called Richard, the owner of South Record Shop, on the way down and checked there wasn't someone else closing in, ready to grab their copy of the Fad Gadget rarity. There wasn't; it was stashed safely when I got there. South is one of the new breed of record shops, having been open only a couple of years and with a healthy online presence. I took a quick look through the racks, and while chatting to Richard he revealed that he was in a band that rarely played live, but the fact that he cited Galaxie 500 as an influence means they could be making an appearance at Tim Peaks next year.

Two hours later we were soundchecking in Brixton. And that was meant to be that.

Except it's a false ending – like one of those songs that carries on after you think it's finished.

I arrived at Brixton Academy, having found each of the fifty-one albums – one of them, John Grant's, twice – and only one person hadn't managed to get back to me. But after the soundcheck at Brixton Academy, I headed to the dressing room to see a note on the mirror. It read:

Willie Nelson, *Stardust*.

I knew he'd come through in the end. X

Mick Jones had just phoned. The note was from Davo, our guitar tech and former BAD roadie. It had slipped Mick's mind and he was checking to see whether he was too late. He was but he wasn't.

So Mick had sent his choice, and I smiled as I took it from the mirror. After the gig we drove through the Christmas lights of Oxford Street and the West End listening to *The Globe* by Big Audio Dynamite, drawing up a hit list of where to find the album the following day. Three shops didn't have it, but I headed up to Soho and found a copy in Sounds of the Universe – over the years I'd often headed there to find reggae and dub albums, and I'd whiled away many an hour with headphones on, listening to anything from Senegalese 1970s funk to experimental jazz.

The last album from the last recommender.

We all have those eureka moments when we fall in love and it

248

slaps you around the face from nowhere like a bolt out of the blue – it's a glorious feeling and it's out of our control. We just accept it and go with it, looking for the signs and trying to join the dots. For me, finding a record recommended by Mick Jones had this air of magic. Mick is the smiliest man in rock 'n' roll and has been a hero of mine ever since I first starting collecting records.

I'd bought 'The Cost of Living' EP on a camping trip to France in 1979, and The Clash were the benchmark for any band from then on – not just for the music but for their approach to fans, the risks they took and what they left behind.

Then came Big Audio Dynamite, when Mick's experimentation with hip hop and sampling went into overdrive. With a creative force like Don Letts in the band too, their records and gigs were the perfect mix of movie cuts-ups and the biggest beats, around Mick's gigantic smile.

Stardust was Willie's album of standards that he recorded with Booker T in the role of producer – he felt hemmed in by being seen as just a country singer by the outside world and as an outsider by much of the country-music world.

The lyrics to the title track are the most romantic words imaginable, from 1927 but perfectly delivered by Willie. There's 'Moonlight in Vermont', with its jaw-droppingly hypnotic chord changes and the mood of a 1950s Christmas movie. But it's 'Blue Skies' that reminds me most of Mick: 'I never saw the sun shinin' so bright / I never saw things goin' so right'.

So that was that, the final record being a hybrid of standards written in the 1920s and '30s, recorded by a country legend and produced by a soul master – all recommended by a punk. Maybe that sums up the joy of collecting records more than anything else.

Not so long ago it seemed like record shops might be doomed, with only closures rather than openings and some doggedly hanging on in there. But something happened, and it's continuing to happen. Not only did the closures slow down but new shops began to open. More kids at gigs would be asking me to sign their vinyl copies of albums, and as the physical format for music got ever smaller until it actually disappeared with the MP3, there was a fightback. Supermarkets are stocking vinyl for the first time in years, and each new Record Store Day brings more converts along to support the shops.

We don't need record shops just to keep up sales of vinyl, though. They're where friends meet and bands are formed. Wherever I went in search of the records I'd been asked to find, there was something warmly familiar about each record shop – from Istanbul to San Francisco, from high-street giants to market stalls.

I'd been in touch with friends and heroes and been to shops I'd never heard of before, but I came across characters who were similar to everyone I'd met along the way as a record collector, from starting out at eleven years old to buying bootlegs at fairs to being the guy signing covers behind the counter.

Lots of people need record shops to survive, from the people who press the vinyl to the bands that make the records. We've seen lots of other shops and stores fade away, but let's not let it happen this time. Besides, where would I go before a soundcheck or the day after a gig?

THE RECOMMENDATIONS

ABBA, *ABBA Gold*
Oxfam, Manchester
Recommended by Chris Carter

The Allman Brothers Band, *The Allman Brothers Band at Fillmore East*
Record Parlour, Hollywood
Recommended by Kurt Wagner

Sibylle Baier, *Colour Green*
Discogs
Recommended by Kim Gordon

Beach Boys, *Pet Sounds*
Sound Station, Copenhagen
Recommended by Kevin Shields

Captain Beefheart, *Trout Mask Replica*
Kelly's Records, Cardiff
Recommended by David Lynch

Big Youth, *Dread Locks Dread*
Flashback Records, London
Recommended by Andrew Weatherall

David Bowie, *The Rise and Fall of Ziggy Stardust and
the Spiders from Mars*
Amoeba Records, San Francisco
Recommended by Holly Johnson

The Byrds, *Younger Than Yesterday*
Soundclash, Norwich
Recommended by Grumbling Fur

Lou Christie Sacco, *Paint America Love*
Holt Vinyl Vault, Norfolk
Recommended by Bob Stanley

The Clash, *Sandinista!*
Piccadilly Records, Manchester
Recommended by Freddie Cowan

John Coltrane, *A Love Supreme*
Dusty Groove, Chicago
Recommended by Paul Weller

King Curtis, *Live at the Fillmore West*
Record Detective Agency, London
Recommended by Bill Bailey

The Durutti Column, *Vini Reilly*
Dig, Liverpool
Recommended by Tony Wilson

Echo & the Bunnymen, *Porcupine*
Record Collector, Sheffield
Recommended by Ian McCulloch

Duane Eddy and the Rebels, *Have 'Twangy' Guitar Will Travel*
Jazz Record Mart, Chicago
Recommended by Howard Marks

Fad Gadget, *Fireside Favourites*
South Record Shop, Southend-on-Sea
Recommended by Daniel Miller

Joe Gibbs and the Professionals, *African Dub Chapter 3*
Flashback Records, London
Recommended by Bobby Gillespie

Allen Ginsberg, *First Blues*
Discos Castelló, Barcelona
Recommended by Peter Gordon

John Grant, *Grey Tickles, Black Pressure*
Dennis and Lois's car. Rough Trade, Nottingham
Recommended by Dennis and Lois

The Groundhogs, *Split*
RPM Music, Newcastle
Recommended by Mark Radcliffe and Stuart Maconie

Guided by Voices, *Bee Thousand*
Resident Music, Brighton
Recommended by Paddy Considine

Hawkwind, *In Search of Space*
Reckless Records, London
Recommended by Stephen Morris

Holy Modal Rounders, *The Moray Eels Eat the Holy Modal Rounders*
Holt Vinyl Vault, Norfolk
Recommended by Irmin Schmidt

Hüsker Dü, *Metal Circus*
Rough Trade East, London
Recommended by Chan Marshall aka Cat Power

George Jones and Tammy Wynette, *Golden Ring*
Amoeba Records, LA
Recommended by John Cooper Clarke

Joy Division, *Unknown Pleasures*
Monorail Music, Glasgow
Recommended by Ian Rankin

Love, *Forever Changes*
Probe Records, Liverpool
Recommended by Cosey Fanni Tutti

Sergio Mendes and Brasil '66, *Herb Alpert Presents Sergio Mendes and Brasil '66*
Holt Vinyl Vault, Norfolk
Recommended by Anton Newcombe

The Modern Lovers, *The Modern Lovers*
Rough Trade, Brooklyn, New York
Recommended by Nik Void

Willie Nelson, *Stardust*
Sounds of the Universe, London
Recommended by Mick Jones

Nico, *Chelsea Girl*
Rise Records, Bristol
Recommended by Boy George

Pearls Before Swine, *One Nation Underground*
Record Mania, Stockholm
Recommended by Iggy Pop

Photek, *Modus Operandi*
Sound Station, Copenhagen
Recommended by Jason Williamson

Pick-a-Dub Featuring King Tubby and the Barrett Bros,
    arranged by Keith Hudson
Rough Trade, Brooklyn, New York
Recommended by Richard H. Kirk

Pink Floyd, *Relics*
King Bee Records, Manchester
Recommended by Noel Fielding

Rage Against the Machine, *Rage Against the Machine*
Lale Plak, Istanbul
Recommended by Carl Barât

Lou Reed, *Lou Reed*
Disk Union, Shibuya, Tokyo
Recommended by Lawrence

Roxy Music, *Roxy Music*
Bengans, Stockholm
Recommended by Kevin Rowland

Royal Trux, *Thank You*
Pop Recs, Sunderland
Recommended by Lauren Laverne

Barry Ryan, *The Very Best of Barry Ryan*
Soultrade, Berlin
Recommended by Neil Tennant

The Shadows, *The Very Best of The Shadows*
Truck Records, Truck Festival
Recommended by Paul Cook

Paul Simon, *Graceland*
Waterloo Records, Austin
Recommended by James Corden

Siouxsie and the Banshees, *Join Hands*
GJM Music, Hull
Recommended by Pam Hogg

Elliott Smith, *XO*
Waterloo Records, Austin
Recommended by Tom Sheehan

Alexander 'Skip' Spence, *Oar*
Probe Records, Liverpool
Recommended by Bobby Gillespie

Bruce Springsteen, *Born in the USA*
Freebird Records, Dublin
Recommended by Gary Neville

T. Rex, *The Slider*
Sister Ray, Berwick Street, London
Recommended by Johnny Marr

Tchaikovsky, Symphony No. 6, 'Pathétique'
Crossroads Records, Portland
Recommended by Vini Reilly

Tomita, *Snowflakes Are Dancing*
Kontra Plak, Istanbul
Recommended by Edwyn Collins

Van der Graaf Generator, *H to He, Who Am the Only One*
Vinyl Exchange, Manchester
Recommended by Bill Drummond

Loudon Wainwright III, *Album III*
Sound Station, Copenhagen
Recommended by Sharon Horgan

Clifford T. Ward, *Mantle Pieces*
Tim Peaks Oxfam, Kendal Calling
Recommended by Pete Paphides and Nathan

Junior Wells, *Hoodoo Man Blues*
End of an Ear, Austin
Recommended by Iggy Pop

White Zombie, *Soul-Crusher*
Exiled Records, Portland
Recommended by Iggy Pop